The Journey to
the Promised Land

The Journey to the Promised Land

The African American Struggle for Development since the Civil War

DICKSON A. MUNGAZI
Foreword by Dione Brooks Taylor

 PRAEGER

Westport, Connecticut
London

Library of Congress Cataloging-in-Publication Data

Mungazi, Dickson A.
   The journey to the promised land : the African American struggle for development
since the Civil War / Dickson A. Mungazi ; foreword by Dione Brooks Taylor.
      p.   cm.
   Includes bibliographical references (p.   ) and index.
   ISBN 0–275–96824–3 (alk. paper)
      1. Afro-Americans—History—1863–1877.   2. Afro-Americans—History—1877–1964.
   3. Afro-Americans—History—1964–   I. Title.
   E185.2.M86   2001
   973'0496073—dc21   00–029854

British Library Cataloguing in Publication Data is available.

Library of Congress Catalog Card Number: 00–029854
ISBN: 0–275–96824–3

First published in 2001

Praeger Publishers, 88 Post Road West, Westport, CT 06881
An imprint of Greenwood Publishing Group, Inc.
www.praeger.com

Printed in the United States of America

The paper used in this book complies with the
Permanent Paper Standard issued by the National
Information Standards Organization (Z39.48–1984).

10   9   8   7   6   5   4   3   2   1

To the memory of Medgar Evers, humble man of determination whom I was privileged to meet and know and whose contribution to the development of African Americans is invaluable

I'll see you in the morning, safe in the promised land.

Harriet Tubman, 1850

I have looked over, and I have seen the promised land. I may not get there with you, but I want you to know that we as a people will get to the promised land.

Martin Luther King, Jr., 1968

Contents

Illustrations

Foreword

In this historical account, Dr. Dickson A. Mungazi examines key dimensions in the African American struggle for development during the period from the Civil War to the present. Considering four aspects of this struggle, this study examines the areas of social, economic, political, and educational barriers experienced by African Americans in their quest for equality in the United States.

The issues in this struggle resulted in great debates among key stockholders. Central to the debate are opposing beliefs, juxtaposed between the identity thrust upon African Americans as slaves by their white owners and the manner in which they sought a new identity as a free people.

In this instance that identity is used to represent group identity and rights of individuals as members of the African Americans as a group; aided by the Thirteenth, Fourteenth, and Fifteenth Amendments to the U.S. Constitution, which liberated African Americans from human bondage as slaves, and defended their right to life and liberty without fear of deprivation of due process and the right to become voting citizens. Nowhere else in the world has the institution of slavery been dealt with in a more forthright matter more than in these constitutional amendments.

Although originally intended to promote the development of African Americans, these constitutional amendments served the interests of all Americans. To deny African Americans basic rights to freedom and equal status in society would require the Contitution of the United States to be reframed, an action not likely to occur. These amendments would not have been necessary were it not for the strong resentment expressed by a large number of whites, particularly in the southern states, who wished to maintain slavery to ensure their profitable economic lifestyles.

How are this journey and the ensuing circumstances revealed in this study? Dr. Mungazi discusses the social climate that was prevalent around the time of the Civil War, specifically the divergent attitudes about African Americans adopted by whites in the northern and southern United States. Because the federal courts enjoy unrestricted freedom of thought and action, their rulings became the law of the land. The waxing and waning of progress in the court system reflected the social climate of this period.

The Supreme Court's decision in the Dred Scott Case in 1857 set a precedent that did not change until 1938—a long time for a struggling people to wait. As African Americans struggled to define their place in the emerging American society, the battle lines were at first out of their hands entirely. To reinstitutionalize slavery in a new form, laws were passed under Jim Crow sanctions where perviously there were none. Once the framework of these laws was created, the system facilitated the import of African Americans into a new life of slavery to meet the increasing physical needs of the society.

As the need arose, a new law or code of laws was enacted as a further attempt to control and maintain the level of servitude by African Americans. Consequences for any violation were severe and swift. This study discusses the positions of the Supreme Court and the decisions it rendered over the decades, supporting the continued repression of African Americans—that is, until the late 1920s.

In the context of a people struggling for development, education is a highly important variable that helps determine the success and potential contribution of the individual in the future. In the postslavery era, whites were as concerned about educating African Americans as they were allowing them to bear arms in times of war. In each case the fear of revolt was imminent, which had the potential to equalize the social status of African Americans. When education was finally provided in the late 1800s, a law was passed enforcing segregation of the schools, allowing a withdrawal of federal funding.

Dr. Mungazi comprehensively details the struggles faced by African Americans at this period in history. This debate about access to educational resources continued to be discussed today. There has been not shortage of obstacles faced by African Americans since the Civil War. Each obstacle has served to prevent, diminish, control, or direct the lives of African Americans in the areas of social, economic, political, and educational issues.

Leadership is of particular importance in a journey of this kind. Dr.

Mungazi highlights influential persons and their contributions to leadership of the journey. His presentation and discussion of differences of opinion about the course of the journey, especially between Booker T. Washington and William E. B. Du Bois, are not intended to show that there were irreconcilable differences within the leadership itself, but to sharpen the parameters of the struggle.

It must also be remembered that when people launch a campaign for their salvation, differences of opinion become inevitable regarding various aspects of it. To assume that there is ready agreement on all aspects of that endeavor is to forget the imperatives and lessons of history. Each leader discussed in this book, from Frederick Douglass to Julian Bond, made a unique contribution to the quality of leadership that African Americans needed to make the journey.

Dr. Mungazi's admiration of Dr. Martin Luther King, Jr. is evident in this study as he devotes an entire chapter to King's contributions to the plight of African Americans specifically and to oppressed people generally. Dr. King had been recognized all over the world as a person of rare and unusual qualities, both as a man and as leader. The opportunity that Dr. Mungazi had to interview Dr. Martin Luther King, Sr. in Atlanta, Georgia, in May 1962, when the author was only a sophomore in college, has served well in writing this book.

The social and political climate was right when Dr. King emerged as a leader of the nonviolent movement to equalize the treatment of African Americans in the United States. One must not minimize the leadership role that Harriet Tubman played. It made all the difference in the course and success of the journey The underground railroad that she organized was in effect a form of leadership as were other forms.

Many black and white supporters encouraged Dr. King to follow his calling. Although efforts were made to tarnish his reputation, Dr. King proved that he was a man and leader without reproach. The benefits were considerable and have implications for all mankind. For each of the leaders indentified in Dr. Mungazi's study, there were countless others with less notoriety working to effect desired social change.

In this study, Dr. Mungazi chronicles the events that added dimension to the historical complexities of the United States and Africa during the colonial period. He asks his readers to respond not with guilt for past events in the treatment of both African Americans and Africans, but to recall the journey and work collectively in a new direction inclusive of all peoples, circumnavigating past approaches resulting in deleterious results.

The insights in this study will be important to students of African American history, educators, politicians, and the general reading public alike. As participants in this great country, each has a vested interest in the overall well-being of all its peoples, regardless of racial category. Eliminating strife in matters of racial equality requires ongoing attention, but in doing so, has the potential to strengthen the bonds between citizens in the United States.

Dione Brooks Taylor

Preface

THE PURPOSE OF THE STUDY

The purpose of this study is to trace the struggle of African Americans for development from the end of the Civil War to the present. In seeking to fulfill this purpose the study focuses on social, economic, political, and educational aspects as definite forms of development. These are the principal factors that make it possible for any group of struggling people to launch a journey to the promised land. It also discusses the implications which that journey has had on the national character of the United States as a result of the kinds of programs that have been initiated in these four areas. In order to adequately present components of this struggle, the study begins with a discussion of activities that were initiated relative to the search by African Americans for a new identity from 1865 to 1896.

In this approach the study focuses on specific areas of critical importance, such as the effect of Reconstruction, the role of the courts and the leaders who have been part of it. These are conditions of development that African Americans took into account in searching for that new identity. The influence of political and educational institutions that emerged during this period, the action of the North and the reaction of the South to Reconstruction programs, the efforts African Americans made, the inception of formal education, the nature of American society—all combined to form the thrust for the search of that identity in a way that had meaning to African Americans as they traveled on an uncharted course to the promised land.

By the very nature of that struggle, African Americans were trying to influence American society to address various components of an emerging national character in response to their search for a new identity. They also expected to influence the formulation of a new set of national goals and objectives based on new social values unfamiliar to the existing American social practices, not only for themselves, but also for the country as a whole.

The implementation of these goals and objectives was expected to determine the kind of society that they expected to emerge in which African Americans were cast. This aspect of the African American struggle for development forms a critical component of the study. The effectiveness of their endeavor in seeking to meet their developmental needs and in serving national purpose must be determined by how well African Americans were doing after the end of slavery, especially in areas of economic life, political activity, educational achievement, and social adjustment. These activities form the passageway to the promised land. In this way African Americans hoped to influence the United States to build a society based upon the foundation of that passageway.

The question is whether the United States as a nation and white America as a people could comprehend the magnitude of the problems that they were about to face in responding to a call to regard African Americans as their social equals. Given the spirit of the U.S. Constitution, African Americans had every reason to expect nothing less than what it was intended to accomplish. Whether white America recognized it or not, the fact of the matter is that both the U.S. Constitution and Emancipation set the stage for a new beginning of a new relationship between the two races based on mutual respect for the good of the country.

THE APPROACH

The study begins with an examination of major developments that took place soon after Emancipation. The adoption of the Thirteenth Amendment in 1865, the granting of amnesty by President Andrew Johnson to rebellious southern states, and the adoption of the Fourteenth and Fifteenth Amendments, in 1868 and 1870, the action that was taken by President Ulysses Grant from 1869 to 1877 giving effect to Reconstruction, and that taken by his successor, President Rutherford B. Hayes, to terminate it are among events that would determine the course of that development and the course of that journey.

The ratification of the Fifteenth Amendment in 1870, and the passage of civil rights legislation in 1875 gave new hope to African Americans that the future would be better than the past. However, African Americans fully recognized that in the pursuit of their journey to the promised land, they would encounter major problems that only they would solve to ensure their arriving there. This study is a story of a people struggling for a better future than the past and the transformation of society as a rare dream for all.

During Reconstruction African Americans demonstrated their capability in making adjustments to new situations. Senators, civic leaders, community leaders, and leaders in education all came forth to show that African Americans, if given an opportunity, could be effective and successful in whatever they did. The termination in 1894 of federal funds that were used since Emancipation to support federal marshals, the disenfranchisement of African Americans, the curtailment of the educational opportunity that they had utilized to advance themselves as part of a strategy to shape the course of the journey, and the reversal of social and political progress that they had made—all combined to create a new situation that compounded the problems that African Americans had not anticipated.

Suddenly the national climate that African Americans thought Emancipation had created to enable them to launch their journey to the promised land became a mirage, a phantom figure seen only through the eyes of fantasy. Ten years following the end of the Civil War, African Americans recognized that they had a rough road ahead on that journey. This study traces these developments in relation to the response from white America. It then gives an account of the role of leadership among African Americans themselves. In doing so it answers the following questions: Who are these leaders? What qualifications did they hold? What views did they hold and utilize in trying to become effective leaders? What direction did that leadership take? What was the effect of that leadership? How did white America respond to that leadership?

The study then goes on to discuss the obstacles that African Americans encountered on their journey to the promised land. Among these obstacles are the negative attitudes of some white Americans, the lack of opportunity in important areas of national life, continuing discrimination and segregation, apathy among some African Americans themselves, and a difference of opinion among leaders about programs to adopt and strategy to follow. While the formation of the National Association for the Advancement of Colored People in 1909 was a highly positive development of a new strategy, it also brought division among African Americans themselves because one of its founding fathers, William E. B. Du Bois, wanted its leadership to come out of what he called talented tenth. According to Du Bois the NAACP must be led by intellectuals like himself. However, the NAACP has to this day provided needed leadership for African Americans in their struggle for development without embracing Du Bois's idea of the character of its leadership.

The study then goes on to discuss the era of the civil rights legislation beginning with the Civil Rights Act of 1875 and the effect it had on

African Americans and the nation as a whole. It discusses also the role that national leadership played in that endeavor. The Civil Rights Acts of 1957 and 1964 and the Voting Rights Act of 1965 stand out as monuments to the struggle of African Americans for development. One must not forget that the federal courts, especially the U.S. Supreme Court, played an important role in mapping out the passageway to the promised land. The study also provides a comparative perspective of the struggle of Africans during the colonial period and that of African Americans to see some differences and similarities.

SUMMARY, CONCLUSIONS, IMPLICATIONS

The last chapter summarizes the preceding main features and arguments. It also draws some conclusions and presents some implications. Some of these conclusions are the following: (1) The struggle of African Americans for development came out of the conditions following the conclusion of the Civil War in 1865. (2) The difference between success and failure of Reconstruction, between relevant education and irrelevant instruction for African Americans, between mediocrity and a dynamic system leads to the conclusion that characterized the struggle of African Americans. (3) The response of white America to the struggle of African Americans became a critical determining factor of all national programs, because whatever programs were initiated, they had to take the position of African Americans into account. It was virtually impossible to initiate any national undertaking in any area of human endeavor without initiating response to the position of African Americans. (4) The development of education for African Americans required special attention because it was important to other forms of development. (5) In its efforts to improve technological superiority in a competitive world, the United States had to strengthen its system of education for all students. The thrust for educational development of individuals lay in the thrust for national development. (6) The struggle of African Americans to secure an education must be seen in the context of the belief that education was good for the country because it was good for all people. National development cannot be achieved in a climate of discrimination and segregation.

Acknowledgments

In the process of writing a book that covers the struggle of a group of people over an extended period of time, one must rely on historical materials obtained from different sources. Therefore, the author wishes to thank the Interlibrary Loan System at Northern Arizona University (NAU) for making it possible for him to secure the materials he needed to produce this study; the Library of Congress, the National Archives, and Double Delta Industries for additional materials and photographs included in the study; the Arizona Public Library for allowing him access to public documents that he needed to complete the study; and the NAACP for materials and access to some historical photographs that appear in the book.

The author extends special appreciation to the staff at Cline Library at NAU for readiness to help in securing a variety of materials, and to the Office of Regents Professors at NAU for the financial support he needed to travel to collect materials for the study. Several of the author's colleagues at NAU and members of the National Science Association are thanked for support and encouragement while he was producing the study and presenting papers at professional conferences during the past several years. The idea for the study came out of these papers.

The author also extends his gratitude and appreciation to a variety of individuals who helped produce the study and gave suggestions for its improvement: Betty Russell and George Covington, of the Center for Excellence in Education at NAU, for programming the computer to produce the manuscript more efficiently; Dr. Dione Brooks Taylor of Point

Loma Nazarene University, San Diego, for writing the Foreword; Geraldine Peten, educator in the Phoenix area, for access to the paper she wrote for her graduate class; Linda Gregonis, faithful indexer and proofreader; Katie Chase, the project editor at Praeger Publishers; and to his son, Gaylord "T.C." Mungazi, for his active interest and support and for providing some materials regarding the history of African Americans.

Introduction

THE SETTING

No one has read Alex Haley's *Roots* or watched David L. Wolper's TV production of it without getting an inside story of slavery in the United States. The story of slavery has been told in so many ways. One wonders if it needs to be told any more. However, other aspects of African American struggle for development have not been told as well as the story of slavery. This is why reading Nicholas Lemann's *The Promised Land: The Great Black Migration and How It Changed America* (1991) aroused in this author an intense interest in conducting a study on the metaphor of the promised land as it relates to that struggle. Lemann's book and this study are very different in their treatment of the metaphor of the promosed land. Lemann discusses the migration of African Americans from conditions of economic oppression imposed by the South to the more tolerant North. This study addresses the struggle of African Americans for development since the Civil War. Areas of that development are specifically identified as political, economic, social, and educational. These areas collectively form the metaphorical expression of the promised land. In short Lemann's book is a sociological approach to the metaphor of the promised land, while this study is a historical approach. One can say that while the two studies supplement each other they are also quite different.

When President Abraham Lincoln issued the Emancipation Proclamation on September 22, 1862, to take effect on January 1, 1863, people in the United States knew that it was the beginning of a new hope for a major social change for African Americans and the country. Rapidly moving events began to take place in the context of the fact that none of the Confederate States had, at that point, accepted the offer of immunity from legal action if they laid down their arms.

Americans also knew that in the president's initiative the country was set for an unprecedented social, economic, and political conflict caused by the journey to the promised land initiated by African Americans. In 1865, when the Thirteenth Amendment was adopted to abolish slavery, things began to happen in the direction of change that African Americans envisaged for the future. These events provided a climate that proposed the Fourteenth Amendment, stating that it was illegal to deprive any persons of life, liberty, or property without due process of law. The Thirteenth Amendment was quite precise in its provision and left no room for doubt as to what its intent was. In stating, "Neither slavery nor involuntary servitude, except as a punishment for crime whereof the party shall have been duly convicted, shall exist within the United States, or any place subject to their jurisdiction. Congress shall have power to enforce this article by appropriate legislation." This amendment served as a warning of more action to come from the federal government against the South unless it complied with new conditions.

When, on June 13, 1866, the Congress passed a resolution proposing the Fourteenth Amendment, it put in place a series of events that the South was unable or unwilling to understand and accept as its people tried to maintain the social status quo. This amendment extended equal constitutional protection to former slaves. Then on February 26, 1869, the Congress passed another resolution proposing the adoption of the Fifteenth Amendment, which was ratified by 29 states on March 30, 1870. This amendment extended the right to vote to former slaves, stating: "The right of citizens of the United States to vote shall not be denied or abridged by the United States or by any state on account of race, color, or previous condition of servitude." These three amendments made it possible for the United States to approach the question of the development of African Americans in a radical way in order to give effect to the end of slavery. Reconstruction programs came out of these amendments. They were an enormous undertaking in political, educational, and social areas designed to promote the development of African Americans. Reconstruction programs were also intended to bring about a change of attitude among southern whites in an effort to influence their acceptance of African Americans as citizens with equal rights. Extending citizenship rights to African Americans required equal treatment and equal opportunity. Were the whites able to make this rapid adjustment? How was the United States going to accomplish this task?

In order to initiate any programs under Reconstruction, Congress had to pass special legislation. That is why in 1867 a series of laws was enacted under the Reconstruction Act to divide the ten unstructured states into five military districts, each with a major general to command it for purposes of helping the states under his charge for return to the Union. But African Americans and white Americans were moving in opposite directions in response to Reconstruction programs.

THE PLIGHT OF AFRICAN AMERICANS AND THE ROLE OF THE COURTS

The position of African Americans in the country did not improve significantly during Reconstruction, in spite of efforts made by themselves and by northern whites. Having found elements of a new identity they wished to promote and protect if their journey to the promised land was to be successful, they tried all they could to give structure to the journey. As part of their effort to realize their destination, African Americans turned to the courts, especially the federal courts, to help them find the passageway. But from the *Dred Scott* case of 1857 to the *Gong Lum* case of 1927, the Supreme Court was not helpful at all. However, it began to change its attitudes in 1938 with the *Gaines* case.

Section III of the Constitution defines the Supreme Court as the third branch of the U.S. government and defines its function as relating to the exercise of its functions and power as the Congress may from time to time direct. From this constitutional provision it is quite clear that the courts had tremendous jurisdictional power to decide on all cases. In terms of constitutional provisions, the functions of the Supreme Court were mainly as a court of appeal. There is no doubt that its power was extended beyond that of the executive branch and the legislative branch.

The Supreme Court has original jurisdiction only in cases involving ambassadors, public ministers, and consuls. In all other cases, the Supreme Court has appellate jurisdiction. These cases come either from the lower federal courts or from the higher courts in various states. The Supreme Court may take cases from the states only when a federal law or constitutional issue is in question.

The power that gives unique distinction to the Supreme Court is its authority to render final decisions on the constitutionality of any legislation passed by the Congress. In fulfilling this function the Supreme Court acts as guardian of the Constitution. It is the final arbiter of all constitutional matters. Beyond the Supreme Court there is no other recourse. However, the authority of the Supreme Court to review the constitutionality of legislation passed by Congress is not stated in the Constitution.

In 1803 the Supreme Court asserted this power in *Marbury vs. Madison*. Since that time the Supreme Court has exercised this power as part of its functions. Although some people have protested the use of this power, none have succeeded in bringing it to an end. During the New Deal, President Franklin D. Roosevelt tried to bring about change in the use of this power because he thought that its exercise was infringing heavily upon the economic recovery programs he initiated to combat the Great Depression. But he was unsuccessful. A discussion of representative cases is done in Chapter 2 to give the reader an idea of how the courts first derailed the efforts of African Americans and then helped them in shaping their journey to the promised land.

THE ROLE OF LEADERSHIP

A critical component of the journey to the promised land is leadership among African Americans. One can say that among the most important results of the Supreme Court decisions from the *Gaines* case to the *Brown* case was that those decisions aroused a new sense of purpose and destiny, a new perspective in which African Americans viewed their journey to the promised land. The support that the Court gave them and the success that they achieved in these cases gave them new vision, new hope of arriving in the promised land without spending another 40 years in the wilderness.

African Americans now summoned new courage to stage new endeavors in other aspects of their lives that included housing, equal employment opportunity, and securing political and social rights. They lost these gains during the years following the end of Reconstruction in 1877. They now wanted to know whether it was possible for them to secure education without first securing the right to it. To fulfill these goals which they now identified, African Americans decided that leadership was essential to the attainment of their objectives, to arriving at their destination, the promised land.

With the Supreme Court decisions going against them from 1857 to 1937, how would they find the passageway to the promised land? Even before the *Brown* decision African Americans needed a Moses to lead the long journey from the land of slavery and denial of equal rights to the promised land of freedom and equality in society.

The task was not easy, but it was one that had to be undertaken if African Americans ever hoped to move from the wilderness and find a passageway to the promised land. Leadership is born out of dedication to serve the interests of the group, to put the development of the people above their own security. Leadership demands a willingness to take risks of failure, personal injury or death, or rejection and controversy. Effective leadership comes also from commitment, the strength of personal character, unwavering decision, and thorough knowledge of the issues that need to be resolved.

It is not easy to select perons who, as individuals, have determined the course to be followed. In this book material is presented on several individuals who assumed positions of leadership by virtue of positions they held in other organizations. Others became leaders by their ability to define positions on issues in ways that the people could identify with and support. There are also African Americans who exerted considerable influence on leadership by the quality of their work. All of these individuals will be presented in the chapters that follow.

In spite of dedicated leadership, African Americans encountered serious problems on their journey to the promised land. These obstacles included conflict within the leadership itself, such as the one that broke out between W.E.B. Du Bois and William Trotter and Booker T. Washington. Opposition from white America, activities of the Ku Klux Klan, the indifference of federal officials, and outright resistance to efforts to promote the progress of the journey to the promised land—all made it very difficult for African Americans to reach their destination. But in engaging in these activities, white Americans did not know that they were working against their own interests and those of the country as a whole.

THE PERIOD OF CIVIL RIGHTS

The period of civil disobedience and militant confrontation was born during the months following the Grand March on Washington, D.C in August 1963. African Americans were particularly sensitive to the reality that 1963 marked the centennial of President Lincoln's Emancipation Proclamation. The United States Civil Rights Commission, which was established under the 1957 Civil Rights Act, celebrated the occasion with its report to President John F. Kennedy, stating that the United States needed to do more to promote the advancement of African Americans to avoid major national conflict in the future along the line that Gunnar Myrdal had predicted in 1944 in *An American Dilemma*. The substance of this report was included in the 1968 Kerner Commission on Civil Disorders report presented to President Lyndon B. Johnson, that the country was moving in opposite directions, one white and rich, the other black and poor.

Following the crisis caused by the desegregation order in Little Rock, Arkansas, in 1957, the need for congressional action was dramatized by the Montgomery, Alabama, bus boycott two years earlier. Congress responded by enacting in 1957 a Civil Rights Act, which was the first civil rights legislation since the ineffective Civil Rights Act of 1875. Although the 1957 Civil Rights Act was not far reaching in its provisions, it clearly indicated that Congress was at last beginning to wake up to its responsibilities. The Kerner Commission also raised serious concerns about the need to protect the civil rights of all people. The Civil Rights Act of 1964, the war on poverty, and the Great Society movement came out of this era of civil rights. This study presents essential elements of this aspect of the African American journey to the promised land in a proper chronological order.

One cannot discuss the struggle of African Americans without taking the plight of Africans into account, and vice versa. The inauguration of the Pan African movement in 1919, consisting of African Americans and Africans, and the conference held in London in 1945 and attended by African Americans and Africans, created a bond that has remained strong to this day. This study puts a comparative perspective of the struggle of the two groups into proper perspective.

ORGANIZATION OF THE STUDY

The organization of this study takes these varied elements of the struggle of African Americans into account to present aspects of their journey to the promised land that are unique to a people struggling for development. To accomplish this objective, Chapter 1 begins with a discussion of the origins of events that began to unfold with the Emancipation Proclamation in 1862, which led to the search for a new identity that African Americans needed to launch their journey to the promised land. Without that new identity it would have been quite difficult to have a clear vision of the direction of that journey. Chapter 2 presents a discussion of the role of the Supreme Court in that journey.

Although, in human experience, history teaches us that people do not always learn from history, nations cannot realistically endeavor to initiate national programs without taking lessons from the past into account. We have heard that those who ignore the lessons of history are condemned to repeat errors of the past. The importance of history is to help form perspectives that are important to future endeavors. In 1954 the *Brown* decision took the *Plessy* decision of 1896 into account in a realistic manner as a definite form of taking history into account.

Chapter 3 discusses the role of leadership among African Americans. It presents Frederick Douglass, Marcus Garvey, Booker T. Washington, Harriet Tubman, and Julian Bond as leaders. All provided effective leadership that was needed for African Americans to arrive in the promised land. Chapter 4 is a discussion of some obstacles to the journey to the promised land to stress the importance of leadership. Chapter 5 is devoted entirely to the leadership role of Martin Luther King, Jr., because he seems to be a unique leader. It concludes with the tragedy of his untimely death in April 1968. Chapter 6 presents a discussion of the civil rights period. Chapter 7 is a comparative discussion of the struggle of African Americans and Africans during the colonial period.

CONCLUSION

Finally, Chapter 8 offers an interpretive perspective of the implications of the saga of the journey to the promised land, from Emancipation to the present. The developments that are presented are critical to a new national approach to the struggle of African Americans for development. The fundamental consideration is: What must the United States do to provide an adequate opportunity for development to African Americans that reflects the conditions of today? The answer demands a formulation of theory, not just for the present, but also for the future, to address critical issues they continue to encounter. It is a sad commentary that in April 1997 a federal court in California ruled that affirmative action—one national program that was designed to promote the development of African Americans—is unconstitutional.

This is where the study of history becomes important. The untimely death of Reconstruction led to a setback that lasted more than a century. It must be remembered that white America has nothing to lose in the pursuit of affirmative action, just as it had nothing to lose in Reconstruction. It is virtually impossible to undertake the task of building a country by resorting to practices of the past that did not yield tangible results in the national interest. In approaching this task from this perspective, the United States can hope to accomplish it well. The author hopes that this study provides some important insights into that task, the journey to the promised land. It is a journey that all Americans must join in to arrive at a national destination.

Preparing for the Journey: The Search for a New Identity

I believe, my friends and fellow citizens, that we are not prepared
for this suffrage. But we can learn. Give a man tools, and in time he
will learn a trade.

Beverly Nash, 1868

THE EFFECT OF THE THIRTEENTH AMENDMENT

The history of the struggle for development of African Americans is a
story of how they initiated change in political, economic, educational,
and social conditions to shape their future and that of the United States.
This struggle in turn determined the course and the rate of their advancement. The purpose of this study is to trace the major developments
of this struggle and how they influenced change in the conditions that
have affected their lives since the Civil War. It will also attempt to present the implications that they had in their education as a major factor
of that struggle. The reaction of white Americans to legal action and
court rulings beginning with the *Dred Scott* case in 1857 on issues that
deeply affected them in terms of that development will also be presented.

On May 29, 1856, during a speech to the first Republican state convention in Illinois, Abraham Lincoln, the principal advocate of the end
of slavery, had observed: "We allow slavery to exist in the slave states,
not because slavery is right or good, but from the necessities of our
union."[1] But that effort was costly. It created bitterness that lasted for
the next century. It brought about a new level of racial hostility un-

matched by any other event in the past. It created political chaos that followed a bitter Civil War that lasted for four terrible years, and resulted in the death of the president himself.

At the outbreak of the Civil War on April 12, 1861,[2] "none of the Confederate States accepted the implied offer of immunity from prosecution if they were to lay down their arms."[3] In 1865, the Thirteenth Amendment was adopted to abolish slavery.[4] It was quite precise in its provision and left no room for doubt as to its intent. It stated, "Neither slavery nor involuntary servitude, except as a punishment for crime whereof the party shall have been duly convicted, shall exist within the United States, or any place subject to their jurisdiction. Congress shall have power to enforce this article by appropriate legislation."[5] The end of slavery was the beginning of events that were destined to make sure that this ancient institution had no place in the future of the country. By this time the entire world had come to recognize that slavery had to go. National leaders in the United States had come to accept the inevitability of the end of slavery in the country. In taking action to end slavery, the United States was nearly 56 years behind the action Britain took in 1807 to end it. Why did the end of slavery in the United States take that long after the British action? That is an interesting question.

The Fourteenth Amendment was adopted to prevent states from depriving persons of "life, liberty, or property without due process of law."[6] On June 13, 1866, a congressional resolution proposed the Fourteenth Amendment, which the secretary of state proclaimed ratified by 30 states on July 28, 1868. This amendment extended citizenship rights to former slaves. On February 26, 1869, the Congress passed a resolution proposing the Fifteenth Amendment, which the secretary of state declared ratified by 29 states on March 30, 1870. This amendment stated, "The right of citizens of the United States to vote shall not be denied or abridged by the United States or by any state on account of race, color, or previous condition of servitude."[7] These three amendments made it possible for the United States to launch Reconstruction, an enormous political, educational, economic, and social undertaking designed to promote the development of African Americans and bring about a change of attitude among the southern states and bring them back into the national reunification. How was the United States going to accomplish this task?

It must be remembered that before slavery came to an end, and before Reconstruction was initiated, some alternative plans had been discussed to deal with the issue of slavery. One possible action that was considered seriously was the possibility of repatriating African Americans to Africa. The issue was first raised in 1823 in the famous Monroe Doctrine of President James Monroe (who served as president of the United States from 1817 to 1825). Although the main thrust of the doctrine was to prohibit European nations from coming to found colonies in the Western Hemisphere, there was a clause indicating that African Americans who had bought their freedom could go back to Africa if they wanted to.[8]

The idea of repatriating African Americans to Africa was supported by a good number of people in high places. Among these were Henry Clay and Abraham Lincoln. During his term of office as president of the United States from 1861 to 1865, Lincoln made an irreconcilable decision to free the slaves. The only question was when he was going to do it. On July 16, 1852, during delivery of a eulogy at Henry Clay's funeral, Lincoln gave a hint of what he was going to do about the question of slavery. He quoted Clay as saying, "There is a moral fitness in the idea of returning to Africa her children whose ancestors have been torn from her by the ruthless hand of fraud and violence. Transported in a foreign land, they will carry back to their native soil the rich fruits of religion, civilization, law and liberty."[9] Although by 1847 some African Americans had moved back to Africa, settled in Liberia, and founded Monrovia as the capital city in honor of James Monroe, the idea of repatriating African Americans to Africa on a large scale did not materialize. African Americans would no longer consider Africa their home any more than white Americans considered Europe theirs.

On September 22, 1862, and taking all factors into consideration, including his conviction that slavery must come to an end immediately, President Lincoln issued a proclamation stating that as of January 1, 1963, "All persons held as slaves within any state or designated party of a state, shall then, thenceforward and forever, be free."[10] Thus began the brutal Civil War that almost destroyed the United States. For four years, the rancor, the brutality, the venom, and the killing became the experience of a nation that was searching for its soul and struggling for survival. When it was all over, both the North and the South had paid a heavy price. The damage to the nation was beyond measure. Thousands of young men had been killed. Property had been destroyed. President Lincoln himself lost his life to an assassin's bullet on April 14, 1865.[11]

One cannot discuss Lincoln's role in these tragic events without discussing that of his counterpart, Jefferson Davis, who served as president of the Confederacy during the Civil War. Like Lincoln, Davis was born in Kentucky, but moved to Mississippi as an infant. His father Sam Davis was a veteran of the Revolutionary War. His brother Joseph became a successful planter by utilizing slave labor. Like most whites in the South, Davis regarded slavery as necessary to sustain the political, social, and economic system that was operating in the United States as a whole. As soon as he was able to understand his world, Davis took the position that any threat to slavery would constitute a serious threat to that system.

In 1845 Davis was elected to the U. S. House of Representative as a Democrat.[12] Like Lincoln, he served only one term. When Lincoln was elected president of the United States, Davis resigned in protest his U.S. Senate seat to which he had been reelected in 1857. He hoped to direct the military forces of the Confederacy and to become a chief spokesman of the southern states on the question of slavery. But destiny would choose a different role for him. The convention that met in Montgomery, Alabama, elected him president of the Confederacy, and Davis took office on February 18, 1861. He was inaugurated four days later on February 22. Davis was relentless in advocating the continuation of slavery. Thus, Lincoln and Davis, two former Kentuckians, brought the two opposing sides of an issue and the country into a new phase of unprecedented conflict, each believing that he was doing the right thing for the good of the country. There was no room for compromise. In this context the Civil War acquired new, dangerous dimensions.

On November 19, 1863, Lincoln tried to capture the significance of the envisioned end of slavery and the costly civil war that was under way. He delivered the famous Gettysburg address, in which he said,

Four score and seven years ago our fathers brought forth on this continent a new nation conceived in liberty and dedicated to the proposition that all men are created equal. Now we are engaged in a great civil war testing whether that nation or any nation so conceived and dedicated will long endure. It is for us the living, rather for us to be dedicated here to the unfinished work which they who fought here have thus so nobly advanced. It is rather for us to be here to be dedicated to the great task remaining before us, that from these honored dead we take increased devotion to that cause for which they gave the last full measure of devotion that we here highly resolved that these dead shall not have died in vain, that this nation under God, shall have a new birth of freedom and that this government of the people, by the people, for the people, shall not perish from the earth.[13]

There is no question that the Gettysburg address stands out as a monument to the national spirit that Lincoln was trying to recapture and sustain, not only for his time, but also for the future. The moral high ground that it created was absolute and undeniable. It made it possible for the nation to see the issue of slavery from its proper perspective and the importance of Lincoln's decision to end it. In spite of the heavy losses the nation suffered during the Civil War, African Americans did not consider repatriation to Africa a viable option. They would rather have problems of race solved in the United States as their permanent homeland. Reconstruction was initiated on that basis. Even Lincoln himself quickly abandoned the idea of repatriation to Africa as an option.

PROGRESS DURING RECONSTRUCTION, 1865—1877

In order to make a thrust for various programs under Reconstruction, Congress needed to pass special legislation. In 1867 a series of laws was enacted under the Reconstruction Act to divide the ten unstructured states into five military districts. A major general commanded each district for purposes of preparing the states under his charge for return to the Union. This was done by registering voters. Election boards would register all adult male African Americans and any white Americans who took a loyalty oath to the United States. In the ten southern states[14] it was estimated that there were 703,000 African Americans and 627,000 white Americans registered. Because African Americans were recently in servitude, most of them were illiterate. The aim of these actions was to protect the interests of African Americans and to recreate the spirit of national unity. However, the task of trying to educate them presented a formidable challenge. To compound the problem, southern states ignored the spirit of Reconciliation which the country was trying to extend to them. Instead they enacted their own state or local laws such as Black Codes, which were designed to restore the essential elements of slavery in various forms.

In March 1866 the Congress passed the first Civil Rights Act to counteract the Black Codes. This legislation also tried to prevent southern states from discriminating against African Americans in any way. But President Andrew Johnson, who served as president from 1865 to 1869, vetoed the bill, arguing that it would place too many restrictions on the ability of southern states in discharging their constitutional responsibility. However, Congress overrode the veto and the legislation became law in accordance with the provision of the U.S. Constitution.[15] The congressional elections of 1866 were decisive in giving Republicans an overwhelming majority. This victory gave the radical Republicans more power to introduce Reconstruction programs they believed were consistent with Lincoln's ideas.

With more than two-thirds majority in Congress, radical Republicans quickly moved to put Reconstruction programs in place. In 1867 they passed two pieces of legislation that some people concluded were unconstitutional. The Tenure of Office Act prevented the president from dismissing federal officials, including cabinet members, without the Senate's consent. This measure was aimed at limiting the action that President Johnson was likely to take because he was a Democrat who disagreed with Republicans on Reconstruction programs. The Command of the Army Act also prohibited the president from issuing orders to the army except through the commanding general, who would not be removed from office without the Senate's consent. Both the officials and the army were important because Congress intended to use them in implementing their Reconstruction programs. By 1868 radical Republicans set out to punish their political enemy, President Andrew Johnson himself. He had given grounds for such action by removing Secretary of War Edwin M. Stanton in violation of the Tenure of Office Act. Stanton, who was appointed attorney general by President Buchanan in 1860, was named secretary of war by President Lincoln. Stanton and Johnson disagreed on a number of issues relative to Reconstruction programs.

Taking advantage of the conflict between Congress and the president, southern states imposed serious disabilities on African Americans with respect to ownership of property, legal and constitutional rights, and education.[16] In 1868 President Johnson's general amnesty proclamation resulted in the charges of treason being dropped against Jefferson Davis,[17] president of the Confederate States. Some politicians from the North demanded that the leaders of the Confederacy be punished by terms of imprisonment or even death.

Under this plan Davis and top officials in his administration were arrested. But they were never brought to trial because northern authorities could find no legal grounds for putting them on trial. Besides, few Americans supported the idea of revenge. Most military leaders in the South could not be arrested because they were under military parole. However, the federal authorities executed one Confederate military official, Henry Wirz, commander of Andersonville prison in Georgia, where 12,000 Union soldiers had perished.

The Civil Rights Act of 1875 sought to give the freed slaves greater rights as citizens. President Ulysses Simpson Grant, who served from 1869 to 1877, indicated that he was committed to giving effect to all programs carried out under the Reconstruction. However, his words did not match his actions. He did not think that seeking to achieve social equality was an objective of carrying out these programs Grant explained the reason for his thinking: "Social equality is not a subject to be legislated upon, nor shall I ask that anything be done to advance the social status of the colored man, except to give him a fair chance to develop whatever good there is in him, give him access to the schools."[18] This attitude of the federal leadership sent a clear message to southern politicians that the federal authorities were not serious about Reconstruction programs. Steadily the southern states began to weaken the spirit of Reconstruction, knowing that there was little enthusiasm among federal authorities for its success.

HAYES AND THE DEATH OF RECONSTRUCTION

During the presidency of Rutherford B. Hayes, from 1877 to 1881, the question of Reconstruction, as a basis of African American progress, hung in the balance. Southern politicians were doing everything in their power to weaken Reconstruction and to create dissension among leaders of federal programs. Following the bitterly contested presidential election of 1876, Hayes was picked as compromise candidate over the issue of Reconstruction programs in the South. In order to be elected, Hayes needed support from the South. For this reason he simply let the hold on the South go when he promised to restore to the South control over its own political process and destiny. Hayes stated, "I am sincerely anxious to use every legitimate influence in favor of honest and efficient local self-government as the true resource of those States for the promotion of the contentment and prosperity of their citizens."[19]

In political exchange for support of the South, Hayes was made to believe that African Americans would be better off if the South were left alone to solve its own racial problems. These, and many other similar events, attitudes, and political views of post–Civil War developments had serious implications on the development of education for African Americans during Reconstruction and after. The unfortunate pattern of events that shaped future developments appeared to have been set during the Hayes administration. For Hayes to formulate his "let alone" policy was a recognition that the South was increasingly becoming an important factor in national politics. No longer was the North able to use legislative action to influence the terms of political progress as was the case during and the period immediately following the Civil War. Therefore, from the administration of Johnson in 1865 to the end of that of Hayes in 1881, approach to Reconstruction programs showed southern whites that those who tried to carry them out were not fully committed to their success. They therefore decided to initiate a strategy to reverse the programs at the earliest opportune moment.

The South, far from having "repented" of its sin, became more deeply entrenched in its concept and philosophy of black people as inferior beings who did not deserve equal treatment as citizens of any country. This philosophy was put into practice in Africa when Europeans were founding colonies there. The northern national leaders were vaguely trying to express the idea of racial equality. No national leader ever hoped to be elected without appealing for the support of the South, and the South could not give that support as long as the appeal was made on rights for African Americans. It was clear that the South intended to use its new form of power and influence to its advantage.

The reaction of the South to the end of slavery and the impact of the Thirteenth Amendment came in two forms: adopting a new attitude, and taking action to give effect to that attitude. The South adopted this attitude toward what the North was doing to bring about change and toward what African Americans were doing under Reconstruction programs. What exactly did the North do to bring about this attitude by the South? As early as 1862, the New England Freedmen's Aid Society sent some 70 teachers to Port Royal, Virginia, to teach African Americans to play a different role as free people from the one they played as slaves. At the same time the American Missionary Society, which was founded as an abolitionist society in 1846, remained quite active during the Civil War by sending teachers to the South to meet the educational needs of freed slaves. By 1866 the society had sent nearly 400 teachers to different parts of the South. By this time there were nearly 80 organizations and associations carrying on educational work among African Americans in the South. The Freedmen's Aid Society of the Methodist Episcopal Church opened 60 schools and sent 124 teachers, spending $60,000 during the first two years of its operations.[20]

The attitude of the South toward this enormous undertaking was quite hostile. Most whites in the South felt that the people from the North were carrying out this work, not because they wanted to promote the development of African Americans, but because they sought to punish the South and humiliate the whites further. The number of organizations and associations based in the North that carried out work in the South suggested to southern whites that they were motivated by a desire to inflict as much harm as possible so that the South would never have another chance to rise up again and cause another national conflict. Most whites in the South resented the action that the Freedmen's Bureau was taking to fulfill its functions.

The question may now be asked: What did African Americans achieve during Reconstruction? Because Reconstruction programs were designed to give effect to the Thirteenth Amendment, the Congress created the Freedmen's Bureau to coordinate programs intended to promote the development of African Americans. The bureau furnished supplies to destitute African Americans, supervised contracts between freedmen and their employers, and protected their rights. It also sought to help them in other ways, such as social and community development, building clinics and schools. General Oliver Otis Howard was appointed commissioner and director of the bureau.[21] An assistant commissioner was named for each of the Confederate states. In 1866 Congress extended the bureau's power to allow it to continue its work until 1872, spending over $17 million.

Indeed, the bureau operated with funds obtained from the sale of lands and other property sold or confiscated from white owners. The bureau relocated 30,000 former slaves in areas of the country where they were able to acquire land. It opened hospitals and other forms of services. It kept a record of the number of teachers and schools under its charge. These records indicate that in 1867 there were nearly 1,000 teachers in schools of African Americans in the South. By the following year there were more than 2,900 schools. By 1869 there were more than 9,000 teachers under the bureau's jurisdiction.[22] This development did not sit well with southern whites because they believed that the North was doing this to destroy their heritage. What made the southern whites even more angry was the fact that African Americans fully cooperated with any program that was initiated from the North on their behalf.

However, Democrats in the South severely criticized the bureau's work, arguing that the Republicans were doing this not to honor Lincoln's memory and to promote the advancement of African Americans, but to set African Americans against their former white masters. When Congress terminated the bureau in January 1872, it decided to extend the work it had been doing in promoting education among African Americans because it considered this aspect of their life crucial to their development.[23] When Congress decided not to continue to support the bureau, the American Missionary Association suffered severe limitations in its major function of educating freed African Americans in the South. Throughout the South, African Americans were going through a difficult period of change and readjustment from slaves to free citizens. The change was not easy. However, African Americans looked to the future rather than to the past. Their participation in national economic, social, and political activity took new forms. A new kind of relationship was emerging between African Americans and white Americans. There was "anxious locomotion among Negroes changing homes, moving luggage, hunting places,"[24] and planning for the future. The journey to the promised land was gathering speed.

But African Americans of 1865 were confronted with one serious problem: they were illiterate, and so they were badly exploited by the white businessmen, farmers, and landlords, for whom they worked. This why African Americans felt they had to earn the right to new living conditions. This was not easy to get used to, since slavery had not provided them with the necessary experience to exercise this responsibility. Therefore, sooner than later African Americans realized that to secure the bright future promised by their newly found freedom, they had to attend seriously to the business of different forms of their development, including education. But subsequent events would show that the southern whites were equally determined to deny them this right.

In adopting a hostile attitude toward the response of African Americans to initiatives from the North, southern whites responded in philosophical terms. The fundamental question they asked was: What did the kind of freedom the North was promoting for African Americans mean to the society in the South? They understood that since Emancipation, the North had promoted the idea that African Americans were equal to whites because they were no longer their property. Southern whites concluded that if this was what freedom meant, then it could only mean a loss of status for whites. With support from the North, African Americans could dominate the South. This domination could only become real by retaliation for former injustice.[25]

REACTION OF THE SOUTH

Reaction of the South came in form of action that whites believed must be taken to sustain three operational principles: (1) African Americans must be constrained, (2) they must be controlled, and (3) they must be dominated through segregation.[26] To fulfill these three objectives the South began to pass legislation that imposed the burden of servitude on African Americans. From 1865 to 1866 every state in the Confederacy except Tennessee passed legislation imposing the infamous Black Codes, which had varying degrees of severity. For example, they took away the rights of African Americans to own property. They prohibited any form of relationships between whites and blacks. They imposed new restrictions on blacks' right to vote.

Any African American who married a white person was guilty of a criminal offense. They took away the right of African Americans to serve on juries, to bear arms, to hold public office, and to sign contracts that had not been approved by the white establishment.[27] Henry J. Perkinson suggests the severity of the Black Codes saying, "Mississippi authorized any person to arrest and return to his employer any Negro who quit before the expiration of his contracted term of labor. Georgia warned that all persons strolling about in idleness would be put in chain gangs and contracted out to employers."[28] The fact that African Americans were no longer the property of the white man made them more vulnerable to strategies to hurt them as they did not have any means to protect themselves. The formation of the Ku Klux Klan (KKK) in 1868 shows the extent to which white Americans were determined to put African Americans in their proper place. The rules of the game had changed considerably, affecting the conduct of the journey to the promised land.

What made southern whites more determined to limit the advancement of African Americans was that although education for them had received some attention before the Civil War, it began to take formal shape during the Civil War itself. E. F. Frazier concluded, "As the Union armies advanced into the South, they were faced with the problem of caring for the freed slaves who fled from the plantations and sought refuge in the army camps."[29] The runaway slaves, now freed people, were protected by the Union army, put to work, and were provided with food. The American Missionary Association established day schools for them and hired teachers on a larger scale than before, mainly from the North.

But the South became tensely apprehensive over African Americans getting any form of education because some earlier African American leaders had advocated violence as a means to gain their freedom. These include Gabriel Prasser who, in 1800, planned a revolt and an attack of whites in Virginia; Denmark Vesey who, in 1822, had recruited about 9,000 followers to plot against whites in South Carolina; Nat Turner and his followers who, in 1831 killed a number of whites, including Turner's master and his family. So when moves were made to enable former slaves to acquire some formal education, southern whites were sadly reminded of these acts of violence by African Americans. Southern whites concluded that if African Americans committed these acts as slaves, what more would they do as freed and educated citizens? Southern whites also concluded that they would take the law into their own hands. This was why the South was not too interested in the educational development of African Americans.

The period of African American search for identity began during slavery. As early as 1857 the Supreme Court found itself faced with an unusual case. Dred Scott, a slave, was taken by his master from his place of residence in Missouri into Wisconsin, a free territory. On his return to Missouri Scott brought suit against his master for his freedom. He argued that the trip outside the slave area had actually liberated him. In a 7–2 decision, the Supreme Court ruled that because Scott was a slave he had no right to bring suit against his master, that a slave did not become free by merely going outside the slave area, that Congress and territorial legislatures could not stop slavery in a territory that wished to continue it.[30] However, the clouds of the Civil War were gathering rapidly across the horizon of national changing conditions, and only a few years later was the whole issue of slavery fully resolved. For a slave to bring suit against a white man, and for the Court to find time to hear the case, was a remarkable degree of progress by African Americans. The importance of the *Dred Scott* case underlined, among others, the urgency of the need for education among African Americans.

In spite of the many difficulties that confronted them during the post–Civil War period, African Americans were able to make substantial progress in social and political life during Reconstruction. Their participation in political activity of the country was a revolutionary event. Not a single African American had voted in a southern election since 1835, when only a few states had allowed some free African Americans to vote. Suddenly, 703,000 Negroes out of 1,330,000 persons who qualified to vote under the Reconstruction Act of 1867 could now vote. However, because 90 percent of them were illiterate,[31] many were misled by whites who sought to reverse the gains they had made. However, African Americans saw their shortcomings and were determined to overcome them.

In 1868 Beverly Nash, an illiterate former slave in the South Carolina constitutional convention, put it more clearly when he said, "I believe, my friends and fellow citizens, we are not prepared for this suffrage, but we can learn. Give a man tools and in time he will learn a trade. We may not understand it at the start, but in time we shall learn to do our duty."[32] Nash was certainly speaking for many. The tools that African Americans wanted were in the form of education. By this time African Americans were convinced that they were American citizens who were entitled to the rights previously exclusively enjoyed by whites. Nash's view and hope may have been an indication that African Americans had found the means with which to create a new identity for themselves. The journey to the promised land would be based on that identity.

While this was taking place, African American politicians of Reconstruction took positions of leadership. Many of them were ministers and teachers. Some were better trained than whites for the positions they held during Reconstruction. J. C. Gibbs, became Florida secretary of state from 1868 to 1872, and later became superintendent of schools in that state. Gibbs established Florida's first public school system. He had been a graduate of the famous Dartmouth College. R. B. Elliot was a prominent South Carolina politician. Born in Massachusetts, Elliot was educated at Eton College, Britain. He read French, German, Italian, Spanish and became a distinguished speaker. J. T. Rapier received his education in Canada and had a powerful following in his native Alabama (later the power base of George Wallace). Eloquent P. B. Pinchback attained the highest state office of any Reconstruction African American, when he served as acting governor of Louisiana, where he led the fight for universal suffrage. J. J. Wright became a distinguished lawyer from Pennsylvania and served as associate justice of the South Carolina Supreme Court. B. K. Bruce served as a U.S. Senator from Mississippi between 1875 and 1881. Rev. H. R. Revels, from Mississippi, filled the Senate seat that was held by Jefferson Davis, president of the Confederacy. Other African Americans of varying abilities served as lieutenant governors, state treasurers, justices of the peace, and sheriffs. These examples demonstrate a very important point, that those who, in 1997, opposed affirmative action have no proper understanding of this historical background.

These individuals exerted themselves and a had tremendous influence on the development of education for African Americans. Both races came to recognize what education could do to raise a people from the dark caves of ignorance to the highest level of the light of national service! On the one hand African Americans gradually recognized that for them to get on the road to the promised land, to make a better contribution, to live a life of meaning and purpose they had to exert themselves in every way possible. On the other hand white Americans equally recognized that education for African Americans would be a lethal weapon with which to threaten the privileged position that they had enjoyed for so long. That is why they were determined to do everything in their power to put a stop to this development.

Among the congressmen, many African Americans won respect for their diligence, intelligence, and common sense, coupled with a high sense of goodwill: R. Smalls, self-educated African American, who served five terms in Congress as a member from South Carolina; J. R. Lynch, the speaker of the Mississippi House at age 24, who later became a friend of President Grant; J. W. Menard, a congressman from Louisiana, who showed no anger when whites refused to seat him—all serve as good examples of goodwill among Reconstruction African American leadership, which showed moderation and progress. They also showed a surprising, "amazing lack of bitterness towards their former masters. They often supported efforts to have the government remove political restrictions on leading former confederates."[33]

This was a tremendous progress, and one would have hoped that the stream of this progress would continue. But unfortunately this progress was not to last; the gains acquired were not to continue. The national political events of 1876 set the clock back for African Americans with Hayes as president. The federal government washed its hands of the enormous problems that African Americans had to face. The South now became free to do as it pleased with them. Then in 1878 Congress went on to pass "legislation that forbade the use of troops in matters relating to elections."[34] This took away the protection of voting rights from African Americans.

In 1894 the federal government ended all funds that were used to pay special federal marshals and supervisors of elections. The process of disfranchisement of African Americans was then set in motion. The educational opportunity that they had utilized to advance themselves, the social and political rate of progress that they had maintained, now began to erode away faster than they had gained them. One by one the southern states deprived them of their advancement. They knew that the federal government found itself in a position where it could not do anything to stop the erosion of rights of African Americans in American society.

However, the African American search for identity brought a realization that they had to secure education to enable them to secure in turn the rights of citizenship. After the failure of Reconstruction legislature to provide equal opportunity for education, philanthropic organizations undertook to provide the desperately needed education for African Americans. Soon after Reconstruction came to an end, and federal troops were withdrawn, white supremacy was once again restored and the opportunity for education for African Americans was severely restricted as was the opportunity for political and social activity. Most schools for African Americans were taught by white teachers, who, because they had some influence in their community, were able to obtain local sympathy and some support for those schools. But as time went on, it became less socially acceptable for whites to teach in African American schools.

Therefore, teaching fell to the poorly trained African American teachers. This in turn had most unfortunate influential people of the community sharply divided. The schools became the prey of unscrupulous politicians and the object of bitterness and prejudice. They became badly discriminated against in the distribution of school funds. The school buildings received no proper attention, so they simply became shabby and totally unsuitable and unsafe to occupy.[35]

In short, with the Hayes administration, education for African Americans was dying a slow, painful death. Fourteen southern states and the District of Columbia passed laws that required separate schools for white and black children. The journey to the promised land was being halted in painful ways. A number of states sugarcoated segregated school policies by providing for what they called "equal" facilities in the two systems, including the notion of "equal" fund distribution. It would be unrealistic for anyone to believe that after fighting to stop equality in education as a prerequisite of equality in society, the southern whites were now ready to accept African Americans as their social equals.

Indeed, the South did not live by these criteria. Distinction based on race permeated every level of national life. For African Americans even to hope that someday they would enjoy equal treatment would also be unrealistic. This is why, by 1898, per capita expenditure for education of African Americans was still a very small fraction of the amount spent for white children.[36] The only criterion that the South considered was the preservation of the social status quo. For members of the white community in the South, maintaining this status quo was believed to be in the best interest of the African Americans themselves, and they would resent and oppose anything was calculated to change things. Even change in the way of financing education was considered to have a detrimental effect on what was considered to be a proper relationships between the races. Table 1.1 shows how these funds were distributed during this period.

During this time some states like Florida passed laws that made it an offense for any community to enroll both black and white students in the same school. It was quite clear that with a segregated school system a new kind of problem was created, especially in the area of black education! The financial burdens of separate school systems, the plight of African American children, the adversities and the odds under which African Americans had to obtain an education for "real life"—had all to remain a pattern, a way of life for African Americans for years to come. The philosophy of separate but equal then became solidly established, and this appeared to be a permanent order of things.

Table 1.1
Distribution of Funds for Education by Race per Child, 1898

State	White school	African American school
Dist. of Columbia	$14.82	$10.64
N.C.	$1.17	$1.07
Florida	$5.92	$2.27

Source: R. E. Potter, *The Stream of American Education* (New York: American Book Company, 1967), p. 350

To alleviate the difficulties imposed on African American education by segregated school systems, some philanthropic organizations, mainly based in the North, tried with some degree of success to give financial support to the African American schools. One example is the Peabody Education Fund, which was established in 1867 by George Peabody, a wealthy Massachusetts merchant and banker. He gave about $3.5 million "to be used in those states which had suffered from the destructive ravages and disastrous consequences of civil war."[37] Mississippi and Florida did not accept these funds because this would provide African Americans with some opportunity for better education, and this would not be in the best interest of whites in the South, although Peabody made provision for using the funds in general educational developments, including education for whites.

African Americans were once again aware that because their education was so vital to their future and that they had to secure it somehow, they just did not lose heart though the odds were heavily against them. For them it was better to struggle along the unbeaten path to the future, rather than look back to the dreadful past and its horrors. They recognized the injustices of the philosophy of the "separate but equal" systems, but they became prepared to make the best of the existing situation. Ten years following the end of the Civil War, schools for African Americans began to get better organized. Colleges and universities for African Americans began to appear all over the country. Although many of these institutions took care of the large part of primary and high school education, their entrance requirements were as high as any college in the nation. These colleges offered a general education program as well as professional, technical, and industrial training, which was badly needed to enable African Americans to acquire the skills that American society needed as a result of the great industrial revolution of the 19th century.

Table 1.2 gives a sample of black colleges founded during this period and later in Alabama, Arkansas, and Delaware. The founding of these colleges was made possible in part by the collective effort of some philanthropic organizations and the federal government. In addition to

Table 1.2

Predominantly Negro Colleges and Universities in Alabama, Arkansas, and Delaware

Institution	Location	Date of Founding	Enrollment in 1967	Type
ALABAMA Alabama A. & N	Normal	1875	1,222	Coed
Albama A. & M. offers a liberal arts and general programs, as well as teacher-preparatory and terminal-occupational training leading to the master's and or second professional degree.				
Alabama State	Montgomery	1874	2,082	Coed
Alabama State offers a liberal arts and general program, as well as teacher-preparatory training leading to the master's and/or second professional degree.				
Daniel Payne Jr. College	Birmingham	1889	312	Coed
Daniel Payne is a two-year college with a three-year professional school.				
Miles College	Birmingham	1907	816	Coed
Miles College offers a liberal arts and general program, as well as teacher-preparatory training leading to the bachelor's and/or first professional degree.				
Oakwood College	Huntsville	1896	410	Coed
Oakwood College has a liberal arts program, and offers A.B. and B.S. degrees.				
Selma University	Selma	1878	224	Coed
Selma University is a junior college and school of religion owned and operated by the Alabama State Baptist Convention.				
Stillman College	Tuscaloosa	1876	522	Coed
Stillman College offers a liberal arts and general program, as well as teacher-preparatory training leading to the bachelor's and/or first professional degree.				
Talladega College	Talladega	1867	413	Coed
Talladega College offers a liberal arts and general program, as well as teacher-preparatory training leading to the bachelor's and/or first professional degree.				

Table 1.2 (*continued*)

Tuskegee Institute	Tuskegee	1881	2,482	Coed

Tuskegee Institute offers a liberal arts and general program, and has a number of professional schools which grant the master's and/or second professional degree.

ARKANSAS Arkansas Agr. Mech. & Normal College	Pine Bluff	1873	2,490	Coed

Arkansas A., M. & N. offers a liberal arts and general program, as well as terminal-occupational training leading to the bachelor's and/or first professional degree.

Philander Smith College	Little Rock	1868	614	Coed

Philander Smith College offers a liberal arts and general program, as well as teacher-preparatory and terminal-occupational training leading to the bachelor's and/or first professional degree.

Shorter College	Little Rock	1886	216	Coed

Shorter College, a two-year college with a three-year professional school, offers a liberal arts and general program leading to the bachelor's and/or first professional degree.

DELAWARE Delaware State	Dover	1891	788	Coed

Delaware State offers a liberal arts and general program, as well as teacher-preparatory training leading to the bachelor's and/or first professional degree.

Gibbs Jr. College	St. Petersburg	1957	762	Coed

Gibbs Jr. College offers a liberal arts and general program, as well as terminal-occupational training in a two-year college-level curriculum. No degrees are granted.

Hampton Jr. College	Ocala	1958	375	Coed

Hampton Junior College offers a liberal arts and general program, as well as teacher-preparatory and terminal-occupational training. No degrees are granted.

Johnson Jr. College	Leesburg	1962	282	

Table 1.2 (*continued*)

Johnson Jr. College offers a liberal arts and general program, as well as terminal-occupational training. No degrees are granted.				
Lincoln Jr. College	Fort Pierce	1960	122	Coed
Lincoln Jr. College offers a liberal arts and general program, as well as terminal-occupational training. No degrees are granted.				
Roosevelt Jr. College	West Palm	1958	183	Coed
Roosevelt Jr. College offers a liberal arts and general program, as well as teacher-preparatory and terminal-occupational training. No degrees are granted.				
Rosenwald Jr. College	Panama City	1958	113	Coed
Rosenwald Jr. College offers a liberal arts and general program, as well as teacher-preparatory and terminal-occupational training. No degrees are granted.				

George Peabody, Andrew Carnegie gave $10 million in 1902 toward African American schools and education. General Education Board, enriched by John D. Rockefeller, the Rosenwald Fund, and the Anna T. Jeanes Fund all played a major role in the founding of many African American schools. J. S. Roucek and T. Tierman concluded that as the 19th century wore on, some groups started to emphasize the need for more adequately trained ministers, teachers, or tradesmen at many schools regarded as normal, institute, academy, seminary, college, or university. Many of these schools survived, but some changed their names or purpose, and others were absorbed by the states. However, some lived as landmark institutions.[38]

Roucek and Kierman also concluded that the literacy rate was improving fast as a result of self-determination among African Americans, as shown by the following figures, and not due any significant action by the whites: in 1860 literacy was 5 percent, by 1890 it had increased to 60 percent, by 1910 it had gone up to 70 percent, and in 1940 it had gone up to 92 percent.[39]

H. A. Ploski and R. C. Brown concluded in 1967 that the 30 years between 1860 and 1890 saw a revolutionary change in African American education as a reflection of the importance that black Americans themselves attached to education as a means to secure their full citizenship rights, granted to them by the Fourteenth and Fifteenth Amendments.[40] But this remarkable progress was short-lived. The whites were gaining ground in their effort to put an end to African American social and political advancement, although the number of African American institutions of learning increased. The unfortunate events of the 1876 national politics played into the hands of white southern strategy.

The Democratic candidate for president, Samuel Tilden of New York, was believed to be the winner in the election until Republicans in some southern states accused the Democrats of intimidating black voters to give Tilden a victory margin. A complicated, confused investigation was then conducted and in the end the Democrats agreed to let Republicans introduce subsidies for southern railroads, a southern postmaster general, to allow removal of the federal troops from the South, and, most important of all, not to interfere in the manner in which the South would handle the Negro question. This political deal has become known as the compromise of 1877. To fulfill his part of the deal, Hayes withdrew federal troops from the South and Reconstruction thus came to a close.

This tragic development set a new stage for the South to strip African Americans of their gained and earned advancement. Southern whites, who now had a free hand to do as they pleased, now turned to violence as a machinery to achieve this end. First, several schemes were introduced to make it harder or impossible for African Americans to claim or cast their votes in any election. Changes in the polling places, complicated ballots, long and difficult literacy tests, and physical obstruction, were all used to discourage blacks from voting.

As northern and federal support for the education of African Americans declined, violence of major proportions increased. During a visit to the southern whites in 1880, Hayes indicated that the federal government might "let it alone" to determine the nature and course of development for African Americans. The whites cheered Hayes wildly, and labeled him with yells of "let alone" wherever he went. Hayes seemed to enjoy it, as this was how he had come to power. Yet, by the end of his administration in 1881, Hayes regretted that the South, when "let alone," would never seek to give support to general development schemes among African Americans. It was too late, the damage had been done, and his "let alone" policy set a tragic pattern that was to cost the nation heavily in its efforts to change over many years to come.

Nearly a hundred years had to pass before the tragic pattern was changed. By the time of his death in 1893, Hayes might not have known the extent of his damage and disservice to African American advancement, his harm to the national cause and mission to bring the two races true freedom and equality—rights so greatly cherished that Lincoln chose the passage to national conflict to bring them about to all Americans.

The setbacks that blacks suffered during the Hayes "let alone" policy were a signal that more was to come. Tennessee became the birthplace of the Ku Klux Klan, the dreadful organization that was to cause so much terror and suffering among African Americans until about 1968. S. W.

Webster sums up the activities of the KKK and other similar organizations: these groups were usually secret societies and had as one of their prime goals the subjection of African Americans and non-Christians. The most commonly used means of oppression included murder, physical violence, intimidation, arson, and ostracism in business or social affairs.[41]

These organizations were not restricted to the South. Most states made some effort to control the activities of such organizations as the KKK, but they were not very successful. The inability of the states of the South to deal with terrorist organizations led to the passage of federal legislation designed to halt such anti-civil rights activity as was taking place in 1893 leading to the *Plessy* decision three years later. The main goal of organizations such as the KKK was the preservation of white supremacy. To do this they realized that they would have to prevent blacks, who were quite a number in most states of the South, from voting.

The U.S. Congress, seriously weakened by the Hayes "let alone" policy, appeared powerless to act decisively and promptly, though it tried. In 1890 Congress considered two seemingly important bills that were designed to restore the vote to African Americans by seeking to improve public education so that more black voters would qualify for the deliberately-made-difficult literacy tests. The second bill was meant to supervise national elections, so that anti-Negro frauds would be reduced. These bills had the support of President Benjamin Harrison, who served as president from 1889 to 1893, and appeared to have a good chance of success.

However, aware of the power and influence they now exercised, the southern politicians reacted violently and with great bitterness against such legislation. Senator James Z. George of Mississippi spoke against the bill in very strong terms and tone that seemed to represent the southern attitude toward African Americans in general. Said George, "If you will not stop this 'Force Bill' then, remembering the history and traditions of our race, we give you notice of your certain and assured failure, it will never come to pass in Mississippi, in South Carolina, or in any other state in the South, that the neck of the white race shall be under the foot of the Negro, or the Mongolian or any created being."[42]

This threat of possible renewed sectional violence, as well as a number of other political problems, sadly led to the defeat of both bills and, despite campaign pledges, Harrison and the Republicans were forced to abandon the fight for the constitutional rights of the blacks. In 1891 Mississippi had shown disregard and contempt for federal intervention and interference in its state affairs by calling a special constitutional convention for the sole purpose of disenfranchising the state's remaining black voters.

A new amendment to its constitution required that African American voters pay a poll tax of $2.00 as a condition and price for voting and refused the vote to any African American accused (not convicted) of some minor criminal offense and those who could not read or interpret a section of the Mississippi constitution. Since the literacy test was always administered by a white judge, it could be used to disqualify educated blacks without embarrassing or reducing the rolls of the uneducated, ignorant white people. Soon other Southern states followed the Mississippi example.

By 1900 the U.S. Congress was so silent, so weak, so afraid to do anything that the southern congressmen openly boasted on the floor of Congress about their unlawful, unconstitutional, and criminal nations. Benjamin Pitchfork of South Carolina stated in the Senate that his state had disenfranchised all the Negroes it could. He went on, "We have done our best. We have scratched our heads to find out how we could eliminate the last one of them. We stiffed ballot boxes. We shot them. We are not ashamed of it."[43]

Pitchfork was not joking, he meant what he said. While Congress failed to act, blacks were being lynched at the rate of three per week during the last two decades of the 19th century. Between 1882 and 1900 alone, some 3,011 blacks were lynched in the nation. Behind all this despicable cruelty and senseless violence was a white desire to put the black people back in their original place as second-class citizens. But African Americans were fully aware that although fate had seemed to turn against them, someday they would overcome these imposed difficulties.

While this was happening some black people began to wonder whether there was room for them in the white American society. If the U.S. Congress could not give them protection under its laws, where could they turn to? They were more determined than ever to save themselves from destruction, from returning to a new form of slavery, from second-class citizenship. They looked to the future more boldly than ever before. But they also recognized that the path to this cause would be slow, costly, and painful, but it seemed the only path to follow on their long march to the promised land.

SUMMARY AND CONCLUSION

The purpose of this chapter was to present some developments that followed the conclusion of the Civil War in 1865 and how they affected the position of African Americans. Among these events were the Fourteenth Amendment in 1868, the Fifteenth Amendment in 1870, and the Civil Rights Act of 1875. These three important actions initiated by Congress were meant to give African Americans a more secure feeling as citizens and greater protection. The Fourteenth Amendment states:

All persons born or naturalized in the United States and subject to the jurisdiction thereof, are citizens of the United States and of the State wherein they reside. No state shall make or enforce any law which shall abridge the privileges or immunities of citizens of they United States, nor shall any state deprive any personal of life, liberty or property, without due process of law, nor deny to any person within its jurisdiction the equal protection of the law.[44]

Then, the Civil Rights Act of 1875 stated:

All persons within the jurisdiction of the United States shall be entitled to the full and equal enjoyment of the accommodations, advantages, and privileges of inns, public conveyances on land or water, theaters and other places of public amusement, subject only to the conditions and limitations established by law, and applicable alike to citizens of every race and color, regardless of any previous conditions of servitude.[45]

These official actions combined with the determination of African Americans themselves to give them the means to search for a new identity. But these laws proved ineffective as the violence described in this chapter increased toward African Americans after 1877. Therefore, what purpose did their existence serve? They reinforced the determination of African Americans to intensify their search for a new identity. They knew that the federal government was not totally able to enforce its own laws, they knew that more suffering was to come. Nonetheless they were prepared to try to change the course of events in the things that deeply affected their lives. Their search for an identity lay in the kind of environment that emerged from these conditions.

Meanwhile, African Americans were being subjected to other forms of psychological, social, physical, and economic humiliation. The Jim Crow movement was now having a great influence on the attitudes of whites on African Americans in general, every effort was being made to portray African Americans as creatures less than human beings, with less intelligence and less ability than whites. But still they looked forward to the day when they would arrive in the promised land. In order to make that journey a success they needed to carve a new identity that would provide inspiration and courage to face the formidable obstacles they were certain to encounter. This was not an easy task. It was not an easy task for the children of Israel. It is never easy for any group of people, but it is a journey that every group of people in the position that African Americans found themselves in must undertake.

NOTES

1. John Gabriel Hunt, *The Essential Abraham Lincoln* (New York: Random House, 1993), p. 105.

2. Historians have not reached agreement about the causes of the war. Some say that it was caused by the issue of slavery. Others say that it was caused by differences in social status of the industrial North and agricultural South. But they agree that it started on April 12, 1861, when Confederate troops attacked Fort Sumter; but President Lincoln did not respond until April 15 when he called for troops. It came to an end officially on May 26, 1865, when the last Confederate troops surrendered, following General Robert Lee's surrender to General Ulysses Grant on April 9, and President Lincoln's assasination on April 14.

3. Richard Bardolph, *The Civil Rights Record: Black Americans and the Law, 1949–1970* (New York: Thomas Crowell, 1970), p. 20.

4. The record shows that the secretary of state proclaimed the amendment ratified on December 18, 1865, when it was ratified by 27 states; Kentucky and Mississippi rejected it.

5. Pathfinder Publications, *The Constitution of the United States with the Declaration of Independence* (Boston: Pathfinder, 1973), p. 33.

6. Ibid., p. 34.

7. Ibid., p. 35.

8. In 1845 President James Polk referred to the Monroe Doctrine in a dispute that broke out between Britain and the United States over Oregon. In 1895 President Grover Cleveland used the doctrine to threaten to declare war on Britain if the British government did not agree to arbitration over dispute with Venezuela. Both President Theodore Roosevelt and President Woodrow Wilson used the doctrine to protect American interests in Latin America from interference from European nations.

9. Hunt, *The Essential Abraham Lincoln*, p. 69. One wonders how Clay would have reacted to the brutal civil war that ravaged Liberia in 1994.

10. Ibid., p. 279.

11. History says that John Wilkes Booth entered Lincoln's private box at about 10 p.m. at Ford's Theater, where he was watching a play. "Our American Cousins" on that day and shot the president in the head. Lincoln died the next day. April 15. Booth jumped on the stage and shouted, "Sic semper tyrannis!" (Thus always to tyrants). The audience thought this was part of the play. Booth, who was believed to be mentally imbalanced, was killed in a shoot-out with the police in Bowling Green, Virginia, a few days later.

12. Davis held other important positions in both the U.S. government and the state of Mississippi. For example, in 1853 President Franklin Pierce named him secretary for war. In 1860 he actively supported Stephen A. Douglas's candidacy for president of the United States.

13. Hunt, *The Essential Abraham Lincoln*, p. 300. History says that the next day, November 20, Lincoln received no less than five requests for hand-written copies of the two-minute speech. Indeed, the speech has gone down in history as one of the great speeches of all time. The quote here is not the full text of the speech.

14. These were Virginia, Tennessee, North Carolina, South Carolina, Georgia, Alabama, Mississippi, Arkansas, Louisiana, and Florida.

15. Andrew Johnson was a Democrat from Tennessee. He wanted to carry out Lincoln's program, but he faced a Republican Congress controlled by men who wanted to punish the South. Congress passed a series of legislation over his veto,

including the Civil Rights Bill of 1866. The conflict between Johnson and Congress eventually led to his impeachment on February 24, 1868.

16. Bardolph, *The Civil Rights Record*, p. 25.

17. In 1881 Davis published *The Rise and Fall of the Confederate Government* as an answer to his critics.

18. Bardolph, *The Civil Rights Record*, p. 30.

19. Ibid., p. 31.

20. Henry J. Perkinson, *The Imperfect Panacea: American Faith in Education, 1865–1990* (New York: McGraw-Hill, 1991), p. 14.

21. Howard University, a predominantly black school founded in Washington, DC, in 1867, is named after him. Founded by an act of Congress, Howard University is funded by the federal government. Its entrance requirements were "nearly equal to the smaller New England colleges" (*Report of the U.S. Commissioner of Education for 1901*, p. 833).

22. Perkinson, *The Imperfect Panacea*, p. 15.

23. Robert E. Potter, *The Stream of American Education* (New York: American Book Company, 1967), p. 352.

24. R. S. Henry, *The History of Reconstruction* (Gloucester, MA: Free Press, 1963), p. 143.

25. This is a typical response among a group of people who have inflicted harm on another group. It was a typical reaction to the end of colonialism in Africa. The latest example is what happened in South Africa in 1994, when the notorious system of apartheid was forced to an end. Whites feared retaliation by Africans.

26. Perkinson, *The Imperfect Panacea*, p. 17.

27. Ibid., p. 18.

28. Ibid., p. 17.

29. E. F. Frazier, *Bourgeoise: The Rise of the New Black Middle Class* (New York: The Free Press, 1965), p. 61.

30. S. W. Webster, *The Education of Black Americans* (Berkeley: University of California Press, 1974), p. 11.

31. R. E. Dennis, *The Black People of America* (New York: McGraw-Hill, 1970), p. 139.

32. Ibid., p. 140.

33. Ibid., p. 143.

34. Webster, *The Education of Black Americans*, p. 17.

35. Potter, *The Stream of American Education*, p. 349.

36. Ibid., p. 350.

37. Ibid., p. 341.

38. J. S. Rouceck, and T. Kierman, *The Negro Impact on Western Civilization* (New York: Philosophical Library, 1970), p. 207.

39. Ibid., p. 217.

40. H. A. Ploski and R. C. Brown, *The Negro Almanac* (New York: Bellewether Publishing Corporation, 1967), p. 487.

41. Webster, *The Education of Black Americans*, p. 14.

42. Dennis, *Black People of America*, p. 168.

43. Ibid., p. 19.

44. Bardolph, *The Civil Rights Record*, p. 49.

45. Ibid., p. 55.

2

The Courts and the Search for a Passage

We conclude that in the field of public education the doctrine of "separate but equal" has no place.
                        Earl Warren, Chief Justice, U.S. Supreme Court, 1954

THE SUPREME COURT IN PERSPECTIVE

It is not possible to discuss any measure of success that African Americans achieved in political, social, and economic areas of their struggle for development without relating their efforts to educational attainment. But that educational attainment was a reflection of how the courts, especially the U.S. Supreme Court, ruled in some critical cases that came before it.[1] In doing so the Supreme Court defined the parameters of the journey that African Americans launched to the promised land. To understand why the Supreme Court ruled the way it did in these cases, one needs to understand its background. This chapter focuses on the kind of education that African Americans received as a result of the decisions reached by the courts in their effort to secure education as part of their passage to the promised land.

Section III of the U.S. Constitution describes the Supreme Court and its functions as the third branch of the U.S. government. The Constitution goes on to add that judicial power would be extended to courts in all cases, in matters of law and equity, within the framework of the law. Judicial power of the United States would be vested in the Supreme Court and in lower courts as the Congress may from time to time decide to establish. Judges, both of the Supreme Court and lower courts, would hold office during good behavior, and would, at stated times, receive for their services salaries which would not be diminished during their continuance in office.[2]

COURTS AND THEIR FUNCTIONS

This section of the Constitution went on to add that the laws of the United States, or which would be made under their authority in all cases affecting ambassadors, other public officials, to all cases of admiralty and maritime jurisdiction were to be observed by all parties. The laws were also intended to resolve all controversies to which the United States would be a party, as well as controversies between two or more states, between a state and citizens of another state, between citizens of different states, between citizens of the same state. In all cases the Supreme Court was authorized to have appellate jurisdiction, both as to law and fact.[3]

From this constitutional provision it is quite clear that the courts had tremendous jurisdictional power to decide on all cases. Because the Supreme Court functioned mainly as a court of appeal, its power extended far above and beyond the level exercised by the executive and legislative branches.[4] The question now is: In defending its right to judicial review, was the Marshall Court giving itself more power than was intended by the Constitution? Nobody has been able to provide a clear answer to this question. Today the only thing that some people express as a concern is that individuals appointed to serve on the Supreme Court must not legislate from the bench. There is no assurance that the individuals named to the court will operate under this principle, because the Supreme Court is free to interpret the Constitution in any way it sees fit.

It is important to understand the background of the Supreme Court before ones tries to understand its functions. The Congress ordained and established a federal court system by the Judiciary Act of 1789. Although there have been amendments to this legislation, its original intent has remained the same. Section II of the Constitution states that the president "shall nominate, and by and with the advice and consent of the Senate, shall appoint ambassadors, other public ministers and consuls, judges of the Supreme Court, and all other officers of the United States."[5] Advice and consent of the Senate require that the president submit the name of the person he wishes to serve on the Supreme Court to the Senate Judicial Committee, which decides by vote to send the name to the Senate floor for debate and final vote. Once the individual is confirmed he or she is pretty much responsible to his own beliefs, conscience, and views based upon his or her understanding of the law.

There are two other provisions relating to the courts. The first provision is that all judges shall hold office for life, unless they are removed from office by impeachment for criminal behavior or conduct considered unbecoming a judge.[6] The second provision is that the salaries of judges cannot be reduced while they remained in office. These two provisions were made to free the judges as much as possible from political and financial pressure that may impede their ability to discharge their responsibility in a fair and unbiased manner. The rationale behind these provisions was that judges might be unwilling to make a decision that would displease Congress if they knew that it was likely to remove them from office or reduce their salary. But, as we shall see later in this chapter, judges are human beings with biases just like anyone else. This bias became evident in the court decisions they made relative to the position of African Americans.

The Constitution does not specify the number of justices to serve on the Supreme Court. The first Supreme Court had six members, the chief justice and five associate justices.[7] In 1801 the Congress reduced the number to five. But in 1807 the Congress increased the number to nine, and then to ten in 1863. In 1866 the Congress reduced the number to seven once more. However, since 1869 the number has remained at nine members, a chief justice and eight associate justices. The decisions of the Supreme Court are made by vote following debate. Because the Constitution does not specify qualifications of judges, members are not required to have demonstrated experience as judges or lawyers. Any citizen can hold office if he or she is nominated by the president and is approved by the Senate. However, in practice only those who hold training as lawyers and have had considerable experience have been appointed to the Supreme Court.

It is quite interesting to note how the Supreme Court operates. Cases are argued before the court each year from October to June in the Supreme Court Building in Washington, DC, very close to Capitol Hill. All justices are expected to attend, except in case of illness or absence from the city made necessary by compelling circumstances. A case may be heard if no less than six justices are present. Since the Supreme Court is generally an appeal court, the decision of the lower court stands in case of a tie vote of the Supreme Court. Cases in the Supreme Court are argued by attorneys who are specially licensed to argue before it. Before an attorney is allowed to argue cases before the Supreme Court he or she must be presented by another attorney who is already admitted to practice before it. Nobody is qualified for admission to practice before the Supreme Court unless he or she has been in good standing for three years as a member of the American Bar Association or the bar association of the state in which he or she resides or of the District of Columbia.

After hearing a case, the justices discuss it further at their regular meetings, usually held on Saturday. In this manner the justices appear to fulfill the role that is normally fulfilled by the jury in lower courts. After the vote is taken, the chief justice, if he is in the majority, will ask one of the justices in the majority to write the opinion. This is a formal statement of the Court's reasons for its decision. But if the chief justice is in the minority, the senior justice in the majority will write the opinion. In the terminology of the Supreme Court this is called the majority opinion. The chief justice usually writes opinions that address important constitutional issues. For example, in 1857 Chief Justice Roger B. Taney, appointed by President Andrew Jackson in 1836 and served until 1864, wrote the majority opinion on *Dred Scott vs. Sandford* to address the constitutionality of slavery. In the same way in 1954, Chief Justice Earl Warren, appointed by President Dwight Eisenhower in 1953 and served until 1969, wrote the opinion on *Brown vs. Board of Education of Topeka* to address the constitutionality of segregation in public schools. The reason the role of the courts comes early in this study is that they were involved early in the struggle of African Americans in their journey to the promised land.

A practice developed in the late 18th century which meant that each of the justices was assigned to one or two judicial circuits in which the country was divided. The justice used to "ride the circuit," meaning that he was responsible for cases in his circuit which he visited from time to time to see the conduct of courts. The Supreme Court's functions are defined by the Constitution. Cases may come to it in several ways. Some may be directed there when constitutional issues are to be resolved. That is what happened in the *Brown* cases of 1954 and 1955.

The power that gives unique distinction to the Supreme Court is its authority to render final decisions on the constitutionality of any legislation passed by the Congress. In fulfilling this function the Supreme Court acts as guardian of the Constitution. It is the final arbiter of all constitutional matters. During a visit to Washington, DC in 1976 this author was privileged to visit the Supreme Court and had interaction with Justice Potter Stewart, who remarked that the Supreme Court was not final because it was infallible, but that it was infallible only because it was final.[8] This suggests that beyond the Supreme Court there was no other recourse. However, the authority of the Supreme Court to review the constitutionality of legislation passed by the Congress is not stated in the Constitution. This is why in 1803 the Supreme Court asserted this power in *Marbury vs. Madison*. Although some people have protested the use of this power, none have succeeded in bringing it to an end. During the Great Depression President Franklin D. Roosevelt tried to bring about change in the use of this power because he thought that its exercise was infringing heavily upon his recovery programs. But he was unsuccessful.

Many people agree that the power that the Supreme Court exercises to declare any legislation unconstitutional is important to the preservation of the nation. Some argue that without a referee over state action, national interests might be sacrificed. Local legislatures may be motivated only by local interests that may not be in the best interest of the country as a whole. In principle every legislation passed, either by the U.S. Congress or by a state legislature, is subject to review by the Supreme Court. In all the functions of the Supreme Court, the chief justice plays an important role. It is his responsibility to ensure that all constitutional issues are addressed in cases before it. Apart from the action that Chief Justice Earl Warren took in 1954 to persuade other justices to reach a unanimous decision in the *Brown* case, a chief justice has no special role to play in the outcome of cases. To date 16 men have served as chief justice from John Jay beginning in 1789 to William H. Rehnquist beginning in 1986.[9]

THE PLIGHT OF AFRICAN AMERICANS

To understand why the Supreme Court was involved in the struggle of African Americans in their journey to the promised land, one needs to understand the conditions that controlled their lives beginning with slavery. Highly developed societies existed in Africa for hundreds of years before they were invaded by European adventure seekers in the 15th century. The famous systems in ancient Ghana, from which the modern state has adopted its name, came into flourishing condition in A.D. 700. Other established African systems existed for hundreds of years in Mali, Songhai, the Sudan, and Congo. Conditions varied considerably from one part of Africa to another. Centers of culture and trade also existed for the benefit of all. From 1200 to 1600 an Arab-African institution of learning was located at Timbuktu and attracted scholars from all over the Mediterranean world to learn about science and arts. For thousands of years Egypt served as an example of highly developed civilization related to other civilizations in Africa.

Because most Africans lived under tribal conditions that were considered primitive, Europeans began to take advantage of them. By the time that Vasco da Gama reached the southern tip of Africa in 1487 and Christopher Columbus reached the New World in 1492, Europeans had conceived ideas of exploiting Africans in blatant ways. The fact that Columbus depended on Pedro Alonzo Niño, his African navigator of *Santa Maria*,[10] did not mean much to Europeans because he was black. The fact that when Vasco Núñez de Balboa discovered the Pacific Ocean in 1513, 30 Africans were with him helping him build the first ship to be constructed in the Western Hemisphere,[11] did not mean much either. Social class in Africa existed in various forms. The king, the councilor, the storyteller, the legal expert, the servant, and the ordinary member of the village—all had places of their own within the hierarchical structure of society. By 1600, after the colonists in the New World had failed to induce Native Americans to seek employment within the new economic establishment, a decision was being slowly made to think of the possibility of bringing slaves from Africa.

The Arab traders who had been in contact with different parts of Africa saw an opportunity to increase their margin of profit by agreeing to be part of the infamous trade in human merchandise. Suddenly the Arabs transformed their function from being trade partners with Africans to being agents of European slave traders. By 1618 the fate of the Africans was sealed. The arrival of 20 African slaves, three of them women, in Jamestown, Virginia, in 1619 officially introduced the infamous but highly lucrative trade to the New World.[12] From that time to when President Abraham Lincoln issued the Emancipation Proclamation on September 22, 1862, African Americans were treated as nothing more than the property of the white man. That is what slavery meant for all these years. But, more important still, the social, political, and economic systems in the South were based entirely on the institution of slavery.

During the 50 years from 1700 to 1750, thousands of slaves were forcibly brought to the New World every year. In the South the number of slaves was so great that slaves outnumbered the colonists 2 to 1. By the time of the Revolution beginning in 1770,[13] slaves made up nearly 700,000 of the total population of 2.5 million in the colonies. Nearly 5,000 African Americans served with distinction in the Revolutionary Army. Some were freemen, others were indentured slaves. Some historians, such as John Hope Franklin and Alfred A. Moss, Jr., concluded that Crispus Attucks, a runaway slave, was among those killed in the Boston Massacre.[14] Attucks suggested a strategy of getting rid of the British, saying, "The way to get rid of these soldiers is to attack the main guard."[15]

It is ironic that Africans Americans would serve in the Revolutionary Army and would be killed to set the colonies free from British rule, and yet they were not accorded the same status as whites, and that it would take a brutal civil war to free them from the yoke of slavery. Although, on November 12, 1775, General George Washington issued instructions to army recruiters not to enlist African Americans,[16] many came forward to serve in the struggle for American independence. They would serve with distinction in the Civil War, World War I, World War II, and every other war the United States has fought. On January 1, 1777, the Massachusetts General Court received a petition written by African Americans demanding immediate freedom.[17] The petition came as a surprise to the colonists. But once African Americans decided that they, too, wanted freedom, they were not moved from that objective. The demise of Reconstruction programs in 1877 suggested to them that it was necessary to adopt another course of action. This course of action was resorting to the Supreme Court.

THE SUPREME COURT AND THE SEARCH FOR A PASSAGE

In their continuing search for a passage to the promised land, African Americans, having been disappointed with the inaction of national leadership, now turned to the most important institution in the country, the federal courts. They looked to the courts as the final arbiter and guarantor of their constitutional rights as citizens. They hoped that their rights, so flagrantly violated by state authorities, especially in the South, might be restored. From 1857 to 1927 they did not have much good luck there either. The rest of this chapter examines some of the court actions on cases that have become so important in the history of the struggle for development and for social justice of African Americans as they searched for a passage to the promised land. It will also present some implications of the courts' actions on these cases. It is not possible to discuss hundreds of court cases that have been decided by the U.S. Supreme Court. Therefore, the chapter will take some representative cases to substantiate a point of view consistent with the theme of this study.

The *Dred Scott* decision of 1857 in many ways set the trend that remained until 1938. Between 1857 and 1910 the courts and the American public were so racially conservative that many court decisions during this time went against African Americans. On August 21, 1858, during the first debate with Stephen A. Douglas on the question of slavery, Abraham Lincoln expressed surprise in the way the Supreme Court ruled in the *Dred Scott* case, saying, "I do say that, as I understand the *Dred Scott* decision, if any man wants slaves, all the rest have no way of keeping that one man from holding them."[18] It is quite evident that Lincoln opposed the decision. When he was elected president in 1860 the decision weighed heavily on his mind as he considered ways of ways of bringing slavery to an end. Something in his soul, in his entire physical being, convinced him that slavery was wrong.

Lincoln was not the only high-level U.S. official to oppose slavery. History says that Chief Justice Salmon P. Chase was opposed to the continuation of slavery for most of the time he served on the U.S. Supreme Court. As secretary of the Treasury, Chase laid the foundation of the evolution of the present national banking system. He was so efficient that after he resigned that position in 1864, Lincoln named him chief justice of the U.S. Supreme Court in recognition of his ability, even though he did not like him personally because he was a Democrat. Chase proved himself from 1849 to 1855 as U.S. Senator from Ohio, and as its governor from 1856 to 1860. However, in 1872 he was unsuccessful in seeking the nomination of the Democratic Party for president of the United States. Chase did not share Stephen A. Douglas's views favoring the continuation of slavery. Like Lincoln, Chase did not compromise his views against slavery during the time he served as chief justice of the Supreme Court from 1964 to 1873.[19] He and Lincoln do not appear to have coordinated their strategy, perhaps because they belonged to different political parties. Therefore, his role in fighting against slavery has been lost to history, overshadowed by that of Lincoln. Chase tried with remarkable success to maintain correct trial procedure in the impeachment of President Andrew Johnson.[20]

Unlike Thomas Jefferson, who took the position that slavery was a necessary evil because the economy, the social system, and the political process depended on it, Lincoln, by 1848, was quite consistent in arguing against it. This is why, in 1858, reacting to the *Dred Scott* decision of 1857, he concluded that the Supreme Court made an error in reaching it. Speaking on his metaphor of "A House Divided" on June 17, 1858, to the Republican Convention of Illinois, Lincoln stated, "I believe that this government cannot endure half slave and half free."[21] For the rest of his life Lincoln would never vacillate on his stand against slavery.

Because Lincoln felt that slavery had no place in the United States of the future, he thought that efforts must be made to end it before it became a major cause of conflict between the North and the South. But because African Americans were not legally organized until about 1915, some ten years after the founding of the Niagara Movement in 1905, which became the National Association for the Advancement of the Colored People in 1909, Lincoln lacked an adequate basis on which to formulate his decision and action. However, when the NAACP was finally formed, it established a legal and education defense fund which future presidents would utilize to continue Lincoln's legacy. While in 1857 African Americans had no legal means to respond to the *Dred Scott* decision, they began to see clearly that their journey to the promised land depended upon their own initiative. Although there were other civil rights cases that came before the courts, such as the 1883 civil rights cases, the cases of that year were a result of the suit brought against hotel and other public accommodations for refusing to accept African Americans in violation of the 1875 Civil Rights Act. In this case the Supreme Court simply ruled that the U.S. Congress, in passing the act, did not know what it was doing.

In the *Dred Scott* case Justice Joseph P. Bradley, an associate justice of the Supreme Court from 1870 to 1892, delivered the majority opinion saying, "The essence of the law is not to declare broadly that all persons shall be entitled to the full and equal enjoyment of the accommodations advantages, facilities, and privileges of the inns, public conveyances, and theaters, but that such enjoyment shall not be subject to any conditions applicable only to citizens of a particular race or who had been in a previous condition of servitude."[22] One must note that this strong position by the Supreme Court against African Americans was taken by a vote of 8–1, and that this attitude by the Supreme Court was to prevail well into the 20th century. The one dissenting opinion was Justice John Marshall Harlan, who served on the Supreme Court from 1877 until his death in 1911. Harlan argued:

I cannot resist the conclusion that the substance and spirit of the recent amendment of the Constitution have been sacrificed by a subtle and ingenious verbal criticism. Congress therefore, under its express power to enforce that amendment, by appropriate legislation, may enact laws to protect that people against the deprivation, because of their race, of any civil rights granted to other freedman in the same state.[23]

Justice Harlan went on to say that the U.S. Constitution was color blind, it did not recognize its citizens on racial basis but on constitutional basis. However much good reasoning Justice Harlan put into his argument and opinion, which he based on the Fourteenth Amendment and the 1875 Civil Rights Act, he did not influence the decisions of the Supreme Court much during this era of conservative attitudes, which it used to build a solid and formidable strategy that African Americans were to utilize later. It is possible that if Chase and Harlan had served during the same time, they would have become associates in expressing views against slavery. For now, high emotional feelings expressed by the Court in this fateful decision signaled to African Americans that they were not to expect much from the Supreme Court of the land at that point in their search for a passage to the promised land. This was a period of wandering in the wilderness without clear vision of the direction that passage was likely to take in the future.

Nevertheless, African Americans were not disheartened, nor did they stop from trying. The message of the decision to both African Americans and white people was simply that white society had closed ranks against African Americans, that a new trend was in the making, that white people meant quite serious business in their declared intention to deny them. African Americans decided to fight a difficult battle and war. But they realized that to win the struggle they just had to be prepared for the hard times ahead. There were a number of other cases, important civil rights cases, that came before the Supreme Court for decision. But one by one African Americans lost them all. In education the pattern was the same. For example, before 1899 the constitution of Georgia provided that there would be a thorough system of public schools for the education of children in the elementary years, as nearly uniform as practicable, the expenses of which would be provided for by taxes or otherwise the schools would be free to all children of the state, but separate schools would be provided for white students and African American students.[24]

But for some reason the Atlanta school board ran into financial problems in running the schools, so a decision was reached to close the schools for African Americans and continue to operate schools for white students. But schools for white students would not admit African American students. The African American taxpayers sought an injunction that would require the defendant school board to close the white school system until the board was in a financial position to reopen the schools for African Americans, or to admit African American students into the white schools. One would have thought that the action of the school board was a violation of the equal protection clause of the Fourteenth Amendment. But that is not how the Supreme Court saw the situation.

After appeals through the state supreme court, the case came before the U.S. Supreme Court. Again, the Court ruled against the African Americans, stating that the substantial relief which was being asked was an injunction that would either impair the efficiency of the high school provided for white students or compel the board to close it. The Court argued that if that were done, the result would only be to take from white children educational opportunity enjoyed by them without giving to African American children additional opportunity for the education furnished in the high schools. The African American school children of the county would not be advanced in the matter of their education by a decree compelling the defendant board to cease giving support to the high school for white students. The Court concluded that there was no case to be determined.[25]

The action of the board of education and of the state court of appeals was therefore upheld. But Justice Harlan warned prophetically that segregation by law would inevitably cause racial hatred and create a feeling of distrust between the racial groups. However, the warning fell on deaf ears, and in this case and decision of 1896, the Supreme Court seemed to put the stamp of approval on the principle of separate schools.

It is important to see what action the Supreme Court took in other cases dealing with the education of African Americans. Berea College in Kentucky was started by missionaries from the American Missionary Society soon after the Civil War, mainly for African American students. By 1908 Berea was operating on an integrated basis, disregarding the practices and patterns of segregated schools in the South and in defiance of a state law which made racial segregation mandatory. The state of Kentucky ordered Berea College to segregate, but because Berea saw no reason to do so it brought suit against the state, arguing that the association of African American and white students at the school was purely voluntary.

But the state supreme court established the rule that was upheld by the Supreme Court that the section which forbade mixing of the races in schools was not a denial of equal protection or of due process, but that the "teaching in different rooms of the same building or in a different building, so near to each other as to be practically one, would violate the statute, as it was such intimate personal association of the pupils that was being prohibited."[26] When the case came before the Supreme Court, as it was expected, its decision was in agreement with the Kentucky state supreme court ruling against Berea College. The Supreme Court stated in its opinion that it needed to concern itself only with the inquiry whether the first section of the Kentucky constitution of 1891[27] could be upheld as coming within the power of a state over this own corporate creation. It concluded that it was of the opinion, for reasons stated, that it did come within that power, and on this ground the judgment of the court of appeals of Kentucky was affirmed.[28]

Once again, the lone voice of dissension in the Supreme Court, Justice Harlan, disagreed. In the view which he held as his duty, Harlan felt obligated to express his opinion as to the validity of the act as a whole. He was of the opinion that in its essential parts the statute was an arbitrary invasion of the rights of liberty and property guaranteed by the fourteenth Amendment against hostile state actions. Therefore, the law was based on the principles of freedom and charged with the protection of all citizens alike. The law could not make distinctions between citizens in the matter of their voluntary meeting for innocent purposes simply because of their respective races. Further, Harlan argued that if the lower court was right, then a state may make it a crime for whites and African Americans to frequent the same marketplaces at the same time, or appear in an assembly of citizens convened to consider questions of a public or political nature, in which all citizens without regard to race, would be equally interested. In this opinion Harlan concluded that the judgment should be reserved upon the grounds that the statute was in violation of the Constitution of the United States.[29]

Certainly, the views held by Justice Harlan were good, more in line with the law, and would provide the basis for future important developments. But given the attitudes of the time, given the conservative thinking of the Supreme Court, given the circumstances that rendered the Congress ineffective, unable to do something to correct the deteriorating situation that faced African Americans, the opinions of Justice Harlan were simply a far cry in the wilderness. Time was not yet on his side; he would have to wait for a change of attitudes by both the nation and the Supreme Court itself. This change of attitude would not come in his lifetime.

The effect of the Berea decision extended far beyond the bounds of the South. The concept of equality of even the simplest and most easily seen aspects of the schools was rendered farcical by many northern communities, where segregation became common, especially in big cities because a racially segregated residential system became a pattern of the

American society. In some communities boundaries of school districts were so constructed as to ensure the greatest possible separation of the two races.

Under these conditions the difference between schools for African Americans and those of white students was so great that it was easy to see that the principle of "separate but equal" established by the Supreme Court in 1896 was simply a farce. But some states, like Indiana, New Mexico, Kansas, and Wyoming, allowed local school authorities to segregate students by race, and Arizona made segregation at grade-school level mandatory until 1951, when a new state law made such segregation optional. In short, the Berea decision had a tremendous impact on the character of black education in the country. We will briefly present three cases that show the continuing pattern until the Supreme Court reversed itself in 1938.

THE *PLESSY* CASE, 1896

In 1890 a Louisiana law required that all railway companies provide separate but equal accommodations for African Americans and for whites, either by separate cars or separate compartments. In 1892 Homer Plessy, an African American, attempted to board a coach reserved for whites, and refused to vacate the seat when ordered to do so. He was forcibly removed from the coach and was imprisoned for violating a state law. Plessy took his case all the way to the Supreme Court. In 1896 the Court reached a momentous decision of endorsing the notion of "separate but equal," and this doctrine, which now became the law of land, was destined to remain a constitutional guide until it was reversed 1954.

Deciding against *Plessy* the Supreme Court made particular reference to the school situation. In a majority opinion rendered by Justice Henry B. Brown, a Yale Law School graduate and legal scholar from Michigan, and who served on the Supreme Court from 1891 to 1906 appointed by President Benjamin Harrison, argued that the object of the Fourteenth Amendment was undoubtedly to enforce the absolute equality of the two races before the law, but he concluded that in the nature of things it could not have been intended to abolish distinction based upon color or to enforce social practices, as distinguished from political equality or a commingling of the two races upon terms unsatisfactory to either. The most common instance of this situation was connected with the establishment of separate schools for white and colored children, which had been held to be valid exercise in the legislative power.[30]

Once more the vigorous, prophetic dissenting opinion was written by the far-sighted Kentuckian legal prophet, Justice Harlan, who argued that the arbitrary separation of citizens on the basis of race was a badge of servitude for African Americans totally inconsistent with the civil freedom and the concept of equality before the law established by the Constitution. It therefore could not be justified upon any legal grounds. If any adverse effect would result from the commingling of the two races upon public highways established for the benefit of all, they will be infinitely less than those that will surely come from the state legislation regulating the enjoyment of civil rights upon the basis of race. The country boasted of the freedom enjoyed by all Americans. But it was difficult to reconcile that boast with a state of the law which, practically, put the brand of servitude and degradation upon a large class of our fellow citizens, equals before the law.[31]

Again, Justice Harlan set the tone for future action, but for the time being, this was yet another far cry in the wilderness. The whole nation wildly acclaimed the wisdom of the Supreme Court in its action of legally justifying "separate but equal" laws, and for the segregation of schools. For the next 60 years "separate but equal" became the household word in most aspects of life in the nation. If the "equal but separate" philosophy was applied in daily living conditions and association of people, it was more evident in the schools, where it took a heavy and costly toll in the education of African Americans.

For those 60 years the schools were established and developed according to the notion of separate but equal. The school districts were restructured or redefined, population patterns shifted in accordance with this notion. Transport and related economic and social aspects came into line with the theory of separate but equal. American society was consolidating itself on the basis of the harsh realities of the thinking of separate but equal. This new thinking was being universally accepted.

African Americans appeared to have resigned themselves to the new order of things as they were being forced to abandon their search for a passage to the promised land. Although so far they had not met with success, they kept trying in the hope that with the passage of time the nation would begin to see reason in the views expressed by Justice Harlan. When would that possibility come about? Was it remote and distant, or was there a real chance that change of attitude on the part of the nation and the Supreme Court would come sooner than later? African Americans kept hoping, so they kept working toward the realization of their dream, toward searching for the passage to the promised land, toward their dream of their constitutional rights as promised by the U.S. Constitution, not as Justice Brown saw it, but as Justice Harlan predicted.

THE *GONG LUM* CASE, 1927

In 1927 the Supreme Court delivered yet another blow to the efforts of African Americans to secure equality in education. Gong Lum was a Chinese resident of Mississippi, and lived in the Rosedale Consolidated

High School District, which was a white school. He was the father of Martha Lum, about 12 years of age. In 1924 Martha, then about 9 years old, was sent by her father to attend Rosedale Consolidated High School. At the opening of the school, she appeared as a pupil, and was able to take her seat and place in the school. At noon recess, she was told by the school superintendent that she would not be allowed to return to the school because an order had been issued by the Board of Trustees to exclude her from the school because she was Chinese, and therefore black because she was not white.

Her father took the case to the courts, arguing that there was no school in the district for Chinese children, and there was none in Bolivar County, where Martha Lum would go. Gong Lum, a mercantile businessman, had been paying tax to support Rosedale. Lum pointed out that Martha was not a member of the black race, nor of mixed blood, but pure Chinese. He argued that the 1890 Mississippi state constitution provided for separate schools to be maintained for children of the white and colored races and that distinction classified Martha as a white child. When the Mississippi state supreme court ruled against Gong Lum, he took the case before the Supreme Court for determination. The decision was reached in 1927, and Justice William Howard Taft who served as chief justice from 1921 to 1930, and who had served as president from 1909 to 1913, wrote the majority opinion, saying:

We must assume that there are school districts for colored children in Bolivar County, but that no colored school is within the limits of the Rosedale Consolidated High School District. This is not inconsistent with there being at a place outside of the district and in a different district, a colored school which the plaintiff Martha Lum, may conveniently attend. If so, she is not denied, under the existing school system, the right to attend and enjoy the privileges of a common school education in a colored school.[32]

It was of little help or comfort to African Americans to realize that other racial groups in the country suffered the same fate under the law as they did. It was, however, surprising to them to know that Chinese people were classified as colored people according to the Mississippi constitution for purposes of education, as confirmed by the Supreme Court. Gong Lum, however, was shocked by the fact that he had been paying tax to support the public schools that denied an education for his daughter.

Well, maybe Gong Lum would be reminded, as Justice Taft stated, that paying tax to support a school did not entitle him to send his child to that school. It was the function of the Board of Trustees to determine how the funds would be used without taking into consideration the source of such funds. The county board in Georgia, as we have already discussed, did just that earlier on when African American taxpayers petitioned that a white school be closed until money was found to reopen their schools which had been closed because of financial difficulties.

In that case of 1899, as we have described, the Supreme Court did not see it that way, it did not see it that way either in 1927. But still one would think that judging by the decision of the Supreme Court, there was something basically wrong with the American system of justice at the time. One would ask, what is the difference between taxation to support the schools to which one's children are denied entrance and taxation without representation, a hot issue which was a battle cry during the colonial days, and the main issue that seemed to trigger the American Revolution? Was the Supreme Court suggesting that taxation without representation was tyranny for the colonists but not tyranny for African Americans of the 20th century? It was indeed a strange logic.

However, Justice Taft and the Supreme Court confirmed that the right and power of the state to regulate the method of providing for the education of its youth at public expense were clear. It decided to add that while all would admit that the benefits and burdens of public taxation must be shared by citizens without discrimination against any class on account of their race, the education of the people in schools maintained by state taxation was a matter belonging to the respective states, and any interference on the part of the federal authority with the management of schools could not be justified.[33]

This conclusion seemed to assure the states that they had a free hand in the matter of education for African Americans in their own states. They would do as they pleased, the U.S. Constitution did not mean a thing, as far as this aspect of American life was concerned. Did the federal law mean anything to the states? Did they respect and recognize it as the supreme authority? Could they recognize it when the Supreme Court, which was to give guidance in this area, took a lead in the wrong direction?

THE *LLOYD GAINES* CASE, 1938

Some 11 years after the *Gong Lum* case, an interesting case came before the Supreme Court in 1938. Back in 1935 Lloyd Gaines, an African American student, was graduated from Lincoln University, an institution maintained by the state of Missouri for higher education of African Americans in Jefferson City, the state capital. Gaines then submitted an application for admission to the Law School of the University of Missouri, because Lincoln University did not have a law school or department. The state of Missouri offered to pay Gaines's educational expenses if he applied to law schools bordering Missouri. Gaines declined, arguing that he was entitled to admission in Missouri because he was a resident of the state. When his admission was refused, Gaines sued the state for denying him equal protection under the Fourteenth Amendment.

Finally, after the lower courts had ruled against him, his case came before the Supreme Court. During this time the era of conservative attitudes was now giving way to more realistic views of Justice Harlan. In this case, Justice Charles Evans Hughes, who succeeded Taft as chief justice in 1930 and served until 1941, delivered the majority opinion. Hughes went on to argue that the equal protection of the laws was a pledge of the protection of equal laws. Manifestly the obligation of the state to give the protection of equal laws could be performed only where its laws operated. It was here that the equality of legal rights must be maintained. The curators were entitled under the state law to refuse such an application and in its stead to provide for the petitioner's tuition in an adjacent state. He added that the Supreme Court concluded that in so doing it denied the federal rights which the petitioner set up and the question was to the correctness of that decision before it. Hughes was of the opinion that the ruling was in error, and that the petitioner was entitled to be admitted to the law school of the state university in the absence of other and proper provision for his legal training within the state. The judgment of the supreme court of Missouri was therefore reversed.[34]

It seems that for the first time the Supreme Court, in this decision, was giving notice of possible change of attitude in the future. Was this a representative trend, or was the decision influenced by the nature of the case, the legal education? Hughes, a respected jurist, had been named chief justice by President Herbert Hoover.

In 1930 the country was blaming Hoover for the Great Depression. Although the Hughes Court ruled against the National Recovery Act of 1933 in *Schecter vs. United States* in 1935, Hughes was highly sensitive to the need "to ensure equal protection under the law for citizens and to uphold their fundamental constitutional rights."[35] This was the first time that the Supreme Court had ever shown this kind of thinking. However, Justice James C. McReynolds, who was named to the Supreme Court by President Woodrow Wilson in 1914 and served until 1941, issued a dissenting opinion, saying that the state offered to provide the Negro petitioner opportunity for study of the law—if perchance that was the thing really desired—by paying his tuition at some nearby school of good standing. This was far from unmistakable disregard of his rights and in the circumstances was enough to satisfy any reasonable demand for specialized training. It appears that never before had anyone asked that Lincoln University provide legal instruction. The problem presented obviously was a difficult and highly practical one. A fair effort to solve it had been made by offering adequate opportunity for study when sought in good faith. The state should not be unduly hampered through theorization inadequately restrained by experience.[36]

A few months earlier before the *Gaines* appeal in 1935, Donald Murray, who was denied admission to the University of Maryland Law School, filled complaints in the courts. The Maryland court of appeals ordered the university to enroll Murray on the grounds that the instruction at the black branch of the University in Princess Anne was "far from equitable and equal, and the out-of-state scholarships for blacks would not suffice."[37]

By the time of the *Sipuel* case at the University of Oklahoma in 1946 there was every indication that the walls of the separate but equal philosophy were beginning to show signs of cracks. The decision of the Hughes Court to break with traditions of the past was a tremendous boost to African Americans in their search for a passage to the promised land. Now, Justice McReynolds began to feel the same way that Justice Harlan felt during the height of the era of the conservative attitude. It would have been interesting to see how Harlan and McReynolds would have related to each other had they served on the Supreme Court at the same time. Once the Supreme Court set a new trend it would not be reversed. This trend reached a climax in the *Brown* decision of 1954.

EFFORTS TO IMPROVE EDUCATION FOR AFRICAN AMERICANS, 1940–1952

The *Gaines* decision appeared to have shocked many people, as did the Murray decision. The American people did not believe that the Supreme Court would suddenly decide to recognize the fact that African Americans had rights guaranteed by the Constitution, and that they would not expect a change in the Court's attitude toward this aspect of national life. Many began to wonder if Justice Hughes, in the *Gaines* ruling, reflected a possible change of thinking. Or, was it because the petitions dealt with the topic that it knew best, law school and legal education?

Whatever the real reasons were, the country could no longer base separation of schools on the basis of the notion of separate but equal. Political leaders could no longer capitalize on separate but equal philosophy as they had done over the previous decades. But they could not foresee a day when African Americans would be regarded by law as equal to white people, though indication was evident that such a day was coming. They saw the immediate issue of separate but equal as one that needed improvement in the conditions of schools for African Americans. Therefore, there was a visible effort between 1940 and 1954 to do something to improve schools for African Americans, to avoid court action

Table 2.1
Expenditure on Education, 1940 and 1952 Compared

Item (per child)	1940		1952	
	White	Black	White	Black
Operating costs	$50.14	$21.54	$164.83	$115.08
New Buildings	$4.37	$ .99	$36.25	$ 29.58

forcing them to integrate all schools. Both the North and the South gradually began to recognize that the foundation of segregation and other barriers to racial justice and equality were now standing on loose ground.

However, in order to save face, Northern legislatures and legislators began to enact antisegregation laws which would affect schools and other social institutes. Southern legislatures and legislators, fearing that an integration movement would eventually spread to the public schools, began to work toward removing some of the visible inequalities from the segregated school system. They began to spend more money on African American education and schools than they had ever done before. The change in expenditures on education between 1940 and 1952 reflected the feeling of "too little and too late," which was beginning to show in the political attitudes of the times. Table 2.1 shows efforts to improve education for African Americans in the amount of money spent for the 12 years from 1940 to 1952 as compared to the amount of money spent on white education per child.

The table shows that in 1940 the South spent 43¢ per black child for each $1.00 that was spent on the white child. But by 1952 the African American child received 70¢ for each $1.00 spent per white child. Mississippi, in an attempt to improve African American schools so that the state would avoid petitions or suits on the basis of unequal facilities, spent 34 percent more for African American schools than for white schools. But the difference in the equality of education between the two systems of schools had become so great over the years that to correct it demanded far more than matching expenditures. Further, the South was not in a financial position to afford the cost of the type of crash educational programs that were required and needed in order to produce quality in the physical facilities, by which people could judge the effectiveness of the schools.

If the 1938 the Supreme Court decision in the *Gaines* case was influential in the Southern effort to improve the schools to avoid the scarring suits, African Americans began to recognize other types of inequalities in their schools. They felt that their teachers, who were graduates of poor schools and poor colleges, were not as well educated as white teachers, even if they had the same qualifications as white teachers. They also recognized the negative psychological effect of being segregated. African American leaders now began to speak about the personality factors which were caused by separate school systems.

These effects were at first recognized by leaders of the integration movement; eventually the overall effects of segregation on the character of African American children became increasingly apparent to most people. First, people began to question the entire structure of the separate but equal philosophy. Even if the facilities in African American schools were equal to those of white schools, the mere fact of separate school systems now posed a serious question as to its effects on African American students, who appeared to suffer a general disability as a result.

What must be done? African Americans now recognized that the separate but equal philosophy was in fact a method of keeping African American schools in an inferior position and providing an inferior education. Separate but equal simply did not mean anything; as long as the schools were separate, they could not be equal. Then African Americans began to work toward convincing the courts that the two systems could not be regarded as equal, and so they would have to go. Integration of the schools was the only means to give African American students equality in education. Charles H. Houston championed this cause beginning in 1937. Houston's legal action paved way to the *Brown* case.

THE *MCLAURIN* CASE, 1950

The court case which was to put this thinking by African Americans to test in the courts was the famous *McLaurin vs. Oklahoma State University Board of Regents*, which came before the Supreme Court in 1950. G. McLaurin, an African American citizen of Oklahoma, applied for admission to the University of Oklahoma Graduate School. His application was denied solely because of his race, as specified by the Oklahoma law, which made it an offense to operate mixed schools. McLaurin then filed a complaint, alleging that the action of the school to deny him admission, and the law on which it was based, were unconstitutional and deprived him of the equal protection of the law.

When a U.S. district court reversed the action of the university and stated that the law on which the action of denial was based was unconstitutional, the Oklahoma legislature amended its law to permit the admission of McLaurin and other African American students to institutions of higher learning. However, the amendment provided that the program of instruction on a segregated basis would be maintained for McLaurin and other African American students to institutions of higher learning. McLaurin was then admitted but required "to sit apart at a designated desk or in an anteroom adjoining the classroom, to sit apart at a designated desk on the mezzanine floor of the library, but not to use the desks in the regular reading room, and to sit at a designated table and to eat at a different time from the other students in the school cafeteria"[38]

McLaurin filled suit with the district court to have this form of segregation removed, but that court held that such treatment did not violate the provisions of the Fourteenth Amendment, and so the court rejected the suit. McLaurin then appealed to the Supreme Court in 1950 and Chief Justice Frederick Vinson, who was appointed by President Harry Truman in 1946 and served until his death in 1953, delivered the majority opinion, saying that in the interval between the decision of the lower court and the hearing in Supreme Court the treatment afforded the appellant was altered. For some time, the section of the classroom in which the appellant sat was surrounded by a rail in which there was a sign stating "Reserved for Colored," but these had been removed. He was now assigned to a seat in the classroom in a row specified for students of his race, he was assigned to a table in the library on the main floor, and he was permitted to eat at the same time in the cafeteria as other students, although here again he was assigned to a special table. He could wait in line in the cafeteria and there stand and talk with his fellow students but while he ate he had to remain apart. The result was that the appellant was handicapped in his pursuit of effective graduate instruction. Such restrictions impaired and inhibited his ability to study, to engage in discussion and exchange views with other students, and in general to learn his profession. The Court concluded that the conditions under which the appellant was required to receive his education deprived him of his personal and present right to the equal protection of the laws.[39]

Vinson concluded by saying the court considered these circumstances of McLaurin's admission a violation of the equal protection clause of the Fourteenth Amendment and ordered them removed. For the first time in its history, the Supreme Court referred to the effects of segregation on African Americans. It was recognized and widely accepted that the separate but equal theory had no validity and the sooner it went the better. With each successful court action and decision, African Americans became more determined than ever to rediscover the passage to the promised land by securing the rights of citizenship granted to them by the Constitution. They were beginning to come out of the wilderness when they had spent 40 years unsure of the direction to take to reach their destination.

THE *BROWN* CASES, 1954–1955

All these developments were gradually building to a climax with the famous and historic *Brown* cases of 1954 and 1955. By this time African

Americans had gotten some experience in legal issues and procedures on their journey to the promised land. The NAACP had become well-organized and -informed about the law in reference to their institutional rights. In the *Brown* cases there were five separate cases from the five states of Kansas, South Carolina, Virginia, Delaware, and the District of Columbia. To argue in favor of continuing racial segregation in public schools, the Topeka, Kansas, Board of Education hired a famous and formidable constitutional lawyer, John W. Davis. Davis was the Democratic candidate for president of the United States in 1924, but lost to Calvin Coolidge. But over the years Davis never lost the flamboyance that was part of legal practice. In many ways Davis was the Stephen A. Douglas of his time. Arrogant, confident in his knowledge of the fine points of law, and sure of his legal facts, Davis was highly conscious of the precedence that the outcome of the case would create for the future of the country. He argued that precedence was on his side, meaning that the Supreme Court should not reverse the *Plessy* decision of 1896.[40] The plaintiffs hired a modest but well-informed lawyer, Thurgood Marshall,[41] who kept the argument for desegregation on a simple level to allow all parties to understand the issue involved in the case.

The *Brown* cases began as early as 1952 and all challenged the constitutionality of segregated public schools on racial grounds. "The gravity of the judgment was further acknowledged by the Court's announcement that it was allowing a breathing spell by prescribing that in the autumn of 1954 the court would hear arguments on the nature of the decree by which its decision might best be carried into effect."[42] In short, the Supreme Court went a step further than its 1950 *McLaurin* action by making provision for the implementation of its 1954 decision.

In 1952 African American students in the four states mentioned above and the District of Columbia alleged that whites discriminated against them solely on the basis of race. The parents of the African American students sought the help of the District of Columbia in seeking resolution of the problem, but the lower court dismissed their complaint. Because there was a constitutional question in the petition, the cases were referred to the U.S. Supreme Court for determination. The importance of the decision constituted a landmark in the history of social justice in the United States. We will attempt to reproduce the main current thinking, attitudes, and views of the Supreme Court on the whole question of racial equality, as written by the chief justice himself, Earl Warren, who delivered the unanimous opinion.

Chief Justice Warren, who had been recently appointed to that position by President Eisenhower, appeared deeply disturbed by the racial injustice in the country. Now he felt he was in a position where he could influence an end to it, at least constitutionally. In this unanimous decision the Supreme Court reviewed recent previous cases, including the

McLaurin case. Then Warren concluded by saying that segregation of white and colored children in public schools had a detrimental effect upon African American children. The impact was greater when it had the sanction of the law, for the policy of separating the races was usually interpreted as denoting the inferiority of African American children. A sense of inferiority affected the motivation of a child to learn. Segregation with the sanction of law, therefore, had a tendency to retard the educational and mental development of African American children and deprive them of some of the benefits they would receive in a racially integrated school system. The Court concluded that in the field of public education the doctrine of separate but equal had no place. Separate educational facilities were inherently unequal. Therefore the Court concluded that the plaintiffs and others similarly situated for whom the actions had been brought were by reason of the segregation complained of deprived of the equal protection of the laws guaranteed by the Fourteenth Amendment. The Court announced that segregation was a denial of the equal protection of the law.[43]

The decision was certainly a milestone in the progress of education for African Americans and for their journey to the promised land. It meant that no state legislature could pass laws permitting segregation in public schools any more. It also meant that separate but equal practices in education were over. In short, no form of racial segregation whatsoever could be permitted in public schools. The nation was tired of this meaningless, empty phrase; something more positive, more constructive must take its place.

The Warren decision made it clearer than the decision of the Vinson Court of 1950 in stating the psychological effects of segregation on African American students and that all forms of segregation had to go. African Americans could never be happier. The momentous decision provided them with a new hope, with a bright future. They were going to forget the past and strive towards a new era of racial equality.

If this hope was misplaced, as the decade of 1955–1965 would show, certainly African Americans were not aware of it as successive court actions were generally in their favor since 1938. Table 2.2 shows a summary of the highlights in court action that indicated progress toward granting African Americans their rights. The listing is not exhaustive, it is simply meant to give an idea of the change of attitude the Supreme Court initiated in 1938 toward the education of African Americans as part of their search for a passage to the promised land.

This table shows that the Supreme Court's decisions followed a definite pattern. In similar cases that came after 1954, the pattern was to continue. Once the Supreme Court developed a change of attitude in 1938, it remained the order of things even into the era of the controversial busing issue beginning in 1971. In its own way the Supreme Court first made it difficult for African Americans to search for a passage to the

Table 2.2
Summary of Supreme Court Decisions Affecting African Americans, 1857–1972

	Year of Case	Title of Case	Issue	For or Against
1.	1857	Dred Scott v. Sanford	Slavery	Against
2.	1873	Slaughter House	Privileges	Against
3.	1883	Civil Rights	Rights	Against
4.	1884	Ex. Parte Yarborough	Voting	Against
5.	1896	Plessy v. Ferguson	Facilities	Against
6.	1899	Cummings v. Board of Education	Education	Against
7.	1908	Berea College v. Kentucky	Education	Against
8.	1927	Gong Lum v. Rice	Education	Against
9.	1938	Missouri et rel v. Gaines	Education	For
10.	1948	Sipuel v. Oklahoma	Education	For
11.	1950	Sweatt v. Painter	Education	For
12.	1950	McLaurin v. Oklahoma	Education	For
13.	1954	Brown v. Board of Education of Topeka	Education	For
14.	1972	Furman v. Georgia	Civil Rights	For

promised land. But once it believed it found that passage, it remained committed to it, enabling African Americans to trail it.

SUMMARY AND CONCLUSION

Having been disappointed by the end of Reconstruction, African Americans now turned to the courts to restore their rights. But from 1873 to 1938 the courts, including the Supreme Court, were functioning during a period conservative attitudes. The *Dred Scott* case of 1857 set the stage for the courts to disregard the call from African Americans to restore their rights. In decision after decision the courts enunciated theories that intimately affected African Americans in their struggle for educational development. But once change came about beginning with the *Lloyd Gaines* case in 1938, the courts became persistent in enunciating theory that affirmed the rights of African Americans to education. The evolution of this theory was long in coming. But once it was in place it began to show real results.

NOTES

1. Henry Hampton and Steve Fayer, *Voices of Freedom: An Oral History of the Civil Rights Movement from the 1950s Through the 1980s* (New York: Bantam Books, 1991), p. 36.

2. Quoted in Barnes's Historical Series, *A Brief History of the United States* (New York: American Book Company, 1899), p. 345.

3. Ibid., p. 344.

4. The Marshall Court, from 1801 to 1835, was the first to rule on the constitutionality of laws passed by Congress. In 1935 the Supreme Court ruled in *Schechter Poultry Corporation vs. United States* that the National Industrial Recovery Act of 1933 was unconstitutional. During the crisis caused by the Watergate scandal of the Nixon presidency beginning in 1972, Judge John Sirica ruled that President Richard Nixon must hand over certain tapes to a congressional committee that was investigating his role in the scandal that forced him to resign on August 9, 1974. This means that the Supreme Court has more power than the president and the Congress.

5. Pathfinder Publications, *The Constitution of the United States with the Declaration of Independence* (Boston: Pathfinder, 1973), p. 18.

6. During the Warren Court from 1953 to 1969, efforts were made to remove the chief justice himself and William O. Douglas because of their liberal interpretation of the Constitution. But efforts amounted to nothing. For details see PBS, *The Warren Legacy*, a documentary, October 7, 1989.

7. The first Supreme Court was headed by John Jay, who served from 1790 to 1795 and was named by President George Washington. In 1795 Washington named John Rutledge, who had served as associate justice from 1790 to 1791, but the Senate refused to confirm him because he was too extreme in his views about the need to sustain slavery.

8. The author, along with 19 other graduate students from different countries of the world, was in Washington, DC, during a trip lasting one week in May 1976 sponsored by the U.S. State Department.

9. Rehnquist, a conservative Republican, was appointed by President Ronald Reagan in 1986 to replace Warren Burger who retired in that year. For the names of Chief justices and the terms of their office, see Judith Gillespie and Stuart Lazarus, *American Government: Comparing Political Experiences* (Englewood Cliffs, NJ: Prentice-Hall, 1979), p. 437.

10. Sharon Harley, *The Timetables of African American History* (New York: Simon and Schuster, 1995), p. 7.

11. Ibid., p. 8.

12. Ibid., p. 9.

13. Some people, including this author, conclude that the American Revolution started with the Boston Massacre of March 5, 1770, when the British troops fired into a group of protesters, killing three men and wounding eight others.

14. John Hope Franklin and Alfred A. Moss, Jr., *From Slavery to Freedom: A History of African Americans*, 7th ed. (New York: McGraw-Hill 1994).

15. Ibid., p. 69.

16. Ibid., p. 74.

17. Ibid., p. 78.

18. John Gabriel Hunt, *The Essential Abraham Lincoln* (New York: Random House, 1993), p. 132. There were seven Lincoln-Douglas debates on the question of slavery in 1858. The other six were held on August 27, September 15, September 18, September 19, October 15, and October 18. Douglas was an articulate debater. Originally from Vermont, Douglas, a Democrat, moved to Illinois where he was elected prosecuting attorney for his district in 1935. He served on the supreme court of Illinois, as a member of the U.S. House of Representatives, and as a member of the U.S. Senate. However, his performance in the debates dis-

pleased some members of the Democratic Party. He was nominated by Northern Democrats for President in 1661 but Southern Democrats refused to support him. Douglas therefore lost the presidential election to Lincoln.

19. Gillespie and Lazarus, *American Government*, p. 437. History says that on February 21, 1868, the House of Representatives voted 128 to 47 to adopt 11 articles of impeachment against President Andrew Johnson. On March 5 Chase presided with remarkable efficiency and distinction as the Senate began the impeachment proceedings. On September 10, 1998, Kenneth Starr, an independent counsel appointed to investigate the behavior of President Bill Clinton, submitted his report to Congress, which immediately made it public, paving way for possible impeachment for the sex scandal involving Monica Lewinsky.

20. Gillespie and Lazarus, *American Government*, p. 437.

21. Hunt, *The Essential Abraham Lincoln*, p. 115.

22. R. Bardolph, *The Civil Rights Record: Black Americans and the Law, 1849–1970* (New York: Thomas Crowell, 1970), p. 68.

23. Ibid., p. 69.

24. J. Tussman, *The Supreme Court on Racial Discrimination* (New York: Oxford University Press, 1968), p. 9

25. Ibid., p. 11.

26. Bardolph, *The Civil Rights Record*, p. 156.

27. The section of the constitution of Kentucky stated, "every grant of a franchise, privilege, or exemption, shall remain, subject to revocation, alteration, or amendment." This was revised in 1904.

28. Tussman, *The Supreme Court on Racial Discrimination*, p. 12.

29. Ibid., p. 14.

30. Robert E. Potter, *The Stream of American Education* (New York: American Book Company, 1967), p. 363.

31. Bardolph, *The Civil Rights Record*, p. 151.

32. Tussman, *The Supreme Court and Racial Discrimination*, p. 20.

33. Ibid., p. 21.

34. Ibid., p. 28.

35. Gillespie and Lazarus, *American Government*, p. 430.

36. Ibid., p. 30.

37. Potter, *The Stream of American Education*, p. 479.

38. Tussman, *The Supreme Court and Racial Discrimination*, p. 36.

39. Ibid., p. 37.

40. This was the last case Davis argued before the Supreme Court. He argued a total of 140 cases, far more than any other lawyer did. Davis also served as ambassador to Britain from 1918 to 1921. In 1953 Queen Elizabeth II made him honorary knight.

41. In 1967 President Lyndon B. Johnson named Marshall the first African American to serve on the Supreme Court. He was succeeded by Clarence Thomas, named in 1992 by President George Bush. Thomas is known for his controversial and conservative views.

42. Bardolph, *The Civil Rights Record*, p. 277.

43. D. Fellman, *The Supreme Court and Education* (New York: Columbia University Press, 1969), p. 138.

3

The Search for a Moses:
The Effect of Leadership

Someone imbued with the spirit of human freedom from among the
oppressed themselves, has arisen to lead them on to victory.

Frederick Douglass, 1894

NAACP IN A LEADERSHIP ROLE

The founding of the National Association for the Advancement of Colored People in New York City on February 12, 1909, the 100th anniversary of Abraham Lincoln's birth, signaled the beginning of a new era in
the structure of leadership among African Americans as a strategy to
help them arrive at their destination, the promised land. Principal among
those who attended the inauguration of this important organization were
William E. B. Du Bois, who had founded the Niagara Movement a year
before, and Ida B. Wells, a young African American journalist whose
eloquent editorials focused national attention on violence that included
lynchings perpetrated against African Americans by white extremists,
such as members of KKK. Participants of the conference agreed to work
toward the elimination of race violence, end racial segregation, promote
equal educational opportunity, and advance civil rights for all Americans.[1]

In addition to Du Bois and Wells, Henry Moscowitz, Mary W. Ovington, Oswald G. Villard, and William E. Walling decided to lead African
Americans in making a call for their struggle in advancing in their educational, economic, social, and political lives. Today NAACP is a net-

work of more than 2,200 branches covering all states, the District of Columbia, Japan, and Germany.[2] Its activities include economic development, education, health, labor conditions, political participation, legal representation, public relations, and the like. NAACP began to take an active part in legal matters affecting African Americans in a campaign first led by Charles H. Houston, who completely dedicated himself to that cause, eventually leading to the *Brown* decision in May 1954.[3]

In the early years of NAACP, African Americans brought legal suits to the courts in an effort to end racial segregation in all its forms. For example in 1917, in *Guinn vs. United States* the U.S. Supreme Court struck down as unconstitutional the grandfather clauses of state constitutions in the exercise of voting rights under the Fifteenth Amendment. In the same year the Supreme Court declared unconstitutional an ordinance in Louisville that required African Americans to live in certain designated areas of the city. In 1923 the Court declared that exclusion of African Americans from juries was a violation of the principle of the right to fair trial.[4]

In 1919 NAACP launched the first major campaign to persuade Congress to pass antilynching laws. To raise the consciousness of both African Americans and white Americans, NAACP published in that year an exhaustive review of lynching records entitled *Thirty Years of Lynching in the United States, 1889–1918*. NAACP leaders, at great risk to their own lives, concluded from first-hand investigations that racially motivated violence was having a harmful effect on all people. Leadership roles among African Americans of later years came out of the conditions that NAACP had created in its formative years. That leadership had a tremendous effect on the progress of the journey to the promised land.

It is appropriate to give a brief summary of the current president of NAACP to give an idea of the kind of leadership it has provided over the past 90 years. Kweisi Mfume[5] was elected president and chief executive officer of NAACP on February 15, 1996. Mfume gave up his congressional seat in the United States Congress, where he had represented Maryland's 7th congressional district for ten years, to assume the leadership of NAACP at a critical point. Mfume was born, raised, and educated in Baltimore. There his natural talents began to show early in his life as he began to view himself as someone who could play an important role in shaping the character of American society by his dedication to principles of fairness, justice, and equality.

Mfume became politically active in his freshman year in college as editor of the his school's newspaper and as head of the Black Students' Union. After graduating magna cum laude from Morgan State University in 1976, Mfume returned to his alma mater to teach courses in political science and communications. He then studied at Johns Hopkins University, where he received a master's degree in international relations. In

1986 he was elected to the U.S. House of Representatives with an over-whelming majority.[6] Clearly Mfume's qualities of leadership were manifested in whatever he did. This is why in 1996 African Americans felt that he should assume the leadership of NAACP to give African Americans a new thrust on their journey to the promised land.

AFRICAN AMERICAN LEADERSHIP IN PERSPECTIVE

The most significant result of the *Brown* decision was that it aroused a new sense of destiny, a new perspective in African Americans' journey to the promised land. The success that they had scored so far gave them new vision, new hope of arriving in the promised land. African Americans now summoned new courage to stage a new endeavor in other aspects of their lives that included housing, employment opportunity, and securing political and social rights which they lost during the years following the end of Reconstruction. They wondered whether it was possible for them to secure education without first securing the right to it. To achieve the goals they now identified, African Americans decided that leadership was essential to the attainment of their objectives. Who then were the leaders of the journey to the promised land for African Americans?

What were some of their strategies and how did they influence the direction of the journey? With the Supreme Court decisions going against them from 1857 to 1937, how would they find the passageway? Even before the *Brown* decision, African Americans needed a Moses to lead the long journey from the land of slavery and oppression to the promised land of freedom and equality in American society. The task was not easy, but it was one that had to be undertaken if African Americans ever hoped to move from the wilderness of uncertainty and confusion and find a passage to the promised land.

It is important to note that African Americans did not collectively elect their leaders. Leadership was born out of individuals who had a vision of the future different from the past. These individuals identified issues and causes which they persistently addressed to alert their people of the need to launch an endeavor that would help them realize their objectives. They became leaders by their ability to address issues that were critical to the development of their people, by the strength of their conviction, by the power of their persuasion, by their ability to invoke a response, and by their personal sacrifices in putting their own lives in danger to promote the cause of the group. Leadership among a struggling people is often born out of dedication made by individuals to serve the interests of the group, to put the development of the people above their own security. Leadership often demands a willingness to take risks of failure, personal injury or death, or rejection and controversy. Effective leadership also comes from commitment, the strength of personal character, unwavering dedication, and thorough knowledge of the issues that need to be resolved or addressed.

It is difficult to select any persons who, as individuals, have determined the course to be followed by the group. In the journey to the promised land, some individuals assumed the position of leadership by virtue of the position they held in other organizations. For example, Booker T. Washington was president of Tuskegee College from 1881 until his death in 1915. Martin Luther King, Jr. was president of the Southern Christian Leadership Conference from 1963 until his death in April 1968. Others have become leaders by their ability to articulate positions on issues in ways that African Americans could identify with the support. Frederick Douglas was that kind of leader. W. E. B. Du Bois became a leader by the power of his intellect.

History is full of names of leaders among African Americans from Crispus Attucks, the African American martyr of March 1770, through Martin Luther King, Jr., the African American martyr of April 1968, to Kweisi Mfume and Julian Bond. In between there are leaders ranging from Roy Wilkins, Benjamin Hooks, and Medgar Evers to Kwame Toure and Jesse Jackson, from Constance Baker Motley to Angela Davis and Maya Angelou. This chapter discusses the contribution of selected leaders whose commitment to African American social evolution has had profound influence on the development of the journey to the promised land. In doing so, the chapter runs the risk of eliminating some leaders who have made major contributions to the development of African Americans. The leaders discussed in this chapter are Frederick Douglass, Marcus Garvey, Booker T. Washington, William Trotter, Harriet Tubman, and Julian Bond. The leadership of Martin Luther King, Jr. is discussed in Chapter 5 in an attempt to relate his role to seeking solutions to the obstacles that African Americans encountered as discussed in Chapter 4. The leadership role that Du Bois played is also presented in Chapter 4. These leaders related their philosophy and activity to a variety of issues relevant to the struggle of African Americans which gave direct bearing and relevance to their journey to the promised land.

There are also individual African Americans who exerted considerable influence by the quality of their work. Two examples come to come mind. The first is that of George Washington Carver. In 1894 Carver, a former slave born in Diamond Grove, Missouri, graduated from Iowa State College with a degree in botany. While he was still a baby he and his mother were abducted by thieves. Later his mother's master bought him back in exchange for a horse. He never knew his father, and his mother had vanished. Born in 1864, a year before the ratification of the Thirteenth Amendment ending slavery, Carver endured the pain and suffering of not knowing his parents. A brilliant and dedicated student,

Carver applied himself to learning in a manner that surprised those who knew him. He showed an intense interest in plants. Upon his graduation from Iowa State College he was persuaded to remain there as director of the greenhouse. He began immediately to collect varieties of plants that numbered 200,000 by the time he moved to Tuskegee in 1896. In 1916 Carver was named Fellow of the Royal Arts in London in recognition of his work in botany. Carver soon began to formulate his theory about converting peanuts into many products that we take for granted today. In 1923 he received recognition for his contribution to the evolution of theory of botany. In 1939 he received the Roosevelt medal for many of his inventions and contributions to the study of botany. Just as Carver defined theory as the mother of invention, one can define it as the origins of human endeavor. In this regard Carver was a powerful leader among African Americans on their journey to the promised land.

The second example is Daniel Hale Williams. In 1913 Williams was named the first African American member of the American College of Surgeons for his contribution to the theory of medical science. Beginning in 1896 Williams was the first to formulate a theory of plasma, the straw-colored liquid part of blood that remains when the red and the white blood cells are removed. Williams discovered that plasma contains water, salts, proteins, and other food materials. He discovered that plasma carries dissolved food materials to all parts of the body and picks up waste materials produced by the body cells and carries them to the organs that remove waste materials from the body. Williams concluded that plasma can be used for blood transfusions when whole blood is not needed or cannot be obtained. He advanced his theory that plasma can be used during surgery to combat shock, and that it can successfully be used to restore blood volume lost during severe bleeding. Williams also concluded that plasma generates antibodies that help destroy germs and help prevent infection. Today a variety of uses of plasma is part of the medical practices utilized to save lives that would otherwise be lost. In this connection Williams exercised effective leadership in medical science. What he did contributed to the progress of the journey to the promised land.

FREDERICK DOUGLASS

Frederick Douglass was born in Maryland in February 1818 into the lowest position of his society, slavery. The actual date of his birth is not known because accurate records of slaves were not kept. He was the son of a slave woman and her white master, a practice very common during slavery.[7] In 1841 he became involved in the African American community in New Bedford, Massachusetts, and began to show qualities of leadership. In that same year William Lloyd Garrison, the great abolitionist, recognized Douglass's speaking ability and offered him $450 a year to be an antislavery speaker. Four years later, in 1845 the Massachusetts Anti-Slavery Society persuaded him to publish his autobiography, *Narrative of the Life of Frederick Douglass: An American Slave Written by Himself*, which was a great success. Appropriately Douglass invited William Lloyd Garrison to write the preface. Garrison considered it an honor and readily accepted, saying on May 1, 1845, as the manuscript was ready to go to press, "Mr. Douglass has very properly chosen to write his own narrative in his own style. It is, in my judgment, highly creditable to his head and heart. He who can peruse it without a tearful eye, a heaving breast, an afflicted spirit, without being filled with an unutterable abhorrence of slavery and all its abettors must have a flinty heart."[8] After publishing *The North Star* in 1847 Douglass knew that he had what it took to become leader. He emancipated himself mentally and intellectually and, in the process, become an orator, an abolitionist, an editor, a politician, a leader, and a prophet.

At the time of his birth, slavery was at its peak, and slaves were not allowed to read, as events of 1831 would show, when Nat Turner and his followers revolted and murdered their white masters. But in spite of all the difficulties imposed on slaves, Douglass managed to lift himself by his own efforts and became one of the great names in an age that was characteristic of greatness. From 1845 to 1865 he was the foundation of the African American protest movement. In 1845 Douglass described some of the conditions that controlled his life as a slave and his determination to overcome them, saying that he was seldom whipped by his old master, and suffered little from anything more than hunger and cold. He said that he suffered much from hunger, but much more from cold. During the hot summer and coldest winter, he was kept almost naked— no shoes, no stockings, no jacket, no trousers, nothing but a coarse linen shirt reaching only to his knees. He had no bed. He must have perished with cold, but on the coldest nights he used to steal a bag which was used for carrying grain to the mill. He would crawl into this bag, and there sleep on the cold, damp clay floor with his head in and his feet out.[9]

Douglass's ability to speak took him to different parts of the country, including Massachusetts and Maryland, where he learned early in life that knowledge and education were power. The wife of his master, who was also believed to be his father,[10] was impressed with his intelligence and wanted to teach him the letters of the alphabet. But her husband did not allow it, saying, "Give a Nigger an inch and he will take it all. Learning would spoil the best Nigger in the world."[11] This attitude is quite similar to the one adopted by colonial officials in Africa. For example, Ethel Towse Jollie argued in the legislature in colonial Zimbabwe in 1927, "We do not intend to hand over this country to the Natives or to admit them to the same position that we ourselves enjoy. Let us make no pretense of educating them the same way we educate whites."[12] Douglass, not yet ten years old, got the message and concluded that words, properly put into use, become a formidable weapon with which to fight the injustice of slavery. So he became more determined to acquire knowledge, the instrument that he would later use to exert great influence on the struggle that lay ahead.

In 1838, at the age of 20, Douglass escaped from slavery and went to New York, where he later married charming Ann Murray, a free African American woman from Baltimore. He changed his slave name from Augustus Washington Bailey, the name of his master, to begin a new life as a free man under the name of Frederick Douglass, by which he is known to history. Good looking, tall, well built, and highly intelligent, Douglass began to embrace the ideas of *The Colombian Orator* (a radical magazine that promoted emancipation of slaves), subscribed to Garrison's *Liberator*, and attended meetings held by local abolitionists. In 1841 Douglass was a leader of the African American community because of his commitment to abolition and his ability to represent their wishes in his speeches. Later that year Garrison was so impressed with Douglass's speeches about the abolitionist movement that he offered him a permanent position in the Massachusetts Anti-Slavery Movement. Douglass saw an opportunity to put his views across to the people and so he accepted gladly.

Throughout his career Douglass would not isolate himself from the masses. He bitterly criticized free African Americans whom he saw as indifferent to the antislavery cause. Free African Americans, Douglass warned, were not separate from slaves because they were chained together, and would rise or fall together. He pleaded that it was more than a figure of speech to say that African Americans were as a people chained together. They were all one people, one in general complexion, one in common degradation, one in popular estimation. As one rose, all must rise, and as one fell, all must fall. Every one of them should be ashamed to consider himself free, while his brother was a slave. Correcting the wrongs of their brothers was their constant theme. There should be no time too precious, no calling too holy, no place too sacred to make room for the cause.[13]

Douglass related his activities to the education of African Americans in as powerful a way as he opposed slavery. In 1850 he staged a school boycott in Rochester, New York, and other places. He explained later that his children were not allowed in the public schools; the district in which he lived, owned property, and paid taxes compelled his children, if they went to public school, to go over to the other side of the city to an inferior school for African Americans. He hardly needed to say that he was not prepared to submit timidly to this proscription, so he had them taught at home for a while. Meanwhile he went to the people with the question and created a considerable agitation. He sought and obtained a hearing before the board of education, and after repeated efforts with voice and pen, the doors of the public schools were finally opened to African American children who began to attend them in common with children of other races.[14]

While Douglass appreciated the support from liberal whites, he became scornful of the missionary psychology of some white abolitionists. He would say,

The relation subsisting between the white and black people of the country is the vital question of the age. A man must be hot or accounted cold, or perchance, something worse than hot or cold. The lukewarm and the cowardly will be rejected by earnest men on either side of the controversy. The cunning man who avoids it to gain the favor of both parties will be rewarded with scorn and the timid man who shrinks from it, for fear of offending either party, will be despised. To the lawyer, the preacher, the politician, and the top man of letters, there is no neutral ground.[15]

Douglass urged all people, black and white, slave and free, to come forward to work for the salvation of a nation by promoting the salvation of African Americans because, he argued further, the country was not free until African Americans were free. The cause of African Americans was the cause of the United States itself.

For the oppressed people in a colonial rule, such as in Africa, Douglass had some advice in 1860:

The history of oppressed nations will confirm to us in this assertion that if we are ever elevated, our elevation will have been accomplished through our own instrumentality. No people that has solely depended upon foreign aid or rather, upon the efforts of those in any way identified with the oppressor, to undo the heavy burdens ever stood forth in the attitude of freedom. Someone imbued with the spirit of human freedom, from among themselves, has arisen to lead them on to victory. They have dashed their fetters to the ground.[16]

The founding of the Pan-African movement in 1919 by both Africans and African Americans was based on this fundamental philosophy. If Douglass had been there in 1919 he would have become an influential leader.

Douglass rejected the notion that would have some people identify the race problem as the black problem. The real problem, he argued, was the white problem, the determination of the whites to benefit from the cheap labor that African Americans provided. The only answer was African American struggle against this injustice. Douglass urged African Americans to pool their resources in a massive crusade against racism.

While he considered the ballot highly essential, he would not neglect economic and political power. He saw the African American worker as an elevator of his own race. Every house that African Americans built became a symbol of a strong tower against the host of racial prejudice.

Despite the intense economic crisis of the 1850s which pushed African American workers out of their means of earning a living into which many whites moved, Douglass rejected the back-to-Africa plan of Martin Delany, another pioneer African American nationalist of the time. Douglass reflected on this subject, stating that it all did not make sense to talk about the removal of 8 million African Americans from their homes in America to send them to Africa. The expense and hardships, to say nothing of the cruelty caused by such a measure, would make success impossible. While he thought that white America was cruel, he did not think whites were that foolish as well. He argued that white America would hardly be disposed to pay the costs involved, to say nothing of the injustice which the measure demanded. He said that the destiny of African Americans was the destiny of America itself. The allotment of providence seemed to make the black people of America the open book out of which the American people in general were to learn lessons of wisdom, power, and goodness. In the extreme difference of color and features of African Americans and Anglo-Saxons would be learned the highest ideas of sacredness of man, and the fullness and perfection of human brotherhood.[17]

Douglass was infuriated by the American failure to make meaningful response to the abolitionist complaint. He let loose his frustration and anger with the fire and eloquence of an Old Testament prophet. Speaking in Rochester, New York, on July 5, 1852, Douglass accused every structure of power in America of treating African Americans poorly:

What to the American slave is your 4th of July? I answer. A day in the year that reveals to him more than all other days, the gross injustice and cruelty to which he is constant victim. To him, your celebration is a sham, your boasted liberty, an unholy license, your national greatness, swelling vanity, your sounds of rejoicing are empty and heartless, your denunciation of tyrants, brass, frustrated impudence, your shouts of liberty and equality, hallow mockery. Your prayers and hymns, your sermons and thanksgiving, with all your religious parade and solemnity, are to him more bombast fraud, deception, impiety and hypocrisy, a thin veil to cover up crimes which would disgrace a nation of savages.[18]

While Booker T. Washington would not adopt such an attitude, Douglass, as well as other African American thinkers and philosophers of the time, played a leading role in shaping the development of the national crisis that finally led to the Civil War. His speeches aroused the conscience of some leading citizens, who felt that the nation could no longer afford to remain silent to the issue of slavery. Douglass, like Martin Luther King, Jr. of the 1950s and 1960s, was a blend of idealism and practicality. This is evident by his confrontation with John Brown, a committed radical abolitionist, on the eve of the Harper's Ferry raid in October 1859.

Brown tried to persuade Douglass to go with him to launch the raid, but Douglass declined because he felt that the raid was not practical and would not succeed. Long arguments followed between the two men, and hard feelings between them resulted. They went their separate ways, never to meet again. Douglass went toward life, to make other accomplishments; Brown went toward rendezvous with death, cutting short his crusade and the opportunity to make a greater contribution to a great cause than he had made at that point. But somehow both men served in their different ways, both decided to take the same cause, but took up different ways to do it.

During and after the Civil War Douglass castigated Lincoln as a "Slow Coach." Long before Lincoln saw it, Douglass was saying that the war was a struggle to give America a new birth of freedom, that African Americans were deeply involved in the root cause of the war, that the war could not be fought or ended without coming to terms with the aspirations of African Americans and the emerging meaning of the country. Douglass recognized that the purpose of the Civil War was not to free the slaves, but to preserve the Union. Since the end justifies the means, Douglass correctly predicted that after the Civil War was over, African Americans would still encounter problems of denial of equal opportunity. He suggested that massive educational programs were needed to train new leaders to restructure the African American family— that fundamental institution to all human progress and the essential basis of social development and stability.

Soon after the Emancipation Proclamation in September 1862 (which is believed to have been influenced by Douglass), Douglass himself pushed for extensive educational programs for African Americans, and demanded integrated schools to bring the former slaves into the American mainstream. He also demanded land, ballots, and Bibles. He argued that as one learns to swim by swimming, the African Americans must learn to vote by voting. By 1883 Douglass was bitter at the Supreme Court action in denying African Americans their civil rights.

Douglass labeled the Court's action as a stupendous fraud, a fraud upon the world. He was angry because he felt that the rights of African Americans were ignored, defrauded, swindled, and cast out. He warned that this action was simply courting social disorder. It was impossible to degrade African Americans without degrading the social fabric of America. The perversion of legal process was bound to fail and force African Americans to fight against socially organized conspiracy to oppress them, because, he concluded, "hungry men will eat, desperate men will commit crime, outraged men will seek revenge."[19]

Douglass then turned his attention to urge African Americans to fight for their rights for education and economic progress. These were the vehicles they needed to get to the promised land. In a speech in Washington, DC, in 1885 Douglass concluded that the present was a critical moment for African Americans because their fate was worse than it was in the past. Now it hung in the balance. No man could tell which way the scales would turn. There was not a breeze that swept to them from the South, but one that came laden with the wail of their suffering people. Now, the American people were once more being urged to do from necessity what they should have done from a sense of right, and of sound affairs, in which other rulers did wrong from choice and right from necessity.[20] African Americans, as Douglass would see it, were quite prepared to pay the price in order to become full citizens and fulfill their hopes of reaching the promised land. In 1894, a year before his death, Douglass concluded that the presence of deprived citizens in any section of the United States—constituting an aggrieved class smarting under terrible wrongs, denied the exercise of the commonest rights of humanity, and regarded by the ruling class of that section as outside of the government, outside of the law, outside of society, having nothing in common with the people with whom they lived the sport of mob violence and murder—was not only a disgrace and scandal to that particular section, but a menace to the peace and security of the entire country.[21] If Douglass had lived through the civil rights era of Martin Luther King, Jr., he would have reminded the leadership of the national government that "I told you so" as his foresight and vision projected the order of things to come.

One might ask: What did Douglass achieve? Up to the time of his death in February 1895, a year before the momentous Supreme Court decision on the *Plessy* case, Douglass waged an endless fight for African Americans to gain true freedom. But at a time when American society was starting again to identify itself, the results of his efforts are clearly a visible legacy of leadership. During Reconstruction Douglas made moves to influence Rutherford Hayes as he is reported to have done with Lincoln. He was a force for unity among African Americans, to whom he gave the leadership that they desperately needed. Douglass helped them become more aware of themselves and their destiny. He mapped out the passage to the promised land. Some 50 years after he died, Mary Church Terrell, a great African American woman leader, writing in *Ebony*, called Douglas the greatest of all Americans. Since that time Douglas has become the central figure, the unifying symbol of African American liberation movement, a Moses of the children of Israel marching out of their bondage to the promised land.

MARCUS GARVEY

Between 1916 and 1927, a wave of nationalism and self-determination welded the masses of African Americans into a unique protest movement led by Marcus Garvey, who became the leading spokesman for a new philosophy of the back-to-Africa movement. Garvey's Universal Negro Improvement Association (UNIA) reached its peak in 1920 by capturing the imagination of African Americans whose position had scarcely been improved by the NAACP, which tended to regard the UNIA as an agency of intellectuals, upper class African Americans, and white liberals.

The UNIA was designed at first to solve economic problems among black people everywhere, but soon it developed into a nationalistic scheme to recapture Africa from European imperialists by moving black people from the United States back to their fatherland, where a nation could be established on the pattern of Liberia. Garvey's publicity agents "dramatized Africa as a promised land to a people solely beset by discrimination, humiliation and injustice."[22]

A native of Jamaica, Garvey got involved in this movement soon after arriving in New York in 1916 at the invitation from Booker T. Washington. He toured some 38 states to study at first hand the conditions under which black people lived. He was enthusiastically received everywhere he went, and his audience contributed large sums of money to the movement. He repeated his double theme of "Africa for Africans, and asked the white South in a religious tone to let my people go!"[23] He developed a vision of a new role for black men to build new empires upon civilizations of the past and create a new light to shine down upon the entire human race. He wanted to unite black people into one great body, to establish a country and a government absolutely their own in Africa. Garvey would preach his gospel forcefully, powerfully, and convincingly.

In 1921 he reminded all black people of the greatness that awaited them in Africa, saying that when Europe was inhabited by a race of cannibals, a race of savages, naked men, heathens and pagans, Africa was peopled with a race of cultured black men, who were masters of art, science, and literature, people who were cultured and refined, people who were like gods. Why, then, he asked, should black people lose hope? He encouraged people to remember that they were once great, and that would be great again. They should not lose courage, or faith, in their ability to save themselves. They should look to the future with confidence. If they must have justice in the United States they must be strong, if they must be strong they must come together, if they must come together, they could only do so through a system of organization. Garvey warned them not to be deceived, there was no justice but strength. Might was right and if they must be heard and respected they needed to accumulate nationally in Africa. Those resources would compel unjust men to think twice before they acted.[24]

Within two years the UNIA was one of the largest black movements in the United States. In 1920 Garvey used his experience as a newspaper man to found the *Negro World*, which had a circulation of 200,000 in the ghettoes in 1921. By 1923 Garvey would claim some 6 million followers. To his followers Garvey gave parades, uniforms, pageantry. Liberty halls for African Americans were erected all over the country. For his women followers there was the Black Cross Nurse organization. For men there was the African Legion. Flags flew in the halls; they were red (for blood of the race), black (for the color of the race), and green (for the hope of new life for the race).

The Garvey movement also organized a chain of cooperative grocery stores, restaurants, factories, publishing houses, and some form of education designed to create more awareness, more clearly stated objectives toward the long journey to the promised land. They would become more open to the evils that the white people were imposing on the shoulders of the black people. The movement reached its peak in 1920 with an international convention which drew some 25,000 persons to Madison Square Garden in New York City. During this convention Garvey declared himself provisional president of the African Republic. In a speech to the convention Garvey said on behalf of all black people of the world that they would say they were striking homeward toward Africa to make the big black republic and that in the making of Africa a big black republic, what was the barrier? The barrier was the white man, who had settled in Africa as his home and they would say to the white man who now dominated Africa that it was in his interest to clear out of Africa immediately because black people were coming not as in the time of Father Abraham, but 200,000 strong. He argued that they were coming also 400 million strong, and that they meant to retake every square inch of the 12 million square miles of African territory belonging to them by divine right. He concluded that black people were out to get what had belonged to them politically, socially, economically, and in every other way.[25]

If Garvey were speaking some 50 years later his speech would have had tremendous influence on the independence movement in Africa, which was trying not to kick the white man out of Africa, but to gain political power that colonialists had enjoyed since the 18th century. Nevertheless, "Nearly every work on African nationalism, thought and politics and on the Negro freedom movements in the United States is a grand movement to be admired as an indication of a new and vigorous race-conscientiousness determined to assert itself in the postwar world.[26]

Like all men, Garvey had his faults and human weaknesses. He became vain, autocratic, and assertive. These negative qualities, as well as pressures which were generated by his black and white adversaries, led him into a series of mistakes and errors, which finally doomed his venture. In 1925 he was convicted of mail fraud in a complicated scheme to finance his Black Star Steamship Line, and a black factory corporation designed to stimulate economic independence among black people as a preparation and readiness to launch his bigger schemes in his back-to-Africa effort. He was sentenced to serve five years in the federal prison at Atlanta. While there he wrote to advise his fellow black people to assure them that he had planted well the seed of black nationalism, which could not be destroyed even by the foul play that he said had been meted out to him. When he was dead they should wrap the mantle of the red, black, and green around him, for in the new life he would rise with God's grace and blessing to head the millions up to the heights of triumphs with the colors that they would know. He encouraged them to look for him for with God's grace, he would come and bring with him countless of millions of black slaves who had died in America and the West Indies and the millions in Africa to help them in the fight for liberty, freedom, and new life.[27]

Two years later, in 1927, Garvey was pardoned by President Calvin Coolidge, who succeeded Warren Harding as president in 1923. But Garvey was deported in the same year as an undesirable alien. He settled in London, with his hopes and dreams shattered, without having set foot on the continent of Africa. Garvey died in London in 1940, lonely and forgotten. But his impact on the African American movements of succeeding generations in the United States has remained.

Like Douglass before him, Garvey succeed in his undeclared mission to bring to the black people the courage, unity, self-determination, and self-awareness to face the odds that lay ahead on their journey to the promised land. Garvey's legacy left deep, serious implications for the development of African American social, economic, political, and educational struggles. Succeeding African American leaders picked up the mantle of the black cause, left by Garvey, not in broken pieces, but in a solid, unified form and state. Garvey had made his contribution, played his part well, now it was the duty of other African American leaders to pick up the banner and raise it high on their journey to the promised land. A new Moses was needed, and a search for one was to continue.

BOOKER T. WASHINGTON

One of the greatest leaders among African Americans in the development of education was Booker T. Washington. Much has been written about him, and in this study an attempt is made to examine what impact his life and philosophy had on education and life of African Americans. Washington tells us of his early childhood, saying that his life had its beginning in the midst of the most miserable, desolate, and discouraging surroundings. Of his father, he said he knew even less than he knew his mother. He did not even know his name.[28] However, he had heard reports to the effect that he was a white man who lived on one of the plantations nearby. Whoever he was, Washington never heard of his taking the least interest in him or providing in any way for support. But he did not find special fault with him. He was simply another unfortunate victim of the institution which the nation unhappily had grafted upon it at that time.[29] About his education Washington stated that he had no schooling whatever while he was a slave, though he remembered on several occasions that he went as far as the schoolhouse door with one of his young mistresses to carry her books. The picture of several dozen boys and girls in a schoolroom engaged in study made a deep impression upon him, and he had the feeling that to get into a schoolhouse and study in that way would be about the same thing as getting into paradise.[30]

This indicates clearly that the simple things that some people took for granted were the ambition of others. For Washington a number of events and observations that were a characteristic feature of the white people would set the goals for his life ambition and achievement. He goes on to say that he remembered that at one time he saw two of his young mistresses and some lady visitors, eating ginger cakes in the yard. At that time those cakes seemed to him to be absolutely the most tempting and desirable things that he had ever seen, and he then and there resolved that if ever he got free, the height of his ambition would be reached if he could get to the point where he could secure and eat ginger-cakes in the way that he saw those ladies doing.[31]

Another example is that in the midst of his struggles and longing for an education, a young African American boy who had learned to read in the state of Ohio came to Malden, West Virginia. As soon as African Americans found out that he could read, a newspaper was secured, and at the close of nearly every day's work this young man would be surrounded by a group of men and women who were anxious to hear him read the news contained in the papers. How Washington used to envy this young man! He seemed to be a young man who ought to be satisfied with his attainments.[32]

Such is the background of life experiences that provided Washington with the realization that with education, one could do almost anything one wanted, including read newspapers and eat ginger-cakes. These two things, among others, to Washington symbolized the extent to which education could serve the needs of individuals and society. As a result of the young man from Ohio reading a newspaper, some African Americans began to discuss the possibility of starting a school in this area. There was excitement and great interest. But in the midst of this great excitement and hope there was a serious problem of finding a teacher. The young man from Ohio was simply too young to teach. After a search, the community found another man, a former soldier; it was agreed to hire him and the parents took turns providing him with food in addition to a small salary. The whole idea of organizing people for education purposes was the starting point for the long march by blacks to the promised land. It was from this Kanawha Valley school project that Washington set himself on the course to secure an education that was to enable him to leave his name in the annals of black education in the world.

Washington, like many other young men in quest of education, worked during the day, and went to school in the evening. He applied himself to learning with ambition, vision, foresight, and purpose, a combination of qualities rarely known in the history of man's quest for knowledge. The years from 1865 to 1871 seemed to shape Washington's future. This period paved the way for his other greater achievements, as shown in his biography, which includes these main highlights: for two years until 1872 he worked as a household boy in the home of Mrs. Lewis Ruffner where he gained experience as a responsible servant. From 1872 to 1875 he attended Hampton Normal and Agricultural Institute, from which he graduated with honors. He went back to teach in Malden, West Virginia, between 1875 and 1878, and was deeply saddened by the death of Reconstruction in 1877, and he held President Rutherford Hayes responsible for the tragic developments that followed Reconstruction.

From 1878 to 1879 he attended Wayland Seminary in Washington, DC. He then went back to teach at Hampton Institute until 1881, the historic year in Washington's career, because that year he founded Tuskegee Institute in Alabama. The following year he got married to Fannie Smith, a local home girl from Malden. In 1889 Washington delivered his first major speech, before the National Educational Association at Madison, Wisconsin. For some ten years Washington had established himself as the most sought-after black speaker in the nation, and was regarded as the leader and spokesman of African Americans.

In 1895, the year that Douglass died, Washington delivered the famous address as an African American representative at the opening of the Cotton States and International Exposition at Atlanta, Georgia. The *Plessy* decision upholding state segregation laws appeared to have convinced Washington that African Americans had better accommodate themselves to the philosophy of the white people if they had to have a future. In the same year Washington spoke at Harvard University Commencement and received an honorary M.A. In 1898 President William McKinley visited Tuskegee, at its 17th anniversary. The following year Washington visited Europe.

Back home from Europe Washington organized the National Negro Business League in 1900. The following year he published *Up from Slav-*

ery, and received an honorary doctorate from Dartmouth College, the school made famous by the Supreme Court decision of 1819, upholding the existence of private institutions of higher learning. In 1903 William E. B. Du Bois published his *Of Mr. Booker T. Washington and Others*, which severely criticized Washington's philosophy of the place of African Americans in American society. In 1911 Washington published *My Larger Education* to be followed in 1912 by *The Man Furthest Down*. He died in 1915 in Tuskegee.

With this brief outline of Washington's biography as background, let us now attempt to examine his philosophy as he put it into practice and as it affected the education of African Americans. With reference to his days at Hampton, Washington said "I learned what education was expected to do for an individual. I not only learned that it was not a disgrace to labor, but learned to love labor, not only for its financial value, but for labor's own sake and for the independence and self-reliance which the ability to do something which the world wants done brings."[33]

When he went back to teach at Hampton in 1879, Washington was assigned to undertake an immense responsibility. General Armstrong, the amiable principal of the school, had long been worried. He explained the reason for his worry, saying that the earnest desire for education on the part of the many African Americans who had no means of meeting even a small part of their expenses was a major concern. In case after case it was the same: a willingness to do anything to earn the necessary money, but a shortage of self-help jobs. Selecting a few of the most promising applicants, Washington offered them work in one of the Institute's industries during the daytime and had them attend school in the evening. The money they earned would pay their current expenses and a little more; the surplus would be credited to their account in the treasury when after a year or two they had built up enough credit, they would be transferred to the day school.[34]

The details of this complicated plan were left to Washington, and his outstanding success, as well as an earlier success in the project that he was asked to handle to help Indian students, brought Washington to national fame almost immediately. Of this venture in education of African Americans, Washington observed that the students showed so much earnestness both in their hard work during the day, as well as in their application to their studies in the evening, that he gave them the name The Plucky Class—a name which soon grew popular and spread throughout the Institute. After a student had been in the evening school long enough to prove what was in him, he gave him a printed certificate which read something like this: "This is to certify that James Smith is a member of the Plucky Class of the Hampton Institute, and is in good and regular standing." The students prized these certificates highly and they added greatly to the popularity of the high school. Within a few weeks the department had grown to such an extent that there were about 26 students in attendance. Washington followed the course of many of these 26 men and women and they held important and useful positions in nearly every part of the South. The evening school at Hampton which started only with 12 students now numbered between 300 and 400, and was one of the permanent and most important features of the Institute.[35]

WASHINGTON AND TUSKEGEE

It is true to say that while Washington's contribution at Hampton brought the school to national attention and fame, it was Hampton that made Washington a national figure—each was important to the other. The relation between Washington and General Armstrong was vital to each of them. General Armstrong was solidly convinced that a man of Washington's talents, ability, intelligence, and character ought to be given a greater opportunity to serve his own people. How then did Washington come to start the greatest educational venture in the history of education among blacks at Tuskegee?

Washington went on to explain, saying that during the time that he was in charge of the Indian School and evening school at Hampton, he pursued some studies himself under the direction of the instructors there. One of these was the Rev. Dr. H. B. Frisell, then principal of Hampton Institute, General Armstrong's successor. In May 1881, near the close of his first year, the opportunity he had not dared expect opened for him to begin his life work. One evening in the chapel, after the usual chapel exercises were over, General Armstrong referred to the fact that he had received a letter from some gentlemen in Alabama, asking him to recommend someone to take charge of what was to be a normal school for African Americans in the little town of Tuskegee. These gentlemen seemed to take it for granted that no African American was suitable for the position and they were expecting the general to recommend a white man for the place. The next day General Armstrong asked Washington to his office, and much to his surprise, asked him if he thought he could fill the position in Alabama.[36]

It was the decision by General Armstrong to recommend Washington as a suitable person to start the later famous school for African Americans that made Washington's name, because during the few years that he spent at Hampton, Washington received and enjoyed the confidence of General Armstrong, who felt that Washington had the potentiality for great leadership in the area of education for black people. On arriving at Tuskegee, Washington had expected to find a schoolbuilding and some kind of school equipment to enable him to make a start. But he was disappointed to find nothing of the sort.

However, Washington found one great asset which no costly schoolbuilding or equipment could give: the hundreds of empty, earnest black students who were in search of knowledge. To him Tuskegee appeared an ideal place to start the school. After a careful search for a suitable place he found an old shanty near a black Methodist Church, which he utilized to make a start. During the first few months that Washington taught in this old church building it was in such poor condition that whenever it rained one older student kindly offered to hold an umbrella over Washington's head while he listened to recitations of the other students.

During the formative years of his career at Tuskegee, Washington made some important discoveries about his students, and on the basis of these discoveries he formulated his philosophy of education that helped place his name in the history of education of African Americans. He tells us about the problem he saw among his students, saying that they first seemed to be fond of memorizing long and complicated rules in grammar and mathematics, but had little thought or knowledge of applying these rules to everyday affairs of their lives. One subject which they liked to talk about and tell him that they had mastered in arithmetic, was banking and discount. But Washington soon found out that neither they nor almost anyone else in their neighborhoods ever had a bank account. While they could locate the Sahara Desert or the capital of China on an artificial globe, the girls could not locate the proper places for the knives and forks on an actual dinner table or where the bread and meat should be placed.[37]

In a paper he wrote for a graduate seminar on "Problems of National Development" at the University of Nebraska, this author observed,

Because Booker T. Washington believed that 85 percent of African Americans in the Gulf states depended heavily on agriculture to earn a living, he concluded that Tuskegee's main educational effort must be directed at turning out graduates who were sufficiently trained to engage in agricultural occupation. He also wanted students at Tuskegee to have depth of character, humility, discipline, obedience and religious values. In this manner Tuskegee became something more than a training ground for manual labor and religion. The education that he was providing his students sought to provide a balance between training the mind and training the hand. However it was also increasingly becoming so controversial that it is was hard to measure its real impact on the developmental efforts that African Americans in general were making to arrive at their destination, the promised land.[38]

Along with the "tooth brush" education that Washington was trying to give his students came emphasis on the clean collar, the use of the nightgown, polished shoes, and, of course, the daily bath. He wanted to see them own decent homes, and the homes were not decent or complete unless they contained good, comfortable bathtubs. Of the two, Washington believed that he would rather see them own bathtubs without houses than houses without bathtubs. Staff members stood by to scrutinize the appearance of the students as they marched in for each meal and for evening prayers, taking out of the line for correction any student who failed to meet the standards. A boy or girl who was late to the dining room went without the meal.[39]

These and many other standards that Washington was trying to instill in his African American students were designed to help them become acceptable to white Americans as civilized and decent people. He was looking for something to make this possible. He was trying to develop an opportunity to impress visitors to every department in the school. At the blacksmith and wheelwright shop visitors could see wagons, small tools, spring wagon seats, and other articles; in the carpenter's shop, wardrobes, tables, wash stands, book cases, bedsteads, and chairs; in the printing office, checks, note catalogs, convention minutes, annual reports, letterheads, and invitations; at the laundry, freshly ironed bedding, dresses, collars, cuffs, shirts, underwear, table linen and towels; and in the sewing room, clothing for men, women, and children. Some 120,000 bricks stood ready for firing at the brickyard, and stacks of lumber attested to the activity of the sawmills. The farm and poultry yards exhibited vegetables, hogs, cattle, chickens, turkeys, guineas, geese, eggs, and honey; while the cooking classes had prepared cakes, jellies, yeast bread, meat of different types, especially roast pork.[40]

The overall impression was that this was a model school for blacks and all these developments took place only seven years after the school's founding. By 1889 the endowment of Tuskegee was valued at $80,000. These developments were made possible by Washington's ability at making speeches, the ability he had developed since assuming his responsibility at Tuskegee. To get money and other support from influential whites, he had to play the music according to their tune. He had to tell the white audiences what they wanted to hear about the role of the educated black people in American society, and Washington knew best how to do just that. The first occasion came in 1884 when Washington spoke about "The Educational Outlook in the South" before the National Education Association, in Madison, Wisconsin.

In that address Washington said that any movement for the elevation of the Southern African Americans, in order to be successful, must have, to a certain extent, cooperation of the Southern whites because they controlled the government and owned property. Whatever benefited African American people also benefited white people. The proper education of all whites would also benefit African Americans. He observed that the governor of Alabama would probably count it no disgrace to ride in the same railroad coach with African Americans, but the ignorant white man who cared for the governor's horse would turn up his nose in disgust. Brains, property, and character for African Americans would settle the question of civil rights. He concluded that the best course to pursue in regard to the issue of civil rights in the south was that it would settle itself.[41]

If Washington believed this, he certainly was alone in his belief, as events of the years to come and the views of his African American contemporary leaders failed to prove him right. Until 1968 Southern whites had no intention of accepting African Americans as equals, and it was not until 1975 that African Americans began to feel they had a future and only because the federal government decided to do something more demanding and more direct since the 1954 laws.

About this speech in Madison Washington would later say that there must have been not far from 4,000 persons present. "Without his knowing it, there was a larger number of people present from Alabama, and some afterward frankly told him that they went to this meeting expecting to hear the South roundly abused, but were pleasantly surprised to find that there was no word of abuse in the address. On the contrary, Washington gave credit to the South for all the praiseworthy things that he said it had done.[42]

As a result of this speech, many invitations began to come to Washington for more speeches from all over the country. In 1893 he was invited to speak at the Christian Workers meeting in Atlanta, but because he had already accepted another invitation to speak in Boston, he was forced to decline. Between 1884 and 1915 Washington gave a number of speeches that laid his philosophy of education, race relations, and black advancement. He gave interviews, wrote newspaper articles, and published a number of other books—all on these subjects.

The visit of President William McKinley to Tuskegee, the well-publicized dinner in 1901 at the White House with President Theodore Roosevelt, the 1896 Harvard commencement address and his honorary M.A. degree from there, and in 1901 the honorary doctorate from Dartmouth College—all helped to give Washington a place among world leaders and statesmen. But his 1895 address at the Cotton States and International Exposition at Atlanta has given Washington the distinction that he has deserved. At that important meeting Washington was introduced by Governor Bullock, who remarked that Washington was a representative of Negro enterprise and civilization.

Washington said that in no way had the value and manhood of all African Americans been more fittingly and generally recognized than by the managers of the magnificent exposition at an early stage of their progress. He concluded that his invitation was a recognition which he said would do more to cement the friendship of the two races than any other occurrence since emancipation. Not only this, but the opportunity here afforded would awaken among all Americans a new era of industrial progress. It did not look strange that in the first years of the emancipation of African Americans, new life began at the top instead of at the bottom, that a seat in Congress or the state legislature was more sought than real estate or industrial skill, that the political conventions or stump speaking had more attractions than starting a dairy farm or truck garden.[43]

In response the *Boston Transport* noted, "The speech of Booker T. Washington at the Atlanta Exposition this week seems to have dwarfed all other proceedings and the Exposition itself. The sensation that it has caused in the press has never been equaled."[44] President Grover Cleveland wrote a letter to Washington to say, "Your words cannot fail to delight and encourage all who wish well for your race and if our colored fellow-citizens do not learn from your utterance to gather new hope and form new determinations to gain every valuable advantage offered them by their citizenship, it will be strange indeed!"[45] Certainly, Washington was enjoying the ride on the crest of the wave of his fame as an educator and leader of the black people.

But then one may ask: What dictated Washington's views and philosophy? Did he really believe in what he was telling the white people or the black people? Or did the conditions of the times shape his mind because he felt he owed his position of leadership to the white people? What determined his stance? Washington lived during the period immediately before and after the Civil War to the time the First World War broke out. This was a period of vast material growth and economic change.

It was the era of "big business," of the Rockefellers and Carnegie, it was the age of social Darwinism, which preached the gospel of survival of the fittest in social, political, and economic competition and the struggle that had been symbolized by the Civil War. It was a time of the philosophy of the right of men of suitable ability to amass as much wealth as they could, but which also stressed their obligation to give to philanthropic organizations. It was the era of the writings of Horatio Alger, who publicized the stories of poor boys who eventually made fortunes and emphasized the moral that opportunity for success was available to anyone who was prepared to work hard, although one would note that Alger's heroes were always white boys.

When Washington was 20 years old, a crucial age for a black boy of the post–Civil War period, Reconstruction died suddenly that fateful year, 1877. Washington must have watched the compromise that Hayes was making with his northern Republican supporters and which brought to an end the efforts that were made as a result of the function of political rights: the abandonment of federal intervention in the South, the end of Reconstruction, and the belief that the South should be free to resolve its own problems without outside interference created new problems.[46] It later became clear that if left alone the South would return to its old ways of treating African Americans as second-class citizens. The beginning of the civil rights movement in 1957 proved the accuracy of this conclusion.

The obvious result was that there was a period of reconciliation between the whites of both sections of the country, who gradually began to share the belief that black people anywhere were inherently inferior, much against Washington's admonition to the contrary. Large amounts of literature began to appear to support this new attitude by whites. Newspapers, political speeches, sermons, social scientists, and psychologists like A. Stanley Hall—all began to warn about the disastrous effects of giving the black people any rights at all. Such books as *The Negro: A Menace to American Civilization* and *The Negro: A Beast* were widely read.

There also appeared a period of European nationalism. In 1936 Germany had taken on the idea of the white race as a superrace to an extreme view, as Adolf Hitler implanted into the German people the thinking that Germans were a superrace. But in that same year this idea was badly shattered by Jesse Owens, an African American athlete from Ohio, at the Berlin Olympic Games and embarrassed Hitler so badly that he became so aggressive on the European international scene as to sow seeds of the European confrontation three years later.

Also the decisions of the U.S. Supreme Court from 1883 to 1896 advanced further argument that African Americans must be better left to seal their own fate in the South. The Civil Rights Act of 1875 was meaningless. In 1898 the Supreme Court upheld the Mississippi constitution that sought to disenfranchise African Americans by means of a biased testing system. The white extremists in the South, who were now firmly in control of southern politics, began to preach strongly that segregation and the elimination of African Americans from any participation in politics would improve race relations by removing causes of friction. But the reverse was actually the result as racial conflict began to increase.

Lynching and brutal murder and other forms of violence carried out by whites reached, as we have noted, a new peak between 1890 and 1910. Contrary to Washington's prediction of African Americans remaining humble, law-abiding, and patient, race riots occurred in several southern cities in the wake of campaigns to rid African Americans of any rights of their citizenship. By all counts while Washington was acclaimed the greatest African American leader by the kind of speeches he was making and by his philosophy of education, seen in the Tuskegee programs, race prejudice was more intense during the latter part of the 19th century and the first decade of the 20th century than any other previous period. Many people observed that the position of African Americans had taken a turn for the worse.

Under these and other circumstances, Washington sought the help of white people to see the importance of their role in building Tuskegee on a more solid financial foundation. He received what he asked for because by the time of his death in 1915, Tuskegee had property and endowment valued at $2 million. But the whites gave this assistance on one clear understanding: that Jim Crow laws would vigorously be enforced. This, in turn, meant that African Americans were put in their proper place, as "freed slaves." Somehow Washington was not fully aware of what was happening. He was a realist; either African Americans had to accommodate themselves to the kind of treatment that whites could feel free to determine, or they would attempt to stick their necks out and fight it out all the way. This last option was closed to Washington, but future leaders would want to keep it open. Malcolm X, H. Rap Brown, Eldridge Cleaver, Kwame Toure, and Angela Davis are among African American leaders who wanted to have this option kept open.

Washington saw the first alternative as a better choice of the two. So he tried desperately to pacify African Americans and urge them to rely on the "goodwill" of whites, whom he was equally trying to please and appease. In the process Washington failed to achieve his objectives among whites and so lost an opportunity to negate his repudiation among his own people. As late as 1912 Washington was still telling whites: "We are trying to instill into the Negro mind that if education does not make the Negro humble, simple and of service to the community, then it will not be encouraged."[47] He said nothing about the same effect of education on whites.

Not entirely unknown to Washington, the 1895 Atlanta speech aroused a great resentment among African Americans, who began to feel that Washington had sold their cause down the drain for personal reasons and benefit, as well as for the reasons that he put Tuskegee above their interests. African Americans all over the country directly attacked him for accepting social segregation, for giving Tuskegee students a kind of education that made them semiskilled laborers in the white man's society, for indirectly encouraging the South to take measures and make laws that were detrimental to their advancement. They also criticized him for not launching an aggressive political campaign, for concentrating all his educational effort on training students to accept the status quo in which whites were using them as an industrial tool to turn themselves into capitalists, for failing to take a stand against the countless Jim Crow laws that were rapidly coming up in the country.

Among the national newspapers that became Washington's many critics was the *Chicago Times-Herald*, which noted in 1898 after Washington's speech in the city: "He pictured the Negro choosing slavery rather than extinction, rehearsed the conduct of the Negro, and drew a vivid pathetic picture of the Southern slaves protecting and supporting the families of their masters while the latter were fighting to perpetuate slavery."[48]

TROTTER VERSUS WASHINGTON

Equally critical of Washington was the Boston *Guardian*, which was edited by William Monroe Trotter, an African American leader educated at Harvard of the period when Charles Eliot served as president. Trotter felt that Washington had lost sight of his purpose because he was a victim of manipulation by southern whites. Trotter also argued that because Washington was supported by appropriation from the Alabama state legislature as an opportunity to make a name for himself, he sacrificed the cause of African Americans. Trotter opposed the kind of industrial training that Tuskegee was giving African Americans because, he argued, "the idea lying back of it is the relegating of the race to serfdom. That underlying idea, the claimed innate mental inferiority of Negroes, must be admitted to be the reason why industrial education for Negroes is more popular with the general white public than advanced or classical education."[49]

Trotter further argued that African Americans, to prove their quality, as Washington urged, had to seek and succeed in various highly skillful occupations at the highest level of education. But conditions did not permit this to happen. Washington therefore was trying to solve the problem from the wrong direction. Trotter saw political and social issues as the fundamentals for the advancement of African Americans. Trotter concluded that this development could come about only after political and other civil rights had been achieved. Trotter called Washington "this apostle of industrialism"[50] who, he said, started off well but got easily misled by the selfish influential whites who made him their puppet.

The basic difference between Washington and Trotter came over the question of advocacy of the development of African Americans, the acceptance of racial segregation, and the kind of education African Americans must receive. Their far-differing views created bitterness between the two leaders, regrettably at a time when they needed a united approach to fight for the common good of all African Americans. The difference in their background, the manner and style of leadership between the two men added a basic framework for a struggle that in turn added further crucial factors to the bitterness between Washington and other African American leaders of his time.

While Washington came up from the environment of black masses, Trotter was from a white background of Boston. Maybe this is why Trotter was able to have more outward pride in African Americans. Washington liked to entertain his audience with analogies, homely stories about rural African Americans. He was quick to apologize for what he termed mistakes among African Americans during Reconstruction in seeking political advancement before educational attainment. Trotter could simply not tolerate what he called Washington's "crime of race ridicule and belittlement."[51] Trotter was not the only African American leader to oppose Washington's philosophy of education and the place of African Americans in society.

Opposition to Washington's leadership was now gathering momentum for an organized challenge to his assumed role as a spokesman of African Americans. Some African American leaders wondered if a conspiracy did not exist between Washington and the southern whites who were now clearly determined to reduce all African Americans to the level of second-class citizens. Maybe Tuskegee itself was a conspiracy, who would know? Trotter had good reason to wonder because some white-run newspapers "were smothering all those who wished to condemn Tuskegee."[52] Trotter was more blunt in his reaction to the controversy. He wrote in *The Guardian* in 1902 to say that the African American trump card on Washington was his corrupt methods. The real issue about him was his lust for power, his desire to be a political leader, to be czar, his clandestine methods of attempting to crush out all who would not bow to him. Trotter said it was plain that Washington sought to be criticized and if it was within his power, he would get where there was no African American paper to oppose his leadership, and no African American would dare to do so. Trotter concluded that Washington wanted to rule the black race with an iron hand.[53]

Also in 1902 *The Guardian* reported that Washington's daughter, Portia, had dropped out of Wellesley College and went on the say that Washington's children were not taking to higher education like a duck takes to water, and that while their defect in this undertaking was undoubtedly somewhat inherited, they justified, to some extent, their father's well-known antipathy to anything higher than the three Rs for African Americans. A breaking point between Trotter and Washington had been reached. Washington could no longer speak on behalf of African Americans. But he had yet to receive harsher criticism and face greater opposition and challenge from other African American leaders besides Trotter, as we will see in the next chapter.

LEADERSHIP FROM HARRIET TUBMAN TO JULIAN BOND

One cannot dispute or ignore the effectiveness of the leadership of individuals like Dred Scott, Harriet Tubman, Roy Wilkins, Benjamin Hooks, John Lewis, Julian Bond, Myrlie Evers,[54] and Kweisi Mfume, to name only a few. Each of these individuals provided unique qualities of leadership that became a demonstration of their unquestionable commitment to the course and success of the journey to the promised land. History says that after gaining her own freedom, her arrival in the promised land, Harriet Tubman, returned to the South at least 19 times to rescue her own family and more than 300 other slaves. She was so successful that her opponents placed a price of $40,000 on her head.[55] She used her metaphorical philosophy, "I'll see you in the morning, safe in the promised land,"[56] to transmit such a strong appeal to African Americans that it offered them encouragement and determination to continue their journey to the promised land.

In the same way Julian Bond has been a giant in the annals of leadership among African Americans on their journey to the promised land. This author has watched him over the years and is truly at a loss for words to describe the effectiveness of his leadership role. The world knows him as the narrator of the successful television series *Eyes on the Prize*, a presentation of the civil rights movement beginning in 1958. Throughout his adult life Bond has been an integral part of the leadership of the civil rights movement. Bond began to play a leadership role in 1960 when he was still a student at Morehouse College. He was a founding member of the student sit-in and antisegregation organization, the Student Nonviolent Coordinating Committee (SNCC). As SNCC's communications director, Bond was active in protests and registration campaigns throughout the South. Bond was elected to the Georgia House of Representatives in 1965 and served until 1986. His leadership skills were outstanding in every way. As chairman of the board of directors of NAACP at the time this book was being written in 1999, Bond has continued to show rare qualities of leadership in its activities.[57]

SUMMARY AND CONCLUSION

In all movements, especially for people who are struggling for development, the question of leadership becomes very critical. This chapter has outlined the roles that four major African American leaders played in providing the direction that African Americans took in their journey to the promised land. Their views and positions on the question of the future of African Americans commended the attention of both whites and African Americans. But what is interesting in this situation is that of the four leaders discussed in this chapter, Marcus Garvey and Booker T. Washington encountered some problems as they tried to exert their leadership roles. Garvey was implicated in a mail fraud case that resulted in his arrest, trial, conviction, and deportation. One wonders if Garvey were a native-born African American whether he would have met the fate that he actually did. The strength of his conviction, the insights that were part of his endeavor, the belief that manifested his action—all testify to his unquestionable commitment to the cause of African Americans.

Washington was so enthusiastic about the promotion of education for his people that he, too, went out of his way to persuade white America to support his program. The letter he received from President McKinley to support his educational program at Tuskegee proved to him that he was doing the right thing. But in doing so he might have crossed the line, because other African American leaders, William Trotter and W.E.B. Du Bois, rejected him openly because they thought that in his effort to please white Americans he compromised basic values and goals that African Americans had set for themselves. What this means is that any leader can become controversial because he is not absolute in his knowledge of the issues. However, each of these four leaders made a viable contribution in trying to function as a Moses in the African American struggle to continue their journey to the promised land.

NOTES

1. NAACP, "What You Should Know About NAACP" (Baltimore, 1999).
2. Ibid.
3. PBS, *The Road to Brown: Charles H. Houston and the Law* (1989).
4. NAACP, "What You Should Know About NAACP."
5. In Nyanja, the main African language in Malawi, Mfume is a derivative of *amfumu*, and means a polished man or a gentleman above others. In West Africa it is son of a king or someone who belongs to a high class judged by his care and concern for others. Anyone who has met Mfume would readily agree.
6. NAACP, "President's Corner: Kweisi Mfume, President and Chief Executive Officer of the NAACP" (Baltimore, 1999).
7. History has recorded that when his wife Martha died, Thomas Jefferson, the third president of the United States, and Sally Hemings, one of his slaves, became parents to seven children. On November 12, 1998, two African Americans, a brother and sister, and two white Americans, also a brother and sister, appeared on the *Oprah Winfrey Show* to discuss openly the fact that they were descendants of Jefferson. See also, for example, August Meier and Elliott Rudwick, *From Plantation to Ghetto*, 3rd ed. (New York: Hill and Wang, 1976), p. 51.
8. William Lloyd Garrison in a preface to Frederick Douglass, *Narrative of the Life of Frederick Douglass: An American Slave Written by Himself* (New York: New American Library, 1845), p. vii.
9. Ibid., p. 43.
10. About this Douglass says, "My father was a white man. He was admitted to be such by all I ever heard speak on my parentage. The opinion was also whispered that my master was my father. My mother and I were separated when I was an infant, before I knew her as my mother" (ibid., p. 21).
11. L. Bennet, Jr., *Pioneers in Protest* (Chicago: Johnson Publishing Company, 1968), p. 199.
12. Dickson A. Mungazi, *Education and Government Control in Zimbabwe: A Study of the Commissions of Inquiry, 1908–1974* (New York: Praeger Publishers, 1990), p. 12.
13. Bennet, *Pioneers in Protest*, p. 205.

14. Ibid., p. 206.

15. Ibid., p. 207.

16. Ibid., p. 209. This line of thinking is the basis of Dickson A. Mungazi, *Colonial Policy and Conflict in Zimbabwe: A Study of Cultures in Collision* (New York: Taylor and Francis, 1992).

17. M. H. Baulware, *The Oratory of Negro Leaders, 1900–1968* (Westport, CT: Negro Universities Press, 1969), p. 55.

18. Ibid., p. 57.

19. Ibid., p. 59.

20. Ibid., p. 60.

21. Bennet, *Pioneers in Protest*, p. 234.

22. Baulware, *The Oratory of Negro Leaders*, p. 56.

23. Ibid., p. 57.

24. Bennet, *Pioneers in Protest*, p. 236.

25. Ibid., p. 237.

26. S. O. Mezu and R. Desai, *Black Leaders of the Centuries* (Buffalo, NY: Black Academy Press, 1970), p. 185.

27. J. Bennet, *Pioneers in Protest*, p. 238.

28. This situation was quite typical during slavery. It has already been concluded earlier in this chapter that Frederick Douglass did not know both his parents. George Washington Carver, another prominent African American who distinguished himself as a scientist, was removed from his mother as an infant and never knew his father. The institution of slavery had a devastating effect in this regard.

29. Booker T. Washington, *Up From Slavery* (New York: Doubleday, 1916), p. 3.

30. Ibid., p. 6.

31. Ibid., p. 10.

32. Ibid., p. 28.

33. Ibid., p. 72.

34. S. R. Spencer, Jr., *Booker T. Washington and the Negro Place in American Life* (Boston: Little, Brown, 1955), p. 46.

35. Washington, *Up From Slavery*, p. 105.

36. Ibid., p. 106.

37. Ibid., p. 122.

38. Dickson A. Mungazi. "The Interpretation of Booker T. Washington's Contemporaries of His Work." Paper written for Graduate Seminar on Problems of National Development (Lincoln: University of Nebraska, Summer 1977).

39. Spencer, Jr., *Booker T. Washington and the Negro Place in American Life*, p. 79.

40. Ibid., p. 84.

41. E. L. Thornbrough, *Booker T. Washington* (Englewood Cliffs, NJ: Prentice-Hall, 1969), p. 59.

42. B. Washington, *Up From Slavery*, p. 200.

43. Ibid., p. 218.

44. Quoted by Washington himself in ibid., p. 226.

45. Ibid., p. 227.

46. Thornbrough, *Booker T. Washington*, p. 72.

47. Charles E. Silberman, *Crisis in Black and White* (New York: Vintage Books, 1964), p. 129.

48. B. Washington, *Up From Slavery*, p. 254.

49. S. R. Fox, *The Guardian of Boston: William Monroe Trotter* (New York: Atheneum, 1970), p. 36.

50. Ibid., p. 35.

51. Ibid., p. 37.

52. Ibid., p. 38.

53. Ibid., p. 39.

54. In 1995, over 30 years after the assassination of her husband, Medgar Evers, Myrlie Evers was elected chairman of the NAACP board of directors and served with distinction for nearly two years.

55. Charles Johnson and Patricia Smith, *Africans in America* (New York: Harcourt Brace and Company, 1998), p. 322.

56. Ibid., p. 323.

57. NAACP, "Julian Bond: A Biographical Sketch" (Baltimore, June 3, 1999).

4

Obstacles to the Journey: Conflict in the Strategy

> As a rule the one-teacher schools do not give instruction beyond the 5th grade.
>
> W.E.B. Du Bois, 1926

DU BOIS AND THE CIVIL RIGHTS MOVEMENT

Among the African American leaders who opposed Washington was W.E.B. Du Bois, a Ph.D. graduate from Harvard University. Like William Trotter, Du Bois grew up in Massachusetts. After high school he went to the South for three years to attend Fisk University and to teach in Tennessee rural schools during the summers. In 1890 he entered Harvard University, where, for the next three years, he met and knew Trotter, who was admitted into Harvard University in 1891, and whom he described as a stubborn, influential member of his class. Du Bois and Trotter joined a party of African American students who traveled to Amherst to see the graduation of two prominent African American members of their movement. Du Bois then became professor of sociology at Atlanta University, where he began to write extensively on issues of great concern to African Americans following the *Plessy* decision of 1896.

At Atlanta he kept to the college community as much as possible, avoided the embarrassment of being black in the South, and devoted himself to the task of uplifting his fellow African Americans through the establishment of what was known as scientific truth. In the late 1890s his racial philosophy was much like Washington's and it is said that he nearly took a job at Tuskegee. But gradually his thinking became more radical as he came to realize that he could not remain silent and removed from the African American struggle for social justice and equality while African Americans were brutally murdered, lynched, starved, and subjected to other forms of inhumane treatment that they received at the hands of whites, especially the KKK.

In 1902 Du Bois was criticized for remaining silent after some participants of the NAACP annual conference argued that they were manipulated by supporters of Washington to deny him an opportunity for leadership among his people. Maybe it was because of this incident, as well as the 1895 Atlanta Compromise speech that Washington gave and his general philosophy on education and life of African Americans, that Du Bois now took a radical position. He became embattled with Washington's failure to take a definite stand against the crisis and humiliation that African Americans were suffering since the death of Reconstruction in 1877. So he now began to direct his efforts against the institutions of the American society.

In 1903 Du Bois published *The Souls of Black Folk*, which Roy Wilkins called in 1961 "one of the greatest books of our century, a timeless and vital contribution to the understanding of the Negro culture."[1] In this book Du Bois explains why he disagrees with the policies and philosophy of Booker T. Washington about the future of African Americans. He noted that Washington's program of industrial education for African American students, reconciliation with the southern whites, and submission and silence on civil and political rights did not originate with Washington. As far back as 1830 free African Americans in the South had tried to build some industrial schools as a viable form of their education. The American Missionary Association had taught African American students some trades as part of their mission to them.

Du Bois believed that Washington was trying to strengthen his philosophy of industrial education by advocating a system of social conditioning that would perpetuate an environment of slavery by seeking alliance with whites under terms dictated by the South. Washington acknowledged the effect of what he was saying about both the struggle of African Americans and the white community which supported his program. His ideas received more support when he said, "It startled the North to hear a Negro advocating such a program after many decades of bitter complaint, it startled and won the applause of the South, it interested and won the administration of the North, and after a confused murmur of protest it was silenced if it did not convert the Negroes themselves."[2] Du Bois took issue with this approach, arguing that to gain sympathy and cooperation of the various elements compromising the South was Washington's first objective and task, but he soon found out that the white community was not interested in the kind of compromise that Washington was suggesting.

For nearly a decade Washington's wisdom was the only thing that seemed to matter in the perception of southern whites about African Americans. Nothing else appeared as important. The speech he gave in Atlanta was the last word spoken by any African American leader. His view that "in all things purely social we can be as separate as the five fingers and yet one as the hand in all things essential to mutual progress,"[3] was considered the ultimate ability of African Americans to recognize the reality of the power of southern whites to influence African American thought process. But Du Bois was not pleased with what he regarded as Washington's betrayal of the aspirations of African Americans, saying that the Atlanta Compromise was by all counts the most notable thing in Washington's career. The South interpreted it in different ways. Radical elements received it as a complete surrender to the demand for civil and political equality for African Americans.[4]

Du Bois also reacted by stating that he saw nothing wrong with "a lone black boy pouring over his French grammar book deep in the weeds and dirt of a neglected home,"[5] a statement Washington had referred to in his speech, and wondered if the reference was not a reflection of Washington's own misunderstanding of the real concern of African Americans which he was now forcing his students at Tuskegee to endure. Du Bois felt that higher education in the liberal arts was the only way to lead African Americans from the hands of poverty and second-class citizenship that they were being forced to accept.

Du Bois figured that if only 10 percent of African Americans received proper higher education, different from the Tuskegee type, then this talented tenth would lead the African American masses on the journey to the promised land. He argued that the masses needed the training in trade and industrial skills in order to secure employment, but that this must not come first as Washington was trying to do, because this kind of education for former slaves would produce a docile African American working class, which was always at the mercy of the whites who would seek to exploit them.

With the passage of time the difference of opinion between Du Bois and Washington became so intense that African American progress became very difficult to measure. African Americans now began to view Washington's Tuskegee with doubts and suspicion. For a time students chose to go elsewhere because Tuskegee was not what they thought it stood for. Efforts were being made to find some common ground between the two men as some white liberals began to stress the things that they had in common, such as both men appeared to respect each other. L. A. Lacey concluded that although Washington had a power base among whites,

both men fought to get racist laws off the books. Both men favored black nationalism, or racial self help, but Washington's nationalist program tended to be primarily economic, while Du Bois's theories encompassed political and cultural ideas. Both men were deeply committed to the black race, although Washington limited his concern to black America and Du Bois's involvement included black Africans and black West Indians.[6]

The views that Du Bois and Washington had in common were not sufficient to stop the verbal war between the two leaders; great differences still remained strong enough to keep them apart. Du Bois now began to direct his efforts to the civil rights movement. He was solidly convinced that in order for African Americans to obtain a good education, they had to secure civil rights first. Then and only then would they be able to secure other opportunities as their rights. In 1905 Du Bois began to take positive action with the help of some 29 members of the Talented Tenth.

The group worked out what became the first organized civil rights movement, which they called the Niagara Movement. A few other people were invited to attend this important meeting at Fort Erie, Ontario, and there appeared to be quite some excitement and enthusiasm over the establishment of the movement. Many more people were expected to attend the conference. But, according to some rumors, some people declined to attend at the last minute because they were pressured or threatened by some white friends of Booker T. Washington. However, the conference went on as planned and Du Bois was elected general secretary, making him the second most prominent living African American at that time to act as a spokesman of African Americans.[7] He was now recognized by many as the representative of the African American aspiration.

For many Du Bois was then an example of what an African American man was and could do for his people. His educational accomplishments were looked at by many as the goal for all African Americans, and he hoped for a day when all black men would obtain higher education than Tuskegee was giving, so that whites had no way to stop their advancement, their journey to the promised land. But first things must come first, and civil rights came first on the list of their long-range planning.

Du Bois was satisfied that the Niagara Movement would function most effectively with a simple structure, and the executive committee was made up of the chairman of the Movement's State Associations. Committees were established: Finance, Interstate Conditions and Needs, Organization, Civil and Political Rights, Legal Defense (which was destined to play a major role in the civil rights movement later), Rescue and Reform, Economic Opportunity, Health, Education, Press and Public Opinion. Obviously "the mood of the conference was vigorous and the statements that came out of the conference discussion sounded like a call for a new American revolution."[8]

The participants agreed that they were not going to beg for or ask the white people for their legitimate rights, that it was now time to demand them as a right. They would not attempt to appease them with sugar-coated, meaningless speeches made by Booker T. Washington; they would not curry favor with white people by sounding the shortcomings of their people; they would not seek to please the whites at the expense of the progress of their people. So they clarified their demands which fell into eight groups: (1) manhood voting rights, (2) a free black press, (3) freedom of speech, (4) elimination of all forms of class distinction, based on race or color, (5) equal employment opportunity, (6) end of white superiority, (7) the recognition of human brotherhood, and (8) united and wise leadership.

No mention of educational opportunity was made. It is a matter of historical record that Washington tried to put a quick end to the Niagara Movement because he saw its birth and activities as a threat to his popularity among whites as the leader of the black people, and the existence of such Movement would distract the attention he was enjoying. Washington was cunning, he had power and influence. First he tried to exercise leadership, but when that failed, he tried to invite underground spy ring activities against the Movement.

Meanwhile newspapers that were friendly to Washington's philosophy attacked the Niagara Movement leaders by suggesting that they were dangerous subversive individuals whose activity threatened the good relationships that existed between African Americans and whites as a result of Washington's efforts. But all these efforts failed and the leaders of the Niagara Movement strongly believed in their positions and had prepared themselves for a tough fight. Du Bois moved to strengthen the Niagara Movement by seeking an alliance with the Constitution League, an interracial civil rights organization founded in 1904 by John Milholland. Washington did everything in his power to put an end to the union of these two organizations, but again he was unsuccessful. Neither of these organizations was against Washington per se, but according to him, one was with him all the way on his own terms, or one was against him and was his enemy.

Then more things began to happen when the Niagara Movement held its second conference, and a number of resolutions were passed. President Theodore Roosevelt, who invited Washington to the White House dinner in 1901, and Secretary of War William Howard Taft were both condemned for their short-sighted views and negative attitudes toward African Americans. In 1906 race riots broke out in Atlanta, and Du Bois, who was out of town, quickly came back to find that more African Americans than whites had been killed. On the train back to Atlanta Du Bois composed a poem, "A Litany at Atlanta," which was an accusation of the whites for starting the fighting, and indicated that only by implementing the Niagara principles could the two races ever hope to live together peacefully and happily in the spirit of brotherhood and equality.

Meanwhile other developments were taking place during the following year, 1907. The Niagara Movement set out to educate African Americans and white people alike to reject a policy of racial protest, and it demonstrated to the nation and the world that all African Americans were not sold on Washington's ideal and gospel of accommodation and subjection to the Jim Crow and other white attitudes that were sweeping through the country. Du Bois played a major role in this vital strategy; his devoted followers were proud of his efforts and accomplishments.

African Americans were gradually embracing the view that Washington was misleading them, that for them to achieve their goals the educational programs at Tuskegee were far too inadequate, and that a new approach must be made. They became convinced that unless they secured their inherent civil rights, any education they may get would be useless as they would be subjected to the will of an unjust society. So African Americans sought ways of strengthening their new strategy. But in that approach a conflict emerged that seemed to bring sunset on the journey to the promised land. After the success of the 1907 conference, public rallies were held in New York, Cleveland, Minneapolis, Baltimore, and Washington, DC. By 1909 another civil rights organization, run mostly by liberal whites, had been formed, dedicated to similar objectives as the Niagara Movement. The possibility of a merger was discussed, but the two organizations met together in New York in 1909 as a National Negro Conference.

THE FOUNDING OF THE NAACP

During the following year, 1910, the National Negro Conference became the National Association for the Advancement of Colored People, which became the most powerful and enduring civil rights movement ever formed in the United States. Du Bois was the moving force behind this historic development, and the nightmare that Washington had always dreaded as a distant possibility now began to haunt him as a reality. He knew very well that he would no longer command the following that he had enjoyed, that he would no longer enjoy the monopoly of a one-sided view which he had expressed on behalf of African Americans, he knew that his tenure as a leader of African Americans was sadly coming to a close.

Du Bois's philosophy of education was to give way to the new era of modern thinking. Washington's back-door approach to social issues had to give way to more practicable methods that were in line with recent developments and trends. The hoe which had been the main apparatus of his agricultural training at Tuskegee was no longer suitable to the new

African American outlook and attitudes. That entire educational system of African Americans was to be overhauled. The organization became incorporated under the laws of the State of New York. Its purposes were stated as:

1. To promote equality of rights and eradicate caste or race prejudice among the citizens of the United States.
2. To advocate the interest of colored citizens.
3. To secure for them impartial suffrage.
4. To increase their opportunities for securing justice in the courts, education for their children, employment according to their ability, and complete equality before the law.[9]

The signers of the incorporation papers included Du Bois, Mary W. Ovington, Oswald G. Villard, John Helmes, and Walter Sacks. The executive committee members were chairman W.E. Walling, the famous Boston lawyer; treasurer, John Milholland; secretary, Francis Bascoers; director of publicity research, W.E.B. Du Bois. Oswald Villard had a rent-free office in the *Evening Post* building. From the very start the organization and its workers were interracial, its board of directors included eight former members of the Niagara Movement. Within three months, NAACP opened its first local office in Chicago, to be followed by hundreds of other local offices across the country. Within a short time NAACP organized its legal structure on a strong foundation because its leaders knew that the legal battles ahead were more important at the time than the political struggles.

The local work was to have a great effect on American racial patterns. With this background, NAACP was now ready to grapple with the immense problems that confronted the black people in their search for social justice and equality. Soon after its birth, NAACP lawyers filed a petition of pardon for a sharecropper in South Carolina, who had been sentenced to death for killing a police officer. The officer had burst into his cabin after midnight to charge him with breach of contract. The newly formed NAACP launched an intensive publicity campaign by means of press statements and articles which exposed acts of racial injustice and took the opportunity to set forth the objectives of the association, which ran its own official organ, *The Crisis*, which was edited by Du Bois.[10]

As a result *The Crisis* received Du Bois's brilliance and ability as an editor. The paper achieved an unprecedented circulation level among African American readers and attracted the attention of many whites. By the end of its first year *The Crisis* had 12,000 readers. Eventually *The Crisis* became self-supporting, with its staff paid from its own resources, rather than from the association funds. This way it became the only magazine in the country to become devoted to the service of African Americans without depending on subsidy. Its founding, as well as the role Du Bois played in its running, became one of the greatest contributions of the NAACP to the African American cause and the national cultural life.

NAACP knew from the start that in order to secure the desperately needed rights in education, politics, and economic welfare, legal security for blacks must be won first. They had watched their rights eroding away in courts, and the era of conservative attitudes in the Supreme Court had set a dangerous pattern. Therefore they were going to do everything in their power to stop and reverse this trend. It was a tough undertaking, yet it had to be done. Immediately after the legal work was set up, many cases came before NAACP, and *The Crisis* did its best to publicize any unjust elements in each case. For the first time after the death of Reconstruction, black people began to look to the future with some hope.[11]

From the start NAACP handled legal cases too many to list. With each legal success by NAACP, white violence against blacks increased, but for NAACP there was no turning back. In 1912 NAACP successfully intervened to stop the discharge of a black fireman on the Southern Railroad when the white Railroad Brotherhood demanded his replacement. A black man who was denied entrance to Palisades Amusement Park in New York was awarded $300 damages and was given a season ticket to the park. Further, NAACP efforts resulted in swimming pools, dance pavilions, and countless other recreational centers being open to blacks. In 1915, the year of Washington's death, a group of blacks whose newly bought homes were bombed in Kansas City because they were in a white neighborhood brought their case to NAACP. With this case won, NAACP began to lay ground work for future court battles against residential segregation.

In 1917 NAACP filed suit against the State of Oklahoma's "grandfather" clause, which was part of the Southern strategy as enacted laws exempted from rigorous tests persons whose parents or grandparents were eligible to vote prior to 1860. This vicious legislation allowed poor and illiterate whites to vote but denied the same rights to black people because none of their parents or grandparents were eligible to vote because they were still slaves. The Supreme Court invalidated this clause and this action was the high-water mark in the activities of NAACP. The action was hailed as the most important court decision affecting blacks since the *Plessy* case of 1896, when the Supreme Court upheld racial segregation.

But other forces were working against the success of NAACP. Powerful philanthropists, mostly of the Booker T. Washington school of philosophy, gave NAACP no help, financial or otherwise. Some conservative white people and some prominent black people attacked NAACP as a radical organization, whose program of complete racial equality was impossible and utopian. They charged that NAACP policies and principles did relations more harm than good. Few newspapers gave its activities sympathetic encouragement.

In the South *The Crisis* was violently denounced. In some cities the paper could not be sold openly. Lynching and mass murder were intensified. But with these opposing forces NAACP became even stronger. Du Bois was clearly emerging as the new spokesman of African Americans; his fiery editorials in *The Crisis* were quoted more often. The paper began to publicize the voting records of all congressmen on antiblack bills, and all candidates campaigning for national office received from NAACP questionnaires regarding their stand on civil rights. The Washington branch of NAACP was designated the watchdog for any anti-Negro legislation brought before Congress or any hostile action on the part of the president that may be known to exist.

At the end of the First World War, Du Bois was sent to Paris by NAACP to cover the Peace Conference. He then remained in France to participate in the first Pan-African Congress, which he had called to bring attention to peace delegates and the civilized world on the cause of black people all over the world. There were 12 Africans, 16 African Americans, 20 from the West Indies. Du Bois was able to play a leading role at the Conference.

Du Bois's personality, his will and courage, his vision of the real problems of the black people were an asset to the Conference, which formulated resolutions calling for all African Americans to maintain their sense of identity, to work toward a single purpose of giving African Americans a sense of human dignity, self-respect, ability to meet the vexing problems of their oppressive society, and keep hoping that someday African Americans would find the peace of mind, the joy of feeling like truly free human beings with all their inherent rights restored, the glory of arriving in the promised land.

Then came an unfortunate turn in Du Bois's fortune. While he was enjoying his new popularity as leader, Marcus Garvey appeared on the scene of the African American freedom movement. As we have seen, Garvey was frank and inflammatory. He told the black people wherever they were that he could deliver them from the misery of oppression in the land of discrimination to the promised land of freedom in Africa. While NAACP had achieved some impressive court successes, the majority of black people did not seem to have a feeling for court action alone. They had many other physical and material needs, and they were too simple and unsophisticated to understand the legal process that was eventually destined to secure and guarantee their human rights.

During this period of confusion among black people, Marcus Garvey addressed himself to the immediate needs that were their major concerns. He spoke to them in the language that they could understand; the legal language of NAACP was too hard for them. Garvey then mounted a campaign against NAACP and Du Bois became his target. He accused him and his co-workers of deliberately ignoring the masses and of worshipping the white man's symbols of progress. He argued that Du Bois was always confused and misguided because he had white ancestors. L. A. Lacy quoted Garvey as having said of Du Bois, "Sometimes he is French, another time he's Dutch, and when it is convenient, he is a Negro. The man who built the pyramids looked like me and I think the best thing I can do is to keep looking like me."[12]

In spite of these attacks, Du Bois did not retaliate. Such behavior would not have been consistent with the image of refinement that he had of himself, and he called on Garvey to cooperate with NAACP in the great task that the black people were facing together. But Garvey would have none of it. The difference of approach to the same problems had some negative effects on African Americans. Only years after Garvey was arrested, sentenced, pardoned, and deported was NAACP able to command the influence and leadership among African Americans, who by this time were much more aware of what NAACP was trying to accomplish.

Beginning in 1917 NAACP concerned itself with activities which, though viewed from a legal perspective, had some implications for education of blacks. At the beginning of the U.S. participation in the First World War there was no provision for training of black officers. NAACP undertook to correct the situation. Joel Spingarn, the famous professor at Columbia University and an active member of NAACP, led a delegation to Washington, DC, to see what could be done about the problem. Out of his discussion with officials he was told that if 200 college graduates could be found, a training school would be started for them. Some 1,500 names were collected, mass meetings were held, pressure was heavily applied on Congress.[13]

The South rejected any form of higher training for African Americans. Although opposed to segregation in principle, NAACP approved a proposal for a separate school to train African American officials. Later NAACP used such a school to fight segregation. The school was established in Fort Des Moines, Iowa, in the spring of 1917, and 1,250 young black men were enrolled. In October of that year, 639 black officers were commissioned. Clearly NAACP had won a partial victory over military prejudice.

From this time on NAACP won one victory after another as it became better organized and gained experience, but the fortunes of the black soldiers within the U.S. Army were not the best. In that same year, 1917, there was a tragedy in Houston, in which 13 African American soldiers were sentenced to death and 41 to life imprisonment for their part in a riot that left 18 whites dead. *The Crisis* was violently attacked for reporting countless incidents of racial prejudice. Congressman J. F. Byrnes of South Carolina demanded that the paper be investigated.

In 1919 Attorney General Mitchell Palmer labeled a number of black publications subversive. A. Philip Randolph, editor of the *Messenger*, was arrested. In 1920 New York listed *The Crisis* as contributing to revolutionary radical views, and the entire black press was considered dangerous to peace. The KKK became even more violent. In the face of all this, NAACP continued to grow; it had set its course, it had tasted the forbidden fruit of success, it was determined to secure more.

NAACP had mobilized its resources now to fight segregation with any means at its disposal. In addition to legal battles of the first decade of the 20th century, they saw need to embrace political weapons to secure rights for blacks, even if it meant confrontation with the U.S. president. In 1930 President Herbert Hoover nominated J. J. Parker of North Carolina for the United States Supreme Court, and sent his name to the Senate for confirmation. Ten years earlier, Parker had gone on record for referring to political participation by blacks in national politics as "a source of evil and danger to both races."[14]

NAACP vigorously opposed Parker's nomination and urged its withdrawal. When President Hoover refused, NAACP launched a massive campaign to prevent Parker's confirmation. They widely publicized his negative attitude toward blacks, that he was against giving any rights to blacks; and so very strong public feelings against Parker were aroused and in the showdown that ensued, Parker failed to win the confirmation, much to the embarrasment of President Hoover. Clearly NAACP was now a force to reckon with.

DU BOIS'S CALL FOR BETTER EDUCATIONAL OPPORTUNITY FOR AFRICAN AMERICANS

Du Bois and NAACP saw the need for equal opportunity for education as vital to the progress of the black people. As early as 1926 Du Bois wrote his observations of the structure of education and the conditions of black schools in Georgia:

It does not appear that the colored schools enter definitely into the minds of those who are charged with common school education. The data collected from scattered schools over the state show that in 15 counties the schools run less than 6 months, which is legal requirement. The churches and lodge rooms which are used for Negro schools are chiefly old, dilapidated buildings, unfit for teaching purposes. In some cases they have no means of getting light, often there are no desks. In most of the churches and lodge houses, the children sit on plank benches which sometimes have no back to them. In some counties there is not a single school building for colored children. As a rule the one-teacher schools do not give instruction beyond the 5th grade.[15]

Du Bois further argued that there were numbers of consolidated white schools which afforded white children, through transportation, education through the 11th grade. Besides, he said, the white children had an opportunity to attend the district agricultural schools, where they could secure junior college work. There were 275 accredited public schools for white students in Georgia alone, but there were only two for African Americans. The fact that there was great hostility toward the educational development of African Americans was attested by the burning of schools in several areas. From the statistics given on the distribution of school funds, it was apparent how little was spent for equipment.[16]

It was equal opportunity that the NAACP now sought to secure for African Americans during the 1930s and this took a great deal of their time and activities. In 1938 NAACP launched a massive campaign and fought to improve the education of blacks all over the country. The first success came in that year, when the Supreme Court ruled in the *Gaines* case that Missouri had failed to maintain equal school facilities for both black and white, and so had violated black student Gaines his rights of equal treatment. Then NAACP attorney Charles H. Houston,[17] who became chief counsel to NAACP, led the legal struggle for school integration. His equally famous successor, Thurgood Marshall, engineered the cases which culminated in the momentous *Brown* desegregation decision of 1954. In 1967 Marshall himself was elevated to the Supreme Court, where he was able to play a leading role in the black fight for equality.

Due to the organized, intelligent, legal procedures and arguments, NAACP has been able to convince the Supreme Court of the wisdom of change. With the *Gaines* case the Supreme Court was improving some of its attitudes toward black education and beginning to imply that equality could not be measured only in terms of bricks and classrooms or the number of teachers in any school. The 1948 *Sipuel* case in Oklahoma and the 1949 *Sweatt* case, which finally came before the Supreme Court in 1950, as well as the 1950 *McLaurin* case, all show that the Court was entering a new period. In the *Sweatt* case the Court ruled that even though Texas had a separate Law School for Negroes, its education was inferior because it lacked "those qualities which are incapable of objective measurement but which make for greatness in a law school."[18]

The result was that Herman Marion Sweatt was the first black student since Reconstruction to enroll in a white state university in the South. Thanks to the ability of NAACP, the case was a major breakthrough in the fight to discard the "separate but equal" philosophy of the *Plessy* days. Two years after Sweatt was admitted into the University of Texas Law School, Thurgood Marshall, on behalf of NAACP, brought to the Supreme Court five cases involving a basic challenge to segregation in public schools—known as *Brown vs. the Board of Education of Topeka*. Up to this time the Supreme Court had ruled merely on isolated, individual students in graduate schools, and had not officially discarded the *Plessy* philosophy until 1954.

The new approach by NAACP and the challenge it now faced promised to affect millions of schoolchildren all over the country, both black and white. If the Supreme Court accepted NAACP's legal argument, a new chapter would be opened in the annals of the nation's schools. It would make integration a national policy; new programs and attitudes would have to emerge to suit ideals of the new era. The cases finally came before the Supreme Court, which responded by making the momentous decisions which have been described. The cases and decisions of the Court brought Marshall, Nabrit, Jenkins, Tate, and six other African American attorneys who fought the issue to national and world fame. About a year later the Supreme Court undertook to put its rulings into effect by calling on all states and school districts to draw up plans to desegregate schools.

The Court also gave federal courts the power to decide whether the new plans were properly formulated and in the spirit of the ruling. The Court urged and ordered compliance with the Court order "with all deliberate speed." For whites this was too radical a position by the Supreme Court. For them to implement the ruling would require great understanding of the problems facing the black students, and this understanding was not forthcoming. But for blacks the decision heralded the dawn of a new day, a millennium.

While the Supreme Court decided on public schools, the decisions had a far-reaching significance, once the highest court of the nation had accepted that a democratic country which fought for independence, because principles of democracy were at stake, had to do more than mere preaching these principles, they had to be put into practice in respect to all citizens! Later, the principles of desegregation were applied in housing, public accommodation, transport, and many other aspects of American life, where Jim Crow laws had been the order of things. Before long the black people as a whole, not just the leaders, began to shift their fight from polite protest to angry demands. They also began to seek better education, jobs, and other opportunities to which they were now entitled.

As African Americans began to apply themselves seriously to make use of their newly found freedom in education, growth in the number of educated, prosperous blacks also increased. The NAACP spearheaded efforts against Jim Crow in many communities, by providing leadership. The black middle class was emerging. An elite of the African American community was gradually becoming an important influence. Soon bank tellers, cashiers, secretaries, lawyers, professors, and educated preachers were having their influence felt in the country.

Prominent names were to emerge, such as Charles Drew, inventor of the modern blood bank system; John Hope Franklin, noted historian; Richard Wright, novelist; George Washington Carver, famous peanut scientist; Given Brooks, Pulitzer prize winner. Although these and many other blacks had left their mark before 1954, it was only then that their intellectual contribution was now appreciated, as evidence that Jim Crow no longer had any place in America. Of the men who made a lasting contribution to the black search for a Moses, Du Bois played a great role in these great developments. He too has left his mark in the great march to the promised land.

Du Bois is reported to have had an unusually good temper; he reacted with coolness where many would act violently. He never lost faith in education as the best means to improve the position of black people. He gave his time and money to many black causes, including the search for education. His basic philosophy was that the educated few must take it upon themselves to teach the others, by hard work, by good examples in behavior, by becoming and remaining honest in all things, in searching for the truth that is knowledge, in gaining experience that is education, in defining the goals that the black people must work toward, in maintaining the standards and values that have made great men in cultivating habits of decency of personal appearance, in selfless service to all mankind.

SOUTHERN RESISTANCE TO SCHOOL INTEGRATION, 1955–1964

Before we discuss the role of the next black leader it may be appropriate to examine the reaction of the nation to the 1954 Supreme Court decision of school integration during the ten years following the decision. NAACP had played its part well to bring an awareness that black people could not be expected to remain in their subservient position forever. The country also fully understood and recognized at the time that the Supreme Court, in its 1954 decision on school desegregation, was determined to solve the problem once and for all.

It also must have been clear that the alternative to this historic school desegregation order would lead to an inevitable confrontation with the federal authorities. Therefore some white politicians in the South reacted by encouraging understanding, coolness, moderation, and hope for peaceful change. The Nashville *Tennessean* ran an editorial saying, "The decision is not going to bring overnight revolutions, but the South is and has been for years a land of change. Its people of both races have learned to live with change. They can learn to live with this one. Given a reasonable amount of time and understanding, they will."[19]

In keeping with this tone and attitude, four big cities—St. Louis, Baltimore, Washington, DC, and Wilmington—started to move in the direction of public school desegregation, which was quietly effected by the autumn of 1954. Atlanta peacefully desegregated its schools. Oklahoma, Kentucky, Missouri, part of Texas, Delaware, Tennessee, and West Virginia all began to work out plans to desegregate their public schools in accordance with the 1954 requirements. By 1962 many of the school districts of the old Confederacy had permitted African American students to enroll with white students.

While these developments were taking place and proceeding with relative speed in the border states, opposition was being formed and organized in some parts of the Deep South. In Mississippi, White Citizens Councils were preparing themselves to fight to the bitter end this menace of school desegregation. These councils became so powerful, so influential that within a few weeks of the 1954 Supreme Court action they spread to Alabama, Louisiana, and Georgia, as well as six other states. The spokesman for the Councils claimed a membership of half a million within a few months. Even states that had made a genuine effort to desegregate their school systems now seemed doubtful, and appeared to have second thoughts about the wisdom or the benefits of desegregation.

The Councils aimed at fighting desegregation in general and their chief targets were inevitably individual black people who were leading the desegregation movement by participating in petitions or lawsuits to desegregate the schools. The Councils used all kinds of methods. Blacks were fired from their jobs or denied credit at local stores. White liberals who urged acceptance of the Supreme Court ruling faced many possible dangers, ranging from physical violence to boycott or forms of intimidation. Once again the KKK was taking a leading part in the fight against desegregation. Senseless violence was once again resorted to.

Black Americans who tried to maintain their rights against local traditions were brutally murdered or beaten. In Belzoni, Mississippi, a minister of religion was murdered when he tried to assert his right to vote; the leader of a local NAACP, Medgar Evers, whom the author was privileged to meet in Iowa, where he came to give a talk about African Americans' search for their rights, was ambushed and murdered. Evers, as the author listened to him speak a few months before his death, impressed him with his intelligence and moderation. Tall, good-looking, soft spoken, Evers saw the African American struggle as a part of the continuous struggle for human justice and equality.

Emmett Till, a 14-year-old boy, also of Mississippi, was kidnapped and murdered in 1955 for allegedly whistling at a white woman. A nine-year-old child was attached with wire from a moving car and dragged. For all these and many other crimes no one was brought to justice. This was what the African Americans were fighting against, because they felt that their rights were being denied them.

The leadership of the Councils did not come only from the rural hate groups that were prevalent in the South, but they also came from respected and dignified legislators. For example, in Virginia, traditionally an influence of moderation of policies toward the issues, there was an amendment to its constitution to allow state funds to be used to finance private schools which were to remain segregated. At the same time Senator Harry F. Byrd, the most powerful politician in Virginia, urged the South to resist at all costs a federally imposed integration. Senator Byrd claimed, in keeping with the southern practice by authorities on constitutional matters, that the South had a constitutional right to declare what they regarded as illegal any decision made by the U.S. Supreme Court. But no rulings against African Americans on constitutional questions were raised, such as the *Dred Scott* case of 1857.

In Alabama whites were equally determined to put a stop to and reverse the dangerous trend of school integration, set by the unwise irrational decision of the Warren Court. The legislators followed the lead set by Virginia by declaring that the Court decision was "null and void, and of no effect. There is just not one way to defy the Court, but many. The South proposes to use all of them that make for resistance. The decision to use all of them that make of resistance. The decision questioned the Constitution, the South will torture the decision."[20] Then to fulfill its pledge to torture the decision, Alabama members of a terror group went on a campaign of violence against black people. Black churches and other organizations were subjected to violence of untold degrees.

The southern disregard for and defiance of the Supreme Court decision was now spreading rapidly to other areas of the South. A number of white political leaders, who had seen reason for moderation in the integration issue, now made an about-turn and took an extreme position. By March 1956, two years after the historic decision, some 101 of the 128 congressmen from 11 southern states got together and signed the Southern Manifesto, a document which asserted that the Supreme Court had far exceeded the limits of its power and abused its legal authority. The document further rubber-stamped the action taken by the individual states in their declaration of their intention to oppose federally forced desegregation of schools.

These developments, attitudes, and actions by Southern states created a new crisis and set the country on a collision course and confrontation of great magnitude between these Southern states and the federal government. Some people believed this would bring the South and the federal government face to face in the first major struggle since the Civil War. Could this be avoided? Many things had changed since the Civil War, the Supreme Court had also changed a lot of its philosophy, and the Court had no intention of reversing this decision—come what may, the decision had to be implemented.

These were no longer the days of Rutherford Hayes. Both the president and the Supreme Court were in no mood for a new "let alone" policy. The national interests were hanging in the balance, the fate of blacks was inseparably sealed with that of whites, the black people had to come out, once and for all, from the feeling and effects of perpetual servitude. The philosophy and policy of Booker T. Washington had no room in the America of 1954 and beyond, and Southern white segregationists could no longer capitalize on it. It was up to the South to choose between confrontation with federal authorities and compliance with the order to integrate their public schools.

Southern resistance to the Supreme Court to desegregate schools suddenly dashed the hopes of blacks for better education—the course or path to their promised land appeared to have come to a sudden end. Some even feared the federal government would return to "let alone" thinking as a way of escaping from their responsibility to see the blacks through. Some African American leaders felt that the promised land was in sight, they needed one last push, one last thrust, to enable them to cross over the river that separated them from their dream. But their feet were weary, their hearts sank low, the source of their courage was exhausted. But somehow they kept moving. As the southern strategy shifted from the courts to rampant violence, African Americans were faced with a new kind of problem. Nevertheless Uncle Sam was not going to let them down at this critical period; there was no turning back. The new problem of lack of courage seemed to have been solved.

During this crucial period some southern states made the wise choice of compliance with the Supreme Court orders, and integration of the schools took place in the spirit of understanding, a genuine wish to forget the painful past, and with a new hope for racial harmony in the future. But other states chose the unwise alternative road to confrontation. Of these, Arkansas, Alabama, and Mississippi tried to test if the federal authorities had the will and the power to enforce the Supreme Court order. The first showdown came in 1957 in Arkansas.

In the fall of that year, nine black students were going to enroll in all-white Central High School in Little Rock. Their enrollment was in accordance with the Supreme Court order. But Governor Orval Faubus made a sudden and unexpected move. He went on television to denounce the order. He claimed that forced school desegregation or integration was bound to arouse profound fear among whites, because they did not believe that African Americans had values in common with whites. Governor Faubus called out the Arkansas National Guard to stop the blacks from entering Central High, or any other public school in the state. Under a directive from President Eisenhower, the federal court ordered Governor Faubus to withdraw the Guardsmen and things appeared to be quiet. The students were enrolled, and the nation breathed a sigh of relief.

But that hope was short-lived as three weeks later hysterical mobs of white people, who felt that Faubus had let the principles of segregation go down the drain, took the law into their own hands and became determined to direct the course of events, as the KKK and Citizens Councils had done. The mobs did not appear to have taken any other form of organization pattern, but were reacting to set back what was going to demoralize southern resistance to court orders. This would be seen as a major victory for integration forces. The mobs screamed and jeered and forced the nine students to leave Central High amid jubilation of victory among whites and sadness among blacks.

But the federal government would take no chances. President Eisenhower sent 100 paratroopers to Little Rock to enforce the federal order. Only then did uneasy calm return to the tense city. This was the first time that a president had resorted to the use of troops to ensure protection of blacks in the south since Reconstruction. Governor Faubus later requested federal courts to postpone integration, but the courts were in no mood to delay the decision, so they refused to grant the request. Although by 1959 only about six black students were enrolled in previously all-white schools in Little Rock, this major setback for Faubus signaled the end of his political career. His influence in the politics of race, which southern politicians so long capitalized on for their personal glory, was clearly coming to an end.

The Faubus-Eisenhower showdown was a vivid indication that the days of southern resistance to federal court orders to integrate schools were numbered and that any southern politician who made newspaper headlines and sought popularity and reelection on the platform of racial hatred had better start looking for other issues. Governor Ross Barnett of Mississippi did just that. James Meredith, a native of Mississippi, was physically stopped from entering the University of Mississippi in the fall of 1962 on orders of Governor Barnett himself. President Kennedy used military authority to have Meredith enrolled.

About a week later a white mob went on a rampage of violence. They attacked the federal marshals who were protecting Meredith, they fought with gasoline bombs, bottles, iron bars, clubs—anything that would inflict physical bodily harm. During the height of violence two people were killed and some federal marshals were injured. President Kennedy felt that he was impelled to send some 30,000 army troops to restore peace and law and order, to enforce the federal order. Like Faubus in Arkansas, Barnett ducked the real issue, school integration. He then vowed that he would die before he allowed a black student to enroll at "Ole Miss." Again, "not since the Reconstruction had the authority of the United States government been challenged so seriously on the issue of black civil rights!"[21] But all the same, the federal authority had to be respected. Soon Barnett "retired" as governor of Mississippi, and Lieutenant Governor Paul Johnson succeeded him.

About a year before the 1957 Little Rock desegregation crisis in Arkansas, there was in Alabama a case which attracted international attention. An African American girl, Authurine Lucy, was to enter the University of Alabama on court orders. Three days after she was admitted riots broke out and the board of trustees, submitting to segregation pressure, withdrew her from the university temporarily. When Lucy criticized the action, she was then expelled from the school for making accusations against the university officials.

Lucy called a press conference to explain her feelings about the situation and foresaw a day when the university would be integrated. Although the university remained segregated for seven years, the real answer as to who had final authority and responsibility over the welfare of citizens came in 1963 with a federal order requiring admission of two black students to summer courses at the University of Alabama. Governor, George Wallace, trying to play the same old political game, stood personally at the gate of the university to stop their enrollment. He had hoped to use the state National Guard to enforce his authority. But President Kennedy federalized the National Guard and Wallace, after defying the federal law, later tried to run for president on a platform of law and order.

What would these developments mean in terms of black education? The message was quite clear: whites were not at all prepared to give them their fair share of the constitutional pie of education. As soon as the Supreme Court order of integration with all "deliberate speed" was made, whites, in addition to campaigns of violence directed at African Americans, launched a legal campaign to circumvent and delay the court orders. Politicians, governors, and lawmakers worked around the clock to find some legal ways not to implement the orders and to continue segregation as a policy of the southern way of life.

As fast as they could, Southern politicians set up barriers to desegregation. Black parents brought suits to fight the new laws and practices. In South Carolina a constitutional amendment was created to allow the legislature to abolish public education. This followed the 1952 Virginia example of Prince Edward County. Georgia and Mississippi followed suit in 1954. In the same year Louisiana adopted a constitutional amendment that provided for separate racial schools on the basis that this would "promote public health, morals, better education and the peace and order in the state, and not because of race."[22]

Mississippi implemented the order of criminal offense—those who attended or taught in integrated schools were punished—and went further to enact legislation that outlawed any other legislation or court order or suit in order to stop the use of the courts as a means to effect desegregation. In 1955 Georgia, a state which had quietly integrated its school system, now ordered that any teachers who supported, condoned, or agreed to teach in integrated schools would have their teaching certificates or licenses invalidated.

A number of states introduced a new practice of allowing local school boards and authorities to classify pupils according to a social and psychological criteria, which made it virtually impossible for anyone to prove that segregation was being maintained purely by racial considerations. During the decade following 1954, 11 state legislatures in the South approved some 450 acts and other pieces of regulations which were designed to delay implementation of the Supreme Court orders to desegregate the schools.

EVENTS IN VIRGINIA'S PRINCE EDWARD COUNTY

Perhaps a good example of southern attempts to forestall or delay as long as possible the Supreme Court order is in Prince Edward County Virginia, where the district court found black schools inferior "in physical plant, curricula, and transport, but denied the students relief while the schools were being equalized."[23] The local school authorities tried everything in their power to circumvent the court order and the ruling that separate school facilities were not equal.

After failing to find other alternatives to justify continuance of segregated schools, Prince Edward County closed its public schools in the spring of 1959. However, tuition grants were made available to students who wished to attend private schools. Tax relief was extended to taxpayers who generously supported the private schools. Therefore once again, because white people had more wealth than black people, black children were denied an opportunity for education in the county between 1959 and 1963, when a private school was opened for black children, operated from 1959 until 1964, the year of a high-water mark in the development of black education.

Black parents started the long legal battles of petitions, appeals, and suits, disregarding the Virginia law not to do so. The district court warned local school boards against making tuition payments to private schools as long as public schools remained closed on racial grounds. In one case the court stated, "The schools of the county may not be closed to avoid the effects of the law of the land as interpreted by the Supreme Court, while the Commonwealth of Virginia permits other public schools to remain open at the expense of the taxpayers."[24]

When an appeals court reversed this decision, the case went to the Supreme Court, which, of course, reversed the appeals court decision and upheld the district court. That decision severely criticized the efforts and attempts to delay implementation of the Court's 1955 order to comply "with all deliberate speed," and went further to state that there had been entirely too much deliberation and not enough speed in enforcing the constitutional rights, which the Court held in *Brown vs. Board of Education*, had been denied children in the schools of Prince Edward County. The time for more "deliberate speed" had run out and that phrase could no longer justly deny these children their constitutional rights to an education equal to that offered by the public schools in other parts of Virginia.[25]

The Supreme Court then ordered the district court to issue an order which would ensure that the petitioners would get the kind of education that was being given to other sections of Virginia's public schools. Still, southern segregation strategists would not so easily give up the fight to maintain school segregation as a southern way of life. When the public schools reopened in the fall of 1964, some 1,600 students were enrolled. All of them except about seven were black. The rest of the white students continued their schooling in private schools of the Prince Edward School Foundation. One would wonder, since these so-called private schools received the substantial part of their support from the tax funds, through individuals and secretly made, would they still claim to be private?

Although integration of schools in Prince Edward County did not become a reality at the rate of speed prescribed the Supreme Court, the Court insisted on the constitutional rights for blacks to public school education. The thinking of the Court was that extremists who feared ignorance less than they feared prejudice would not be allowed to destroy the public school system by closing the schools and refusing children entrance to these schools. Again the Supreme Court once more emphasized that there was no going back to the days of *Plessy*. The country was to look to the future and provide equal opportunity and equal rights for all citizens.

DESEGREGATION OF SCHOOLS IN THE NORTH

For a long time it was believed that racial segregation was a problem uniquely belonging to the South. Only in recent years have people come to realize that the North has had very complex problems of race. In some big cities segregation in housing has created large sections of racially segregated populations, and so schools that have served these communities are segregated. The general pattern has developed over the years whereby suburban schools, which have had their students from middle-class families, have become predominantly white schools, while inner city schools, which have drawn their students largely from slums and lower class communities, have by practice been black. Those charged with the responsibility of integrating schools in the country recognized the effects of de facto segregation and resorted to busing as a means to desegregate schools.[26]

This kind of problem was particularly great in New York. In 1954 the

Public Education Association made a study of de facto segregation in the schools of New York. The study found no evidence of intentional racial segregation, but showed that black schools suffered serious persisting effects of inferior educational standards. The schools also suffered the effects of crowded enrollment, poor equipment, and being staffed by poorly trained teachers. The Board of Education used the study to improve the situation. One of the efforts by New York City was to transport students from their home district schools to other district schools to reduce the effects of de facto segregation. Many white parents protested about the inferior schools. The controversy over busing appears to have created division among the citizens. However, this was a genuine attempt to correct the injustices of segregation.

SUMMARY AND CONCLUSION

There is a hard factor to recognize in the matter of education for African Americans as a means of overcoming the obstacles on the journey to the promised land. The economic welfare of blacks has become a fundamental problem to the question of school integration. Because of their economic position, many blacks could not afford affluent homes, which would in turn entitle them to sending their children to good public schools. Over the years since 1954, African Americans have suffered the crippling effects of resistance to school integration, segregation in housing, and segregation in income. As a result African Americans entered a new phase of the civil rights movement with a shift of emphasis from protest to agitation for their rights. This new phase brought on the scene a young African American leader, perhaps one of the greatest the South had ever produced. He was in a position where events made history for his name. In these leaders African Americans had finally found a Moses to lead them on their journey to the promised land. Although this Moses, Martin Luther King, Jr., would not get there with them, he was sure that the children of Israel as a people would get there. This is now the subject of our discussion in Chapter 5.

NOTES

1. M. Weinberg, *W.E.B. Du Bois: A Leader* (New York: Harper and Row, 1970), p. 31.

2. Booker T. Washington, *Up From Slavery* (New York: Doubleday, 1916), p. 81.

3. Ibid., p. 91.

4. W.E.B. Du Bois, *The Souls of Black Folk* (Chicago: A. C. McClurg and Company, 1903), p. 43.

5. Ibid., p. 47.

6. L. A. Lacy, *The Life of W.E.B. Du Bois: Cheer the Lonesome Traveler* (New York: Dial, 1970), p. 48.

7. E. M. Rudwick, *Propagandist of the Negro Protest* (New York: W. W. Norton, 1962), p. 154.

8. Lacy, *The Life of W.E.B. Du Bois*, p. 54.

9. Langston Hughes, *Fight for Freedom: The Story of the NAACP* (New York: W. W. Norton, 1962), p. 23.

10. Ibid., p. 27.

11. Ibid., p. 31.

12. Lacy, *Life of W.E.B. Du Bois*, p. 67.

13. Ibid., 71.

14. Hughes, *Fight for Freedom*, p. 74.

15. Weinberg, *W.E.B. Du Bois*, p. 144.

16. Ibid., p. 145.

17. For a more detailed discussion of Charles H. Houston, see *The Road to Brown*, a documentary PBS film, 1990.

18. Weinberg, *W.E.B. Du Bois*, p. 147.

19. R. E. Dennis, *The Black People of America* (New York: McGraw-Hill, 1970), p. 320.

20. Ibid., p. 324.

21. Ibid., p. 323.

22. Ibid., p. 325.

23. Robert E. Potter, *The Stream of American Education* (New York: American Book Company, 1967), p. 485.

24. Ibid., p. 486.

25. Ibid., p. 487.

26. For the crisis brought about by busing, see *Eyes on the Prize*, PBS documentary film, 1990.

Photo 1. Abraham Lincoln, president of the United States from 1861 to 1865. "We allow slavery to exist in the slave states not because it is right or good, but from the necessities of our nation." National Archives photo No. 111-B-4246, 1999.

Photo 2. Andrew Johnson, president of the United States from 1865 to 1869. "President Johnson vetoed the Civil Rights Bill of 1866, arguing that it would place too many restrictions on the ability of South to discharge its constitutional responsibility." National Archives photo No. 111-B-5929, 1999.

Photo 3. Frederick Douglass, leader of African Americans from 1845 to 1895. "Someone imbued with the spirit of human freedom has arisen among the oppressed to lead themselves on to victory." National Archives photo No. 121-BA-74, 1999.

Photo 4. Harriet Tubman, leader of the Underground Railroad. "Tubman guided the cause of 300 African American slaves to freedom using her philosophy, 'I'll see you in the morning safe in the promised land.'" National Archives photo No. 200-HN-PIO-1, 1999.

Photo 5. John F. Kennedy, president of the United States from 1961 to 1963. "The lack of adequate education denies the Negro a chance to get a decent job." National Archives photo No. 64-M-7, 1999.

Photo 6. Dr. Martin Luther King, Sr., provided inspiration to the struggle for the journey to the promised land. "The freedom of Negroes is the freedom of America itself." Photo by the Author, 1962.

Photo 7. Lyndon B. Johnson, president of the United States from 1963 to 1968 with African American Civil Rights leaders reviewing the civil rights bill, 1964. From left to right: Martin Luther King, Jr., James Farmer, Whitney Young, President Johnson, Roy Wilkins. "The only genuine long-range solution to racial disorders lies in an attack mounted at every level upon conditions that breed despair and violence." National Archives photo No. 306-PS-D64-4636, 1999.

Photo 8. Martin Luther King, Jr. speaking at March on Washington, 1963. "I have a dream that one day my four little children will be judged not by the color of their skin but by the content of their character." National Archives photo No. 306-PS-D63-4734, 1999.

Photo 9. Thurgood Marshall, chief counsel for the plaintiffs in *Brown vs. Board of Education of Topeka*, argued before the U.S. Supreme Court in 1954. "There are no recognizable differences from a racial standpoint between children." National Archives photo No. 306-PS-58-14226, 1999.

Photo 10. John Lewis (center) presenting civil rights album, "We Shall Overcome," to the author while an aide looks on. "As president of SNCC Lewis was part of a leadership that demonstrated unquestionable commitment to the struggle for the journey to the promised land." Photo by the Author, 1962.

Photo 11. Julian Bond, chairman, NAACP Board of Directors. "Bond has
continued to show rare qualities in the activities of NAACP since 1960." Photo
supplied by Julian Bond, June 1999.

Photo 12. Geraldine Peten, educator in Arizona. "Racial relationships and values must be interrelated with the subjects in an attempt to identify and eliminate false consciousness." Photo by the Author, 1998.

5

Martin Luther King, Jr.:
Sighting the Promised Land

I have looked over, and I've seen the promised land. I may not get
there with you, but I would want you to know that we as a people
will get to the promised land.

Martin Luther King, Jr., 1968

THE EFFECT OF RELATED EVENTS

The success of the NAACP in influencing the Supreme Court in reaching
a favorable decision in 1954 in the Brown cases planted new hope for a
new life among African Americans. The decision boosted their determination to continue their journey to the promised land. But frustration
and impatience increased as southern white Americans showed clearly
that they were not prepared to recognize the rights of African Americans
as citizens of the United States on an equal basis. African Americans
began to wonder if the U.S. government was in a position to do something to help them in their struggle. Because they would not abandon
the direction and developments of their struggle, they had to play a role
in shaping them in order to make progress on their journey. As they saw
resistance of white Americans to that progress, they utilized the attitudes
of the federal government to work for complete integration in all aspects
of national life.

Educational and economic change did not come easily or as rapidly
as the Supreme Court had hoped for. Residential and school segregation
increased all over the nation. Movements within the African American

communities emphasized the need for rapid solutions to the problems they were facing. But those solutions were also slow in coming. African Americans were convinced that they had not made significant progress since 1954. Therefore, they felt there was need for them to make a call for a new leader, a new Moses.

MARTIN LUTHER KING, JR.: THE NEW MOSES

Martin Luther King, Jr. answered that call. In 1963, some nine years after the Supreme Court reached the famous decision on the *Brown* cases, King made an observation of the conditions of life of African Americans, saying that they had been deeply disappointed over the slow pace of school desegregation.[1] He also argued that they knew that in 1954 the highest court in the land had handed down a decree calling for deseg- regation of schools with all deliberate speed. He said that they also knew that this edict from the Supreme Court had been heeded with all delib- erate delay. He said that at the beginning of 1963 approximately 99 per- cent of southern African American students were attending segregated schools. He concluded that if this pace were maintained, it would be the year 2054 before integration in southern schools would become a reality.[2]

King went on to argue that in its *Brown* decision the Supreme Court had revealed a disturbing awareness that made no room for evading its intent.[3] The phrase "all deliberate speed" did not mean that another cen- tury must pass before African Americans would be released from the narrow pigeonholes of the segregated educational system. It meant, in- stead, a rapid integration of all national institutions.[4] Yet the situations made it absolutely clear that the segregationists of the South intended to remain unaffected by the decision. He added that from every section of the South the announcement of the High Court decision had been met with declarations of defiance of the law. Once recovered from their initial outrage, these defenders of the status quo tried to seize the offensive to impose their own meaning and schedule of change.[5]

King concluded that the progress that was supposed to have been achieved with deliberate speed actually created change for less than 2 percent of African American children in most areas of the South and not even a tenth of a percent in some parts of the South.[6] King had already become a national and international figure by 1963. Who was he? What did he do to capture so much attention of the world? He was one African American leader who approached the question of the struggle by his people toward equality with the magnitude of his personality compa- rable only to few in the history of leadership in the United States.

Born in Atlanta, Georgia, on January 15, 1929, King was the son and grandson of ministers, both pioneers in the African American freedom movement of their day. His maternal grandfather, A. D. Williams, had been one of the first leaders of the Georgia chapter of NAACP. Martin's father led the struggle for equal salary for African American teachers along with Charles H. Houston. At the age of six Martin came into his first personal contact with the evils of segregation. One day his father took him to downtown Atlanta to buy a pair of shoes. Entering the store, they sat down near the window. A white salesman approached them and told that he would be happy to wait on them if they just moved to seats in the rear of the store, saying that was where African Americans sat.

When the salesman saw a reluctance on the part of King and his son to move back, the salesman told them that there was nothing wrong with those seats and stressed in a firmer tone of voice that they would have to move back in order to be served. The angry father continued to sit for a moment, then silently rose up, took young Martin by the hand, and strode majestically from the store, saying that he and his son would not buy shoes in a store that practiced any form of segregation.[7] On the sidewalk he spoke to his son Martin through clenched teeth, "I don't care how long I have to live with this system, I am never going to accept it."[8] The clerk regarded himself righteously with a vexed, impressive look—the look of one who knew his rights under the laws and customs of Georgia. The young King felt deeply hurt by the incident but he also became more inspired by the action of his father. He was also touched greatly by the determination of his father to fight against an injustice.

Another incident occurred when King Jr. was age 11. King's mother told him to wait for a little while in a downtown store in Atlanta, while she went to run few quick errands a block away. While he was standing there waiting for her to return, a white woman, a complete stranger, walked up to him and told him that he was the little nigger that stepped on her foot recently and she threw a dazzling slap on his face. Martin simply stood there bewildered, his only notable reaction was to tell the incident to his mother when she returned. It was an experience that made a significant addition to his informal education about the evils of racial prejudice and discrimination. Both of these incident remained with him the rest of his life, but they reinforced his courage and determination to fight for fairness and equality.

At school Martin was an outstanding student. His college years co-incided with some important events in the history of the country. At Morehouse College he won second prize in the Webb oratorical contest during his sophomore year. In 1941 A. Philip Randolph, president of the Brotherhood of Sleeping Car Porters, called some 100,000 African Americans to march on Washington, DC, in a massive demonstration against racial discrimination in industry, where they were excluded from better jobs. Although the march never took place, it had some effect on President Franklin D. Roosevelt, who issued an executive order establishing a committee on Fair Employment Practices. In 1944 when King entered Morehouse College, thousands of African Americans were working side by side with whites in wartime industries. At Morehouse King studied sociology, giving himself an opportunity to study the racial issue in all its aspects and complexities.

One summer King worked in Connecticut tobacco fields and spent weekends in Hartford, where he enjoyed free access to movies, restaurants, and other public facilities which were closed to African Americans back home in Atlanta. When he went back to Georgia from Connecticut, he decided to see a Jim Crow movie. The contrast with Hartford in the treatment of African Americans was too great for him to take. He kept asking himself why African Americans should settle for less than total equality. He also asked why they fared worse in Atlanta than in Hartford. This was another strong influence that shaped his determination to fight the injustices of the American society all his life.

At Morehouse King searched for "some intellectual basis for a social philosophy. He read and reread Thoreau's *Civil Disobedience*, and concluded that the ministry was the only framework in which he could position his growing ideas on social protest.[9] In 1948 he entered Crazer Theological Seminary in Pennsylvania, where he read the work of great social philosophers: Plato, Aristotle, Rousseau, Locke, Gandhi, Jesus. He was the president of the student body—the first black ever to be so honored, graduated first in his class, and was named the seminary's outstanding student.

King was given an opportunity through a scholarship to go to Boston University for his Ph.D. He studied under Dr. Herald De Wolf,[10] head of the Department of Systematic Theology and a prominent biblical scholar. De Wolf and King remained close friends all their lives. De Wolf was so impressed with King, about whom he once said, "Of all the doctorate students I have had at Boston University—some fifty in all—I would rate Martin Luther King, Jr. among the top five. Scholastically, he was unusually good."[11]

After his course requirements were completed, King began to work on his dissertation, entitled "A Comparison of the Conceptions of God in the Thinking of Paul Tillich and Henry Nelson Wieman." This study gave him discipline and training in the organization of ideas. In 1955 King received his doctorate. He had married Coretta Scott in June 1953, in an impressive garden wedding in Alabama, and at which Martin Sr. officiated. Coretta was a student at Boston New England Conservatory of Music. Now King was ready to go into the world, and play his role in the African American journey to the promised land. He had many offers of pastorate positions all over the country, and had a hard time trying to decide.

Among the offers was the Dexter Avenue Baptist Church of Montgomery, Alabama. It was an upper-income congregation made up of professional African Americans and teachers at Alabama State College, a state-supported institution for African American students. A somewhat intellectual church, Dexter provided an excellent forum for an ambitious young preacher. The departing pastor, Rev. Vernon Johns, had a reputation as an eloquent preacher and orator and as a fearless advocate of racial equality and the end to injustice. One story was told of a time Johns refused to vacate a seat on a Montgomery bus and move to the back.[12]

The angry driver shouted "Nigger, didn't you hear me tell you to get the hell out of that seat?" Johns replied, "And didn't you hear me tell you that I'm going to sit right god-damned here?"[13] The driver, stunned by the rich vocabulary of the well-known minister, retreated in confusion. Repeating this story word for word from his pulpit the next Sunday, the Rev. Johns said he did not believe that God was offended by the unauthorized use of His name.[14] This was the man into whose shoes King was about to step. In January 1954 King went to Dexter to preach a trial sermon, which was entitled "The Three Dimensions of a Complete Life." He addressed love of self, love of neighbors, and love of God, and went on to state that John the Revelator, imprisoned on a lonely, obscure island called Potmas, was deprived of almost every freedom except freedom to think. John was not content to look back nostalgically; he envisioned a new Jerusalem, a truly holy city where the length and breadth and height of life were equal. The length of life was the inward drive to achieve one's personal ends. The breadth was the outward concern for the welfare of others. The height of life was the upward reach for God. Life at its best was a coherent triangle. At one angle was the individual person. At the other angle were other persons. At the tip was the Infinitive Person, God; without the due development of each part of the triangle, no life could be complete.[15]

King went on to explain that one must love oneself, that rational and healthy self-interest is an important part of the individual beneficial to society. All people were commanded to love themselves because that is the length needed to live a productive life. At the same time one loves one's neighbor as one loves oneself. Jesus commanded all of us to do that. That dimension of love added a new breadth of life. But in doing so we must never forget that there is a first and even greater commandment, love the Lord with all our heart, and with all our soul, and with all our mind. This is the height of life. Only by a painstaking development of all three can we expect to live a complete life.[16]

Although one woman remarked after the sermon that the 25-year-old minister was somewhat lost or confused in the pulpit without the presence of his mother, neither the woman nor the Dexter Congregation knew that with King's assuming his official duties there in September

1955 a social revolution of great magnitude was about to begin in the country, and that this Dexter Avenue pulpit was to be the starting point of the greatest freedom and nonviolent movement African Americans had ever known. The state of Alabama of 1954 had some 80,000 whites, and Montgomery had 50,000 African Americans. It became apparent to King for the first time after he had settled there from Boston that to most white people in Montgomery, African Americans were objects, tools, instruments, things to be manipulated, dominated, and utilized to promote the interests of the white community and reinforce their sense of superiority. Without a system of forcing African Americans to the back of the bus, the whites would lose that sense of superiority. Montgomery was a city of beauty and charm. Dexter Avenue Church stood across the public square on which the state capital, a beautiful and impressive white building, had for years become the symbol of white supremacy.

The state capital represented a symbol of unquestionable power. Built in 1851, here Alabama voted in 1861 to secede from the Union when the Civil War began. Here too, on the steps of the capital, Jefferson Davis was inaugurated president of the confederacy. Here the first Confederate flag was made and unfurled. Here, during the tragic years following Reconstruction, a new constitution was drafted in 1868 to reduce the effects of the Fourteenth Amendment that was designed to guarantee African Americans the rights of citizenship. During that turbulent era the Dexter Avenue Baptist Church was erected. These memories rang deep in King's mind as he became more grimly reminded of the deterioration of conditions of life of African Americans.

King remembered that no African American had been in the statehouse for the past 79 years. No trace of Reconstruction remained. The Alabama state flag of the stars and bars of Jefferson Davis's days still remained for everyone to see and to be reminded that even in 1954, Montgomery was still the birthplace of the Confederation. Both local and state government symbolized white power, a form of government of whites by whites for whites only. This is part of the environment under which King was to work.

The experience of Rev. Johns with the bus driver was not an isolated incident involving an individual, and an assertive African American leader. The Montgomery African American community had for years been subjected to a series of humiliating, galling indignities. African Americans had been badly affected by Montgomery City Lines, a bus company owned by a northern firm, which repeatedly insulted African Americans, who contributed about 70 percent of the company's revenue. In 1955 African Americans felt that the climate was now ripe to confront the system and demand fundamental change. King was thrown right into the middle of it as he rose to the occasion to play a decisive role in the developments that unfolded in a rapid succession. He knew that to be effective as a leader he must reject the pacifism of Booker T. Washington, the back-to-Africa approach of Marcus Garvey, and the elitism of W.E.B. Du Bois.[17] He knew that real progress that African Americans would make in their journey to the promised land lay in the involvement of the people themselves.

THE PARKS INCIDENT AND KING'S ROLE IN THE MONTGOMERY BUS BOYCOTT

A practice that had been in existence for years required that African American riders of the transit bus systems took the back seats while whites took the front seats. The drivers were empowered to order African Americans who sat in the front to move toward the back of the buses when more white riders came aboard. Should, however, as it so often happened many times, the back seats of the bus were all taken, either the African American riders would remain standing, even if there were empty seats in front, or they would not ride the bus. But, as was the case also, if seats reserved for whites were all occupied, the driver would order African American riders to vacate their seats so that the white riders would have them if the white riders so wished.

The drivers would refer to African Americans riders as niggers, black cows, or by other derogatory and humiliating terms. African Americans lived with this mental anguish, emotional torture, and social degradation for a long time. Often, too, bus drivers would require African Americans riders to pay their fare at the front door, get off, and reboard the bus through the rear door. But in the process the bus would take off, leaving the African American passengers who had paid their fare stranded in the middle of the street. In 1955 African Americans felt that such a practice must be brought to an unconditional end.

Rev. Vernon Johns and other African American leaders had tried desperately to awaken in their people a sense of realism to the tragic situation that badly affected them, but without success. In this same general place where William Yancy had introduced Jefferson Davis as the man who had come to meet the need of the hour, a new man and a new hour began to find a common meeting place. The man was there, Martin Luther King, Jr., and the hour was slowly coming and finally it was there, on December 1, 1955.[18]

King had long been convinced that "freedom is never voluntarily given by the oppressor, it must be demanded by the oppressed,"[19] and that the apathy that Rev. Johns saw earlier among African Americans would suddenly come to an end when the time was ripe for action. On that day Rosa Parks, an African American passenger, boarded the bus with other passengers to return home after work. When the bus stopped at the next stop, some white passengers came on but, as all white seats were taken, the driver asked Rosa to vacate her seat and give way for a white male passenger.

When Parks refused the driver called the police, who immediately arrested Mrs. Parks for violating city segregation ordinances. The act roused and unified the whole African American community. King transformed the apathy of generations into a formidable force of the new civil rights movement that was to transform American society. African Americans reacted to Parks's arrest with a bus boycott that was to last into 1957. The boycott was organized by King and Edgar Daniel Nixon, head of the local chapter of NAACP, under whom Mrs. Parks worked as secretary, and who posted bail for her. Rev. Ralph Abernathy, an influential man in Montgomery and later an associate of King's, came to the assistance of King. Martin Sr. helped the readers design a strategy to change the system. To Martin Luther King, Jr. this was civil disobedience that he had read about during his school days. Now he had an opportunity to try to prove its effectiveness.

On December 5, 1955, the bus boycott was well organized. King addressed the meeting convened to plan the boycott, arguing that African Americans were tired of being segregated and humiliated. They were impatient for justice. But they would protest with love. There would be no violence on their part. There would be no cross burning. No white person would be taken from his home by hooded African American mobs and murdered. If they did this, if African Americans protested with love, future history would have to say of them: "There lived a great people, a black people, who injected new meaning and dignity into the veins of civilization."[20]

The crowd applauded long after King had taken his seat. In 1954 the Supreme Court had issued an order to desegregate schools with all "deliberate speed." But the South appeared to have been so provoked to anger that a revenge for the order took a heavy toll on African Americans. The murder of Emmett Till, a 14-year-old boy from Chicago visiting relatives in Mississippi, was part of the campaign of revenge that whites launched to oppose the action that African Americans were taking to ensure their rights. Soon the Montgomery bus boycott became better organized, large meetings were to take place from one church to another in support of it.

These meetings were attended by all kinds and levels of people: professors, porters, doctors, maids, laborers, housewives, drunks. All at this crucial moment discarded the once-accepted form of rank, class, or creed. They reached out to each other in a new hope, a new faith, a new crisis. The Negro spirituals, hand-clapping, shouting, even emotional outbursts all found the means of their expression at this hour of decision. As King gained a new experience he realized that the emotional expression among African American church members held enormous reservoirs of psychic and social willpower that had not been fully made use of. Also, King began to accept himself and African Americans as history had made them.

The Montgomery city bus officials, who at first took the boycott lightly, now made a token gesture to give African Americans an impression that it was a problem that affected them as well. King himself was not sure that this people would respond so effectively. But he soon found out that with proper leadership they were quite prepared to pay the price. As the boycott continued, City Lines was losing revenue so fast that they were forced to seek a meeting between King and themselves. But King and his associates were quick to see that "no one gives his privileges without strong resistance and that the underlying purpose of segregation was to oppress and exploit the segregated."[21] These observations were proved correct when in January 1956, Mayor Gayle announced his get-tough policy, stating that the establishment had pussyfooted around on this boycott long enough, and it was time to be frank and honest. He stated that African American leaders, including King, had proved that they were not interested in ending the boycott but rather in prolonging it so that they could stir up racial strife. Gayle added that African Americans had forced the boycott into a campaign between whether the social fabric of the community would continue to exist or would be destroyed by a group of black radicals who had split asunder the fine relationships that had existed between African Americans and white people for generations. Gayle concluded by saying that these radical black leaders were after the destruction of the existing social fabric.[22]

On January 26, 1956, King was arrested for allegedly driving 30 miles per hour in a 25-mile zone, and was thrown into prison with drunks, thieves, murderers, and vagrants. This was the first time that King had ever been arrested, but it was certainly not the last. Soon a large number of blacks began to gather at the prison and the prison officials felt that the racial tension that was fast increasing could be eased by releasing King. When he left prison, one of the prisoners was heard to shout to King, "Don't forget us when you get out!" This was in much the same tone as the thief said to Jesus from the cross.

Two days later King's house was bombed with his family inside, but no one was hurt. A thousand blacks gathered at the house, armed with all kinds of weapons: bottles, stones, rocks, iron rods, knives, sticks, but King simply pleaded for calm, like Christ did to Peter, urging African Americans to understand that they were not advocating violence. He told them that he wanted them to be good to their enemies and let them know they loved them. He reminded them that he did not start this boycott, he was only asked to serve as its spokesman. He therefore wanted it to be known through the length and the breadth of the land that if he was stopped, the movement would not stop because what they were doing was right, just and God was with them.[23]

If anyone had an doubts about King as the leader of his people, no one did after this incident. The bombing suddenly brought King into national prominence as the leader of the black people. The southern liberation movement must have found the Moses that they had been looking for since Emancipation. King become the symbol, at least to millions of African Americans, who were now joining the rank and file of the social revolution that was to grip the country and bring change of immeasurable immensity.

King now began to reshape his own philosophy in the face of the immense task before him. He read more than once Adam Clayton Powell's *Marching Blacks* (1945), and Howard Thurman's *Jesus and the Disinherited* (1949) and after the bus boycott period he visited India in 1959 and then solidified his commitment to the nonviolent cause. Bus violence continued to engulf King and his family, both in Montgomery and wherever he went. King took a close look at himself and prayed hard. He felt discouraged by the force of the opposing side. He saw his own shortcomings as a human being, he recognized that African Americans were looking to him for leadership, and that if he lost hope, they, too, would lose hope. He had to have courage, determination, the strength of character, and the belief and conviction that he was doing the right thing.

By 1957, as in other African American liberation movements before his, King was one of the country's most popular and sought-after speakers. *Time*, a leading white-oriented news magazine, and *Jet*, a leading African American-oriented news magazine, ran cover stories on him. *Jet* went on to say that King was a symbol of divinely inspired hope and a modern Moses who brought a new concept of self-respect to African Americans. Many national newspapers paid high tribute to King's qualities of leadership.

In 1957 King became the youngest person and the first active pastor to win the Spingarn Medal (named after the famous NAACP leader of the early days), which was awarded annually to any person who had made the largest contribution in the field of race relations. In that same year King received the first of his many honorary degrees from his alma mater Morehouse. There, Dr. Benjamin E. Hays, who knew King closely and was a famous educator and president of Morehouse, would deliver with emotion the citation that characterized King's life. Hays reminded King and his audience that he was mature beyond his years, wiser at 28 than most men were at 60, more courageous in a righteous struggle than most men would ever be, living a faith that most men preached about and never experienced.

Hays went on to add that significant, indeed, was the fact that King did not betray that trust of leadership. Instead he said he led the people with quiet dignity, with Christian grace, and determined purpose as his unique hallmark of action. Hays also added that while King was away, his colleagues in the battle for freedom were being hunted and arrested like common criminals. While it was suggested by legal counsel that King could consider the possibility of staying away to escape arrest, Hays heard him with his own ears say that he would rather spend ten years in jail than desert the people in their struggle for equality. Hays said that at that moment, his heart, his mind, and his soul stood up erect and saluted him. Hays concluded that King knew that he was called to leadership for just such a time as the country was going through. On its 90th anniversary, King's alma mater was happy to be the first college or university to honor him in this way.[24]

King began to receive a flood of letters inviting him to speak all over the country at all kinds of occasions. He received offers of pastorateships of large northern white churches, professorships, deanships of major white universities. But King declined; his place was among the black people of the South to whom he owed a duty to serve with vision and sacrifice and suffering and torture by the powers that were above him. At a meeting called at Ebenezer Baptist Church in Atlanta, a new organization was formed in January 1957, and was called the Southern Christian Leadership Conference (SCLC) which called on all African Americans "to assert their human dignity by refusing further cooperation with evil."[25]

King was elected president of SCLC in 1963. Immediately he and his associates planned their strategy for action to give effect to the civil rights movement. On Lincoln's birthday King called on President Eisenhower to enforce the law in the spirit of the Supreme Court decision of 1954 and 1955. Among the many rights blacks were to fight to secure were the right to better education. It was time to act, to put words into action. To many people King was an agitator, to others he was an impatient young leader who tended to spoil the good course of events by his quick action.

By 1963 African Americans no longer waited because, as King himself explained, they had waited for more than 340 years for their institutional and God-given rights. He said that the nations of Asia and Africa were moving with jet-like speed toward gaining political independence, but African Americans were still creeping at a horse-and-buggy pace toward gaining a cup of coffee at a lunch counter. He added that it was easy for those who had never felt the stinging darts of segregation to suggest that they wait and have patience.

But when one had seen vicious mobs lynch one's mother and father at will and drown one's sisters and brothers at will; when one had seen hate-filled policemen curse, kick, and even kill one's African American brothers and sisters; when one saw the vast majority of one's 20 million African American brothers smothering in the airtight cage of poverty in the midst of an affluent society; when one suddenly found one's tongue twisted and one's speech stammering as one sought to explain to one's six-year-old daughter why she can't go to the public amusement park that had just been advertised on television and see tears welling up in her eyes; when one saw ominous clouds of inferiority beginning to pro-tect one's children's personality by developing an unconscious bitterness toward white people; when one had to concoct an answer to a five-year-old son who asked, "Daddy, why do white people treat colored people mean?"—these were the conditions that made waiting impossible at this time.[26]

King went on to provide an answer:

When you take a cross-country drive and find it necessary to sleep night after night in the uncomfortable corners of your car because no motel will accept you because of your race, when you are humiliated every day by signs that read "white" and "colored," when your first name becomes "nigger" and your middle name becomes "boy" regardless of your age, and your last name becomes "John" and your wife and mother are never given the respected title of "Mrs." that provides an incentive to fight. When you are harassed because you are black and you never quite know what to expect next, when you are plagued with inner fear and outer resentment, when you are forever fighting a degenerating sense of lack of identity, then you will understand why it is difficult to wait. There comes a time when the cup of endurance runs over, and men are no longer willing to be plunged into the abyss of despair. A group of people cannot forever live under an abyss of despair. It is up to the oppressed people to convert the abyss of despair into a spring of hope. This can be done by utilizing impatience.[27]

King was clearly on his way to world fame. He had effectively as-sumed the role of a Moses. His activities were no longer confined to the local issues in Alabama, they extended to Mississippi, where he was thrown in prison; they extended to all parts of the country, where Af-rican Americans were suffering the painful effects of segregation. In 1962 he preached to all parts of the country, where the blacks were suffering the painful effects of segregation. In 1962 he preached nonviolence in poolrooms and taverns of Albany, Georgia. In 1963 he remembered that he had been arrested in Montgomery in 1958 on charges of loitering.

In 1964 King was arrested in St. Augustine, Florida, for refusing to leave a segregated restaurant, and in the same year he and Ralph Ab-ernathy had an audience with Pope Paul VI at the Vatican. He received the Nobel Prize in Norway. In 1966 he was hit by a rock in Chicago. King brought a new level of awareness of self to African Americans. He wanted nothing less than absolute equality in all aspects of American life—education, housing, job opportunity, equality of pay, political rights—and they wanted these rights now, they were not going to wait any longer.

The protest phase was building to a climax. The sit-ins, the freedom marches, and protests were peaks in the great mountain ranges of a great movement that captured the imagination of such people as Dr. Eugene Carson Blake, later general secretary of the World Council of Churches, and Dr. Benjamin Spock, the famous pediatrician. As King toured the country he was received with cheers and cries of "freedom now!" In June 1962 King led 125,000 people in a great freedom walk in Detroit, the largest rally King led anywhere at that time, and which dwarfed the 17 pilgrimages to Washington, DC, between 1957 and 1959. As the excitement and fires of crisis spread to engulf the land across the nation, King reached a new point of eminence that no other African leader had ever achieved before.

KING AND THE GRAND MARCH ON WASHINGTON, 1963

Perhaps the success of the Detroit march was the beginning toward the biggest protest march seen on the American continent. Encouraged by their success in Detroit, SCLC, Congress of Racial Equality (CORE), SNCC, NAACP, and the Urban League now got together to plan something more extensive to dramatize the fight in which blacks were engaged. The occasion was the Grand March on Washington, DC, in August 1963. It took weeks to plan the details of the march, and Bayard Rustin, the organizer, had worked round the clock for weeks to ensure its success. If it failed the black cause would fail; the black leaders would be discouraged.

Every little detail was given absolute attention. The march had received publicity such as no previous freedom or protest march had done before. Blacks from all walks of life had come together to pour ideas and thoughts to ensure the march's effectiveness. For days King and other black leaders hardly had any sleep. Their concern for the success of the march was a greater cause than their personal comfort; it came above everything else at this critical hour in the history of black advancement.

But even before the final touches to the preparations were made, people began to arrive in Washington soon after midnight of August 27, 1963. They came by any means. By sunrise thousands had come, by train, plane, bus, motorcade. All kinds of groups, political leaders, and individuals converged upon the Capital of the nation for the same purpose, to demand their rights as citizens of the United States of America, that greatest power on earth, which was denying the rights of its citizens purely on the basis the color of their skin.

The moment was here. As the people began to gather and get ready, one could hear from the distance, "We shall overcome!" Color was all over: banners blue, purple, crimson, carrying "Freedom Now!" were seen against the clear sky. One in five people was white, who seemed more like visitors at a family reunion. At the Lincoln Memorial, a mile away from the Washington Monument where huge crowds were gathering, an organ solemnly played freedom songs as thousands marched toward the Monument and assembled. Thousands continued to stream toward the Washington Monument in readiness for the procession. By 1:00 p.m., 200,000 people sat or stood facing the Memorial. Frederick Shuttlesworth briefly spoke first: "We come here because we love our country, because our country needs us and because we need our country. Everybody in America ought to be free. If the politicians want peace, if the judges want to undo their court calendars, then turn the Negro loose in America. Then we'll all be free."[28]

Those at the Grand March included Dick Gregory, Lena Horne, Sidney Poitier, Marlon Brando, Sammy Davis, Jr., Jackie Robinson, 150 members of Congress, countless other celebrities of American society; A. Philip Randolph, the veteran African American freedom leader; Roy Wilkins, executive secretary of NAACP; John Lewis,[29] president of SNCC; a number of African Americans active in the freedom movement; Rabbi J. Prince, president of the American Jewish Congress; Matthew Ahmannn of the Catholic Conference for Interracial Justice; Malcolm X; Mahalia Jackson; and many, many other prominent people were there to demonstrate their support for the cause of justice, equality, and freedom for African Americans, to whom, for years, freedom was only a meaningless and hollow word. The journey to the promised land was now reaching a critical point.

After a dozen or so main leaders spoke briefly, it was King's opportunity to take the podium. The venerable A. Philip Randoph introduced King as a philosopher of the nonviolent system of behavior, and who was seeking to bring about social change for the advancement of justice and freedom and human dignity. As King began to deliver his famous "I have a dream" speech, he was momentarily drawn in the ovation that he received, as the thousands present chanted, cheered, applauded, waved banners and placards that read "We want freedom now!"[30]

Then King told his listeners:

Five score years ago a great American in whose symbolic shadow we stand today, signed the Emancipation Proclamation. This momentous decree came as a great beacon of light of hope to millions of Negro slaves who had been seared in the flames of withering injustice. It came as a joyous daybreak to end the long night of their captivity. But one hundred years later the life of the Negro is still sadly crippled by the manacle of segregation and the chains of discrimination.

One hundred years later the Negro is still languished in the corners of American society and finds himself an exile in his own land. So we have come here today to dramatize a shameful condition.[31]

King concluded his address by telling his audience about his dream, saying that African Americans of that day must continue to dream of freedom and social equality even though they had to face the difficulties of racial discrimination. He said that it was a dream deeply rooted in the American dream itself. He had a dream that one day the United States would rise up and live out the true meaning of its creed, "We hold these truths to be self-evident that all men are created equal."[32]

King added that he had a dream that one day over the red hills of Georgia, sons of former slaves and sons of former slaveowners would be able to sit down together and discuss the mutual problems of survival; that Mississippi, a state he said was sweltering with the heat of injustice and the heat of oppression, would be transformed into an oasis of freedom and justice for all Americans. He added that he had a dream that his four little children would one day live in a nation where they would not be judged by the color of their skin, but by the content of their character.[33]

At the end of the speech men and women stood, unable to control their emotions, unable to hold their tears back, and began to sob continuously. His speech, to the black people across the world, to the oppressed people of Asia and Africa, had the impact of the same magnitude as Booker T. Washington's speech at Atlanta in 1895 had to the white people. It was a speech to the world, not just to America. At the conclusion of the march King and other leaders had a conference with President John F. Kennedy, who had supported the civil rights movement, and who had remarked that "the cause of 20 million Negroes had been advanced by the program conducted so appropriately before the nation's shrine to the Great Emancipator."[34] The Grand March on Washington was organized partly to support President Kennedy's civil rights bill, which he submitted to a reluctant Congress, and strengthened the cause African Americans were fighting by informing the world that they were still not free in a land that claimed to be free, in a country that had often offered shelter and protection to many oppressed people across the world. Unfortunately Kennedy was assassinated on November 23, 1963, and the civil rights bill that he had submitted to Congress was temporarily shelved.

But African Americans would take no chances. They worked steadily for the enactment of the most comprehensive civil rights legislation since Reconstruction. When President Lyndon B. Johnson assumed office he was to follow the policies of his predecessor, and African Americans appeared to like him, though he was from Texas, which had been a subject of the 1950 Supreme Court decision on *Sweatt*. In the coming months the black freedom movement leaders discovered that President Johnson was a man and national leader they could trust. They began to work with him toward their goal of restoring the rights they had lost under the hands of southern politicians, who always had their own way in both the legislatures of the South and Washington, DC. The Civil Rights Act of 1964 was passed partly as a tribute to Kennedy, partly by Johnson's influence, and partly from pressure from African Americans themselves. During his college days, King had written about his philosophy of education, whose foundation was to teach one to think intensively and to think critically. King concluded that education which stopped with efficiency may prove the greatest menace to society. The most dangerous criminal may be the man gifted with reason, but with no morals. He reminded his listeners that society must remember that intelligence was not enough. Intelligence must be combined with character to form the goal of true education. Complete education gave one power to concentrate on the broad objectives upon which to build character. Broad education would therefore transport to one not only the accumulated knowledge of the significance of race but also the accumulated experience of social living.[35]

King lived this philosophy all his life. There was a consistent pattern of living and life between his philosophy and the way he lived. He was not a man who preached one gospel and practiced another. As King's presence was needed all over the country for one cause or another, he responded steadily, as he saw his role and his participation in the struggle for African Americans as his mission in life. In the spring of 1968, he was invited to Memphis, Tennessee, where he was to support two causes: the Poor People's march, which was protesting against the depressing conditions under which they were working, and the Memphis garbage collectors, who also had demands for better working conditions. There, on April 3, 1968, he spoke to 2,000 people who had come to hear him, and he said that there were some difficult days ahead. But it really did not matter to him at that point in the struggle because, he said, he had been to the mountaintop and he had seen the promised land. Like anybody he would like to live a long life because longevity had its place. But he was not concerned about that now. He just wanted to do God's will. He said that he might not get to there with other African Americans, but he wanted them to know that as a people they would get to the promised land.[36]

On February 4, 1968, exactly two months before his death, King had preached a taped sermon at Ebenezer Baptist Church, where he was serving as associate pastor to his father. He said in that sermon, if any of them were around when he had to meet his day he did not want a long funeral. He said that if any of them got somebody to deliver the eulogy, he urged him to tell him not to talk too long, to tell him not to mention that he had a Nobel Peace Prize. That was not important, and they were not to say that he had three or four hundred other awards because that was not important either. He wanted people to know that he tried to give his life serving others. He said that he would like some-body to say that he tried to love all people. He wanted people to say that he tried to feed the hungry and that he tried to clothe those who were naked. He wanted them to say that he tried to visit those who were in prison. Finally, King wanted them to say that he tried to love and serve humanity.[37]

THE TRAGEDY IN MEMPHIS

Indeed, Martin Luther King, Jr. had preached his own funeral sermon because he died, not from natural causes, but from an assassin's bullet. On April 4, 1968, King's life came to a violent end, tarnishing Memphis's reputation forever. Following hectic activities related to the strike that day, King wanted to spend the evening with his associates and aides relaxing and challenging them to accept the principles of nonviolent strategies. While he was doing that a white man slipped into Bessie Brewer Rooming House across the street from and overlooking the Lor-raine Motel,[38] where King and his associates were staying. As King emerged from his room to go to dinner, he stood at the balcony to chat with aides and well-wishers below. This brought him into the telescopic view of the high-powered rifle from the rooming house. He then leaned forward, and in a few moments straightened up. At that moment a gun-man fired a single shot from the Bessie Brewer Rooming House and hit King.

King fell, blood flowing from the gaping wounds in his right jaw and neck. He was rushed to St. Joseph Hospital where he died about 7:00 p.m. at the age of 39. James Earl Ray,[39] a man with a checkered past, was accused of his assassination. For several months Ray escaped justice, seeking refuge in Canada and Europe. Finally he was arrested in London and was brought back to the United States to stand trial. He was con-victed and sentenced to 99 years in prison for King's murder. At the trial and before any evidence was presented, Ray readily admitted his guilt. But later he recanted his admission, saying that Percy Foreman, the at-torney who was paid $165,000 from public funds to defend him, coerced him to admit guilt to save him from an inevitable death sentence.[40]

Until his death in 1997, Ray maintained the recantation of his admis-sion, raising speculation that there was a conspiracy to assassinate King, a speculation that has raised some questions in the minds of the King family members. These questions led to a meeting between Ray and Dex-ter King, the slain leader's youngest son, in March 1997. During the meeting Dexter asked Ray whether he killed his father and Ray said that he did not. An article written by Jack E. White in *Time* of April 7, 1997, concluded that the members of King's family "have fallen under the hypnotic spell of William F. Pepper, Ray's current lawyer and the architect of a breathtakingly convoluted conspiracy theory about the assassination."[41]

In 1992 Ray wrote a book entitled *Who Killed Martin Luther King. Jr.* in which he stressed his denial of involvement in King's death. Writing the foreword to the book, Jesse Jackson seems to agree with Ray, as do the King family members. Jackson said, "Where I do agree with James Earl Ray is that he deserves a full and fair trial, and the American people deserve to know the truth to the best and fullest extent possible. Denying James Earl Ray a trial and sealing the evidence to the year 2027 does not seem to me the best way for justice to be served. Justice delayed is justice denied."[42]

Jackson might have been thinking about the strange relationship that existed between J. Edgar Hoover, director of the FBI, and Cartha De Loach, his assistant who some people say was assigned to harass King and tarnish his reputation. Hoover disliked King intensely because he thought he was an agitator. Hoover then assigned De Loach to investigate King's assassination. Many people believe that for De Loach to investigate King's assassination is the same thing as asking the crown prince to investigate the conduct of the king. It cannot be done. The question that has remained in the minds of people is whether Hoover was part of the conspiracy to assassinate King because of his personal hatred for him.

Accentuating the controversy are two other developments related to the conspiracy theory. The first development is that two judges who were going to hear Ray's plea for a new trial, Preston W. Battle and William E. Miller, died mysteriously. The second development is that Ray himself was stabbed 22 times at Brushy Mountain Prison were he was serving his sentence.[43] Mark Lane, who wrote the preface to Ray's book, agrees with Jesse Jackson, saying

Ray is clearly the primary victim of federal and state lawlessness in this matter. However, the American people and those throughout the world who care to know who killed Martin Luther King and why he died that day in Memphis are also victims. The truth became a target of the intelligence operations that suppressed the facts, suborned perjury, imprisoned witnesses, and tortured the defendant.[44]

These developments indicate to many, including Jesse Jackson, Mark Lane, and the King family that there was a conspiracy in King's assassination. These are the circumstances that Ray tried to exploit to claim his innocence in the assassination of King.

However, the troubling thing about doubt cast by Jackson and Lane about Ray's guilt is that they have completely ignored that since the age of 16 Ray lived a life of crime and misrepresentation of the facts. He always blamed others for his criminal behavior. Even what would appear to be his best description of "Raoul," Ray admits to being a liar and giving himself a new name, Eric Galt,[45] to conceal his criminal behavior and activities. As one reads his book one is obviously persuaded to reach the inevitable conclusion that James Earl Ray, Eric Galt, and Raoul are all one and the same person. How does one believe Ray's description of Raoul and then cast doubt on his guilt under these circumstances? This author reaches the inevitable and only logical conclusion that Ray's entire book is a fabricated fiction. For Jackson and Lane to doubt that Ray committed this heinous crime by himself is to doubt that the hyena kills fawns whenever he has an opportunity. However, King's violent death helped make him leave his name permanently in the pages of history of the African American struggle to get to the promised land. He had played his role of a Moses well, although he was not able to get there.

SUMMARY AND CONCLUSION

The purpose of this chapter is not based on the assumption that Martin Luther King, Jr. was the only leader among African Americans, but simply to state that he brought new dimensions of leadership to the journey to the promised land. As a Moses of a new era, King exhibited qualities of leadership that made him unique, just as those qualities made other leaders unique. Frederick Douglass, Roy Wilkins, Malcom X, Kwame Toure, Rap Brown, John Lewis—all had qualities that made them unique. The one quality that King shared with these African American leaders was his ability to articulate issues that were critical to African Americans on their journey to the promised land. When he said during the March on Washington, DC in August 1963, "Now is the time to lift our nation from the dark and desolate valley of segregation to the sunlit path of racial justice,"[46] he was demonstrating rare qualities of leadership that African Americans needed to continue their journey to a successful destination, the promised land.

But one must also accept the reality that King was also different from these other leaders by the very nature of his personality. His refusal to resort to violence places him in the same class of leaders that includes Mohandas Gandhi, Paulo Freire, and Desmond Tutu.[47] The world of African Americans of King's time had seen enough violence. This vicious circle of violence had to come to an end. Indeed, although violence is always perpetrated by the oppressor, the oppressed must not respond to the situation of violence with violence. Matching violence with violence simply perpetuates violence and the oppressed are the ones who suffer most. This is why in 1965 King began to speak against the war in Vietnam. He saw it as a detractor of the war on poverty and an enemy of efforts to create the Great Society that President Lyndon B. Johnson was trying to build. King was the kind of leader who saw issues of national development from the perspective of the arrival of African Americans in the promised land.

NOTES

1. Martin Luther King, Jr., *Why We Can't Wait* (New York: New American Library, 1964), p. 18.
2. Ibid., p. 5.
3. Ibid., p. 18.
4. Ibid., p. 19.
5. Ibid., p. 21.
6. Ibid., p. 6.
7. Ibid., p. 27.
8. W. R. Miller, *Martin Luther King, Jr.: His Life, Martyrdom and Meaning for the World* (New York: Weybright and Talley, 1968), p. 8.
9. C. Osborne, *I Have a Dream: The Story of Martin Luther King, Jr.* (New York: Time-Life Books, 1968), p. 17.
10. This author was privileged to meet this distinguished scholar in 1959 when he visited Zimbabwe.
11. L. Bennet, Jr., *What Manner of Man: Martin Luther King, Jr.* (Chicago: Johnson Publishing Company, 1968), p. 48.
12. Ibid., p. 49.
13. Ibid., p. 50.
14. Ibid., p. 52.
15. W. Miller, *Martin Luther King, Jr.*, p. 29.
16. Ibid., p. 30.
17. King, *Why We Can't Wait*, p. 33.
18. Ibid., p. 35.
19. Osborne, *I Have a Dream*, p. 18. This is the theory that made Paulo Freire of Brazil famous. See his *Pedagogy of the Oppressed* (Trans. by M. B. Ramos) (New York: Continuum, 1983).
20. R. M. Bleiweiss, *Marching to Freedom: The Life of Martin Luther King, Jr.* (New York: The New American Library, 1969), p. 67.
21. Bennet, *What Manner of Man*, p. 68.
22. Ibid., p. 69.
23. Ibid., p. 70.
24. Ibid., p. 80.
25. Bleiweiss, *Marching to Freedom*, p. 77.
26. King, *Why We Can't Wait*, p. 83.
27. Ibid., p. 84.
28. Miller, *Martin Luther King, Jr.*, p. 161.

29. In May 1962, when the author visited Atlanta, John Lewis acted as his host. He is currently a Democratic member of the U.S. Congress.

30. Martin Luther King, Jr., Address at March on Washington, DC, August 28, 1963.

31. Ibid.

32. The famous words of Thomas Jefferson stated in the preamble to the Declaration of Independence.

33. Bennet, *What Manner of Man*, p. 161.

34. Ibid., p. 169.

35. Ibid., p. 29.

36. Ibid., p. 31.

37. Ibid., p. 170.

38. In 1989 the author made a pilgrimage to Memphis to pay respect to King. He visited the Lorraine Motel, now a civil rights museum.

39. In March 1997 Ray held a meeting with Dexter, King's youngest son, and told him that he did not assassinate his father. There were reports that Ray was near death and he wanted to correct the record before he died. It seemed at that point that King's family members were in favor of a new trial for Ray, because they felt that there was a conspiracy to assassinate him. For details see *Time*, April 7, 1997, p. 52.

40. Observers concluded that Ray, a habitual liar, blamed the mysterious person he claimed to have met in Canada in 1967 named Raoul whom he described in his book as a man "wrapped in mystery and drifted like fog, a junkie and addict trying to hide needle marks." James Earl Ray, *Who Killed Martin Luther King Jr.* (New York: Marlowe and Company, 1992), p. 63. Reporters and journalists concluded that Raoul was, in effect, a figment of Ray's imagination.

41. Jack E. White, "Family Forgiveness: Martin Luther's King's Son Meets his Father's Convicted Killer, Giving New Life to Wild Theories," in *Time*, April 7, 1987, p. 52.

42. Jesse Jackson, "Foreword," in Ray, *Who Killed Martin Luther King Jr.*, p. 7.

43. Ray, *Who Killed Martin Luther King Jr.?*, p. 128

44. Ibid., p. 12.

45. Ibid., p. 64.

46. King, Jr., Address at March on Washington.

47. For a detailed discussion of this remarkable African church leader in racially troubled South Africa, see Dickson A. Mungazi, *In the Footsteps of the Masters: Desmond M. Tutu and Abel T. Muzorewa* (Westport, CT: Praeger Publishers, 2000).

6

Civil Rights Legislation: Vehicle to the Promised Land

The lack of an adequate education denies the Negro a chance to get a decent job.

President John F. Kennedy, 1963

In far too many ways American Negroes have been another nation, deprived of freedom, crippled by hatred, the door of opportunity closed to hope.

President Lyndon B. Johnson, 1965

THE LEGAL STATUS OF AFRICAN AMERICANS IN PERSPECTIVE

The period of civil disobedience and militant confrontation was born during the months following the Grand March on Washington, DC in August 1963. African Americans were particularly sensitive to the fact that 1963 marked the centennial of President Lincoln's Emancipation Proclamation. The United States Civil Rights Commission, which was established under the 1957 Civil Rights Act, celebrated the occasion with its report to President Kennedy.

The report was devoted to extensive and comprehensive historical review of the role and status of African Americans from the colonial period to the mid-20th century. The report saw the possibility of the existence of a much more complex range of problems and potential than were apparent. The report concluded that the practice of a segregated system would eventually engulf the nation as new bitterness emerged, and as African Americans became steadily aware of the injustices of the American society they were bound to take matters into their own hands, as the reservoir of nonviolent approach may become exhausted. The report indicated that the hundred years since Emancipation were but the beginning of the continuing responsibilities and problems that the nation must face. The country could no longer refuse, as it had done during Reconstruction and after, to ensure the civil rights of all Americans.

Since the *Brown* decision the Supreme Court had addressed itself periodically to the question of desegregation in the schools and in general. A number of cases came before the Court, which was disturbed by the slow process of desegregation. In *Watson vs. Memphis*, 1963, the Supreme Court unanimously denounced the policy of gradual desegregation of the city recreational facilities and ordered their immediate desegregation. In 1964 in *Calhoun vs. Latimer* the trial court was ordered to consider whether the Atlanta school desegregation program was going on fast enough. Then, in *Griffin vs. Prince Edward School Board* of 1964, the Supreme Court ordered the Prince Edward County Schools to reopen on a desegregated basis, and directed the federal district court to raise taxes to enable the schools to run.

THE CIVIL RIGHTS ACT OF 1957

Following the desegregation crisis in Little Rock in 1957 and the Montgomery bus boycott two years earlier, the need for congressional action was dramatized. Congress enacted in 1957 a Civil Rights Act, which was the first civil rights legislation since the ineffective Civil Rights Act of 1875. Although the 1957 Civil Rights Act was not far-reaching in its provisions, it clearly indicated that the U.S. Congress was at last beginning to wake up to its responsibilities, which had been "left alone" or pretty much so to the courts.

Among the provisions of this 1957 Civil Rights Act was the creation of a nonpartisan Civil Rights Commission, which was empowered to collect evidence on voting rights violations. The legislation also authorized the Justice Department to initiate action to counter irregularities in federal elections (Sec. 101.19) There was created in the executive branch of government a Commission on Civil Rights whose function would be:

(a) The Commission shall be composed of six members who shall be appointed by the President by and with the advice and consent of the Senate. Not more than three of the members shall at any time be of the same political party.

(b) The President shall designate one of the members of the Commissions as Chairman and one as Vice Chairman. The disability of the Chairman or in the event of a vacancy in that office,

The Commission shall

(1) investigate allegations in writing under oath or affirmation that certain citizens of the United States are being deprived of their right to vote and have that vote counted by reason of their color, race, religion, or national origin which writing under oath or affirmation, shall set forth the facts upon which such belief or beliefs are based.[1]

(2) study and collect information concerning legal developments constituting a denial of equal protection of the laws under the Constitution, and

(3) appraise the laws and policies of the federal government with respect to equal protection of the laws under the Constitution.

(d) The Commission is empowered and required to submit interim reports to the President and to the Congress at such times as either the Commission or the President shall deem desirable and shall submit to the President and to the Congress a final and comprehensive report of its activities, findings, and recommendations not later than two years from the date of the enactment of this Act.[2]

(e) Sixty days after the submission of its final report and recommendations, the Commission shall cease to exist.[3]

With both the Supreme Court and the U.S. Congress on their side, African Americans began to move forward on their journey to the promised land. They were fully aware that with voting rights secured, any aspiration they might have for political office had to appeal to a sense of power of the elected. Further, African Americans became convinced that they must first secure conscious self-respect and an economic and political power base before they could hope to deal more effectively with the major problems of education. Thus the black power movement was born but its aims and purposes were immediately misunderstood. Comments by Stokely Carmichael, spokesman of black power movement, reflected the sentiments of the times, that some confrontation with white America was necessary because King's philosophy of nonviolence was yielding little result. After King's death the philosophy of black power acquired more influence than it had done in the past.

Even with the Civil Rights Act of 1957, African Americans felt there was still something missing. The attitudes of the South had not significantly changed to make them truly comfortable and enjoy desperately needed peace of mind. African Americans still saw discrimination confirmed by state and local law worse now that they were aware of it. The de facto segregation and discrimination which had characterized so much of American life, both North and South, was taking a heavy psychological toll on African American life. Although they were achieving legal rights, they were yet to win full roles in the social and economic life of the nation. The journey to the promised land was getting harder now than in the past.

A vicious circle of residential segregation, job discrimination, inferior educational opportunity, limited economic mobility, and problems of developing self-image were serious handicaps that the African Americans were now suffering from in their long journey. In essence urban African Americans resorted to a wave of riots and demonstrations. The next decade beginning with 1957 reflected this tone of frustration, which characterized the period, and the federal response went a long way to meet the needs of African Americans. In addition to the action of the courts, Congress began to feel that it had to act as well.

THE CIVIL RIGHTS ACT OF 1960

In 1960 four African American students, David Richmand, Franklin MacCain, Ezell Blair, Jr., and Joseph McNeil, from North Carolina A & T College, decided to sit in at a segregated lunch counter in Greensboro, North Carolina.[4] Warmath T. Gibbs, President of A & T College, an African American himself, did not know how to react. Neither did George Roach, the mayor of Greensboro, or the city council. By this time the civil rights movement was fully established and the sit-in protest methods had also become fully established. Mass demonstrations and rallies were also held as part of the strategy to hasten the journey to the promised land. The constitutional validity of this strategy was later upheld by the Supreme Court in a number of cases. African Americans were profoundly disturbed by the reaction of southern white America to recent developments: the wave of arrests, violence, ill-treatment by local authorities on defenseless African Americans, bombed African American homes, churches and schools. All these developments became identified with the protest or civil rights movement. African Americans once more turned to the U.S. Congress for action to give them direction in their struggle on the journey to the promised land.

The future political composition of the federal government was an open question in the spring of 1960, because President Eisenhower's second term of office had been handicapped by recession and by the success of liberals and Democrats in the congressional elections of 1958. Because of coming presidential elections in 1960, and the need for both major parties to demonstrate ability for positive, decisive leadership, African Americans felt that a political wisdom was needed to enact the second federal civil rights act within three years.

The purpose of the Civil Rights Act of 1960 was to eliminate the possibility of racial conflict, which was probable from the current attitude of the Supreme Court on protest marches and demonstrations. The Justice Department was empowered to take action to protect the right of African American voters and to create federal election records. The powers of the Civil Rights Commission to administer oaths and to take statements of witness under affirmative action was strengthened. Title III, Section 3.1 stated that

every officer of elections was required to retain and preserve for a period of 22 months from the date of any general, special, or primary election of which candidates for office of President, Vice President, presidential elector, member of the Senate, member of the House of Representatives, or Resident Commissioner from the Commonwealth of Puerto Rico were voted for. All records and papers which came into position relating to any application, registration, payment of poll tax or other act requisite to voting in such elections except that when required by law, such records and papers may be delivered to another officer of elections.[5]

With these developments African Americans now began to direct their energies toward securing other rights. By 1962 the whole question of African American attendance at state-supported universities was not an issue in the midterm elections. The Supreme Court had avoided a number of landmark cases on that question during the era of new attitudes from 1938 to 1950. But as it has already been seen, continued disregard of federal court orders brought the behavior of Mississippi Governor Ross Barnett and Alabama Governor George Wallace a new awareness of the problems that were still created when they were thought to have been solved.

The beginning of the academic year in 1962 was also the beginning of problems that James Meredith faced at "Ole Miss" and Vivian Malone and James Hood faced at the University of Alabama. To promote their political agendas Governors Barnett and Wallace prohibited the registration of these African American students into the state universities. This action triggered a crisis between the Kennedy administration and themselves. In 1963 came new determination by the president, Congress, and African Americans themselves to put an end to this last pocket of resistance by white racists. The civil rights movement had become too powerful and advanced to allow the nation to ignore the issue it was raising. President Kennedy would be the first national leader to ensure that all state governments complied with the federal laws.

Following the Wallace-Kennedy showdown of 1963, the president went on national television to deliver a comprehensive, far-reaching scheme designed to eliminate the inferior status of African Americans. He then informed the nation and Congress that he was about to ask for extensive federal legislation which would give him power to act to redress the many injustices that African Americans had suffered. The day following Kennedy's address Medgar Evers was murdered in Mississippi, and Kennedy himself was to die by assassination in the same year. But during that address to the nation Kennedy said on the question of African Americans that he was asking government officials to open hotels, restaurants, theaters, retail stores, and similar establishments to everyone, regardless of color. Kennedy saw this as a basic right. He was also asking Congress to authorize the federal government to participate more fully in lawsuits designed to end segregation in public education. He said that his administration had succeeded in persuading many districts to desegregate voluntarily. Dozens of institutions were admitting African Americans without any violence. He noted that African Americans were attending a state-supported institution in every one of the 50 states. But the pace of their progress was very slow. He added that many African American children who was entering segregated grade schools at the time of the Supreme Court decision nine years earlier would enter segregated high schools that fall, having suffered a loss which could never be restored. Kennedy said that the lack of an adequate education denied African Americans a chance to get decent jobs.[6]

Kennedy went on to add that the orderly implementation of the Supreme Court's decision could not be left entirely to those who may not have the economic resources to carry their legal action or to those who may be subject to harassment. He concluded that legislation could not solve this problem alone. The problem must be solved in the homes of every American in every community across the country. He expressed his hope that every American, regardless of where he lived, would stop and examine his conscience about this and other related incidents that injured the efforts African Americans were making to realize their ambition of reaching the promised land.[7]

Congress was ready to examine its own conscience, when in response, it passed the most comprehensive civil rights law since Reconstruction, but only after Kennedy's death. Between 1963 and 1964 NAACP was involved in lawsuits brought against them by Alabama. The Supreme Court struck down the Alabama law that required NAACP to register with local authorities. A number of civil rights cases, such as *Garner vs. Louisiana, Peterson vs. Greenville, Bell vs. Maryland*, came before the Supreme Court which upheld the rights of African Americans.

THE CIVIL RIGHTS ACT OF 1964

With all this background Congress was ready to enact the latest civil rights law, which had far-reaching results on the American society. This new landmark legislation was passed on July 2, 1964, after the Senate made the bill its main order of business for the previous four months. On June 10, supporters of the bill rallied sufficient votes to end the extended southern filibuster. This was the first time since 1917, when the Senate had initially adopted the rules for limiting debate, that the complicated system of cloture was successfully invoked for civil rights legislation. Cloture had been voted five other times before. In 1964 cloture was made possible by the abandonment by Northern Republicans of Southern Democrats, as Minority Leader Everett Dirksen of Illinois, whose deep rambling voice echoed in the corridors of the Senate chamber, stated that time had come to act, action would not be delayed, it would not be denied.

The new law was structured to ensure the greatest possible rights of African Americans in as many areas of public life as possible. Unlike the Civil Rights Acts of 1957 and 1960, the 1964 Civil Rights Law provided for separate titles on voting, public accommodation, public facilities, education, and employment practices. Again, like the 1960 Civil Rights Act, the power of the Civil Rights Commission was extended and two other agencies were established that would facilitate the implementation of the Act: the Equal Employment Opportunity Commission and the Community Relations Service.

The fair employment provisions were to be made over a period of three years and the Act also made it mandatory that all federally sponsored programs and participants in such programs clearly state their compliance with the nondiscrimination provisions of Title VI. The Department of Health, Education and Welfare was authorized to assist school districts, through funds that were available under the Act, to solve their desegregation problems.

As was expected, and because of the unusual importance of this new, latest civil rights law, the Supreme Court took immediate action to make decisions on cases that were brought before it to affirm the constitutionality of the law, and the authority of Congress to pass such law was upheld some five months later in *Heart of Atlanta vs. United States*. Unlike the previous civil rights laws, the 1964 Civil Rights Act systematically tabulates every detail of its provisions under each title in a manner that leaves little doubt as to clarity of language and meaning as well as purpose. For example, Title I refers to voting rights, Title II refers to discrimination in places of public accommodation, Title III refers to desegregation of public facilities, and Title IV refers to education. Because of the importance of this new law to the progress of black education, relevant parts of Title IV are reproduced from Blanstein and Zangrando: *The Civil Rights and the American Negro*:

Title IV: Desegregation of Public Education

Section 401 of this title stated:

(a) "Commissioner" means the Commissioner of Education

(b) "Desegregation" means the assignment of the students to public schools and within such schools without regard to their race, color, religion, or national origin, but "desegregation" shall not mean the assignment of students to public schools in order to overcome racial imbalance.

(c) "Public school" means any elementary or secondary education institution, and "public college" means any institution of higher education or any technical or vocational school above the secondary school level, provided that such public school or public college is operated by a state, sub-division of a state, in governmental agency within a state or operated wholly or predominantly from through the use of governmental funds or property or funds or property derived from a governmental source.

(d) "school board" means any agency or agencies which administer a system of one or more public schools and any other agency which is responsible for the assignment of students to or within such system.[8]

Educational Opportunity and Technical Assistance

Section 402 required that the commissioner shall conduct a survey and make a report to the president and the Congress, within two years of statement of this Title, concerning the lack of availability of equal educational opportunities for individuals by reason of race, color, religion, or national origin in public educational institutions at all levels in the United States, its territories and possessions, and the District of Columbia.

Section 403 required that the commissioner is authorized upon the application of any school board, state, municipality, school district, or other governmental unit legally responsible for operations of a public school or schools, to tender technical assistance to such applicant in the preparation, adoption, and implementation of plans to the desegregation of public schools. Such technical assistance may, among other activities, include making available to such agencies information regarding effective methods of coping with special educational problems occasioned by desegregation. Individuals who attended such an institution on a full-time basis may be paid stipends on the period of their attendance at such institution in amounts specified by the commissioner in regulations, including allowances for travel to attend such institute.

Grants

Section 405 provided:

(a) The commissioner is authorized upon application of a school board to make grants to such board to pay in whole or in part, the cost of:

(1) giving to the teachers and other school personnel in service training in dealing with problems incident to desegregation and

(2) employment specialists to advise in problems incident to desegregation

(b) In determination of whether to make a grant and in fixing the amount thereof and the terms and conditions of which it will be made the Commissioner shall take into consideration the amount available for grants under this section and the other applications which are pending before him, the financial conditions of the applications and other resources available to them, the nature, extent and growth of its problems incident to desegregation and such other factors as he finds relevant.

Suits by the Attorney General

Section 407 provided:

(a) Whenever the Attorney General receives a complaint in writing

(1) signed by a parent or group of parents to the effect that his or their minor children as members of a class of persons similarly situated, are being deprived by a school board of the equal protection of the law or,

(2) signed by a individual or his parents to the effect that he has been denied admission to or not permitted to continue in attendance at a public college by reason of race, color, religion, or national origin, and the Attorney General believes the complaint is meritorious and certifies that the signer or signers of such complaint are unable in his judgment, to initiate and maintain appropriate legal proceedings for relief and that the institution of an action will materialize further the orderly achievement of desegregation in public education, such complaint to the appropriate school board or college, board or authority has had a reasonable time to adjust the conditions alleged in such complaint, to institute for or in the name of the United States against such court shall pursuant to this action provided that nothing herein shall empower any official or court of the United States to issue any order seeking to achieve a racial balance in any school by requiring the transportation of pupils or students from one school to another or one school district to another in order to achieve racial balance or otherwise enlarge the existing power of the court to insure compliance with defendants such additional parties as are or become necessary to the grant of effective relief hereunder.

(b) The Attorney General may deem a person or persons unable to initiate and maintain appropriate legal proceedings with the meaning intended in this subsection.

(c) When such person or persons are unable, either directly or through other interested persons or organizations, to bear the expenses of the litigation or to obtain effective legal representation, or whenever he is satisfied that the institution of such litigation would jeopardize the personal safety, employment or economic standing of such person or persons, their families, or their property, he or they can seek other services.[9]

Certainly Congress was tired of the southern negative attitude to African American progress. It now wanted to pass a law that would put an end to this age-old problem once and for all. The South knew that the days of resistance were numbered. Some members of U.S. Congress had a feeling that in a way the Civil Rights Act of 1964 may have gone too far, but as it was often the case, the end justified the means and for the first time in many years, the Court and the legislature joined forces to fight the social menace that had plagued America for so long. On June 4, 1965, President Lyndon B. Johnson reflected the mood of the unwillingness by Congress to "let alone" the question of African American progress. At the Howard University Commencement exercises he said that in far too many ways African Americans had been another nation, deprived of freedom, crippled by hatred, and the door of opportunity was closed to their hope. In their time change had come to this nation, too. However, African Americans were acting with impressive restraint. They had peacefully protested and marched, entered the courtrooms and the seats of government, demanding justice long denied. The voice of African Americans that the courts once silenced, and the Congress once restrained, the president and the people once made ineffective, suddenly found themselves as allies to promote a great national cause. Americans had listened carefully and had seen the Supreme Court declare in 1954 that racial discrimination was repugnant to human decency and therefore was unconstitutional.[10]

President Johnson went on to add that from 1957 to 1960, civil rights legislation was needed more in this century than at any other time in the history of the country. He said that as majority leader in the U.S. Senate he helped guide two of these bills through the Senate. And as president he was proud to sign the third. And soon the country would have the fourth new law guaranteeing every American the right to vote, breaking the barriers to freedom for all Americans. So Johnson began his program of war on poverty and the influence of his Great Society philosophy was felt. He was convinced that the 1964 Civil Rights Act and the 1965 Voting Rights Acts were monumental landmarks in the black long march to the promised land. But other matters began to demand national attention: the war in Vietnam was at its peak, the black power movement was at its best in its efforts to seek the destruction of the elements that blacks could accept as a starting point in the endless struggle, the Watts, California, and Newark, New Jersey, riots left their scars on the body of American history. So the question of black progress in the area of education did not receive the attention it was to receive, but the course of a new era had been mapped out.

But African Americans appeared to have been disturbed by the accumulation of a number of factors so that by 1967 there was a national wave of riots and on July 29, 1967, President Johnson announced the appointment of National Advisory Commission on Civil Disorders, which was to find out what happened, why it happened, and what could be done to improve the situation. In 1968 the Commission submitted its recommendations, among them:

If disadvantages are not to be perpetrated we must drastically improve the quality of education in the ghetto. Equality of results with all-white schools is what the Commission recommends.

(1) sharply increased efforts to eliminate de facto segregation in our schools through substantial federal aid to school systems seeking to desegregate either within the system or in co-operation with neighboring school systems.

(2) Elimination of racial discrimination in northern as well as southern schools by vigorously applying Title VI of the Civil Rights Act of 1964.

(3) Extension of quality early childhood education to every disadvantaged child in the country.

(4) Efforts to improve dramatically schools serving disadvantaged children through substantial federal funding of year-round quality compensatory education programs, improved teaching, and expanded experimentation and research.

(5) Elimination of illiteracy through greater federal support for adult basic education.

(6) Enlarged opportunities for parent and community participation in the public schools.

(7) Reoriented vocational education emphasis work-experience training and involvement of business and industry.

(8) Expanded opportunities for higher education through increased federal assistance to disadvantaged students.

(9) Revision of state aid formulas to assume more per student aid to districts having a high proportion of disadvantaged school age children.[11]

Blanstein and Zangrando expressed a popular line of thinking when they wrote that they supported interaction as a priority education strategy because it was essential to the fabric of American society. In the summer's disorders of 1967 they had seen the consequences of racial isolation at all levels, and of attitudes toward race, on both sides produced by three centuries of myth, ignorance, and bias. Blanstein and Zangrando said that it was indispensable that opportunity for interaction between the races be expanded. For many minorities, and particularly for children of the ghetto, the schools had failed to provide the kind of educational experience which could help overcome the effects of discrimination and deprivation.[12]

This was a great observation of the serious problems that faced the black people and the American society as a whole. The solution to these problems would go a long way to help the nation help the black people in their march to the promised land. The 1964 Civil Rights Act was in many ways a monumental piece of legislation. It was comprehensive in its provisions.

THE HEAD START PROGRAM AS A FORM OF CIVIL RIGHTS

At the time the Civil Rights Act of 1964 came into being, it was immediately recognized that de facto segregation had some serious, damaging effects on black children and these effects were traced to their environment. The culturally disadvantaged, as the victims of these effects have become known, had no way of off-setting them after the children were in class. It was observed that when children from disadvantaged family backgrounds entered school, they lacked the necessary experience to make progress and succeed. As result, they began to fall further and further behind until they simply dropped out of school. So in 1964 the Economic Opportunity Act was created. Under this act was the Head Start Program, whose purpose was to provide disadvantaged children with the necessary background and experience at the preschool level to enable them to make progress at formal school.

Head Start did not come into being until 1965, and those school districts which were interested in applying for funds to develop preschool programs for the disadvantaged were to do so under Titles II and III. The initial Head Start guidelines were developed by experts in pediatrics, public health, nursing, education, child psychology, and child development. From June to August 1965, it is said that some 500,000 children across the country attended Head Start classes. In Alaska one program had 10 children, in New York there were 26,000 children. In 1966, 575,000 children attended Head Start schools. President Johnson was so encouraged and so pleased that he announced the continuation of the program with some improvements in the organization of the program. By 1967 new guidelines and rules were formulated to include:

(1) Federal assistance was not to exceed 8% of the total cost of the program.

(2) 90% of the total enrollment of Head Start students must meet the poverty guidelines as stipulated by the Act.

(3) All Head Start programs were to comply with conditions of Title IV of the Civil Rights Act of 1964.

(4) One hot meal and a snack were strongly recommended as a part of the daily program.

(5) A central policy advisory committee was to be developed and at least 50% of its members were to consist of Head Start parents. Parent involvement was continually stressed and emphasized for all Head Start programs.

(6) A medical director was required for all Head Start programs.

(7) A career development program was required in order to upgrade personnel as well as to provide staff incentives.

(8) Transportation was required for all children living beyond walking distances.[13]

In 1966 Head Start was considered the most successful of the antipoverty programs, but the cost was astronomical, a total of $95 million, which worked out to be about $168 for each child. Lady Bird Johnson, the president's wife, supported the program when she said, "Head Start will reach out to one million young children lost in a gray world of poverty and neglect and lead them into the human family."[14]

But some experts on education had some doubts about Head Start, because they felt that the question of poor people in American must be looked at from the perspective of the influence of the home, which plays an essential part in the education of the child. Some observers, while agreeing that Head Start had made a good, pleasing effort in many places, also noted that if one side of the river is seen as a gray world of poverty and neglect and the other as a bright world of affluence and virtue, then the child's parents have been condemned and rendered worthless.[15]

Vice President Hubert H. Humphrey stressed the future challenge of Head Start, that successful outcome from the war on poverty depended on educational opportunity, which was contained in economic opportunity as outlined by the Economic Opportunity Act. A number of suggestions were made to improve the effectiveness of Head Start, such as reducing the pupil-teacher ratio, increasing the use of teaching aides, tutorial assistance, and social services to the poor. The various suggestions were made to improve the benefits of pupils as they made the change from home or family background into primary school. In 1968 plans were being made to move Head Start from the Office of Economic Opportunity to the Office of Health, Education and Welfare. At this point controversial discussions began to take place among various members of the American society as to the real value of Head Start.

We will not go into this controversy, but it would be wise to look at the positive side of Head Start, as well as the implication of the 1964 Civil Rights legislation on black education and economic and social progress. President Johnson, a former schoolteacher, a wealthy Texan, solidly believed that the black people could make positive contributions to American society if they were given a chance to improve themselves. The alternative to recognizing this right for blacks would be serious confrontation with the blacks who, over the years, had gradually become aware of their position, and had patiently waited for a day when their dream would come true.

The report of the Commission on Civil Disorders clearly put the position as one that required immediate attention if this confrontation was to be avoided. In 1975 black people enjoyed tremendous freedom and opportunity in education and jobs. Federal law prohibited discrimination in any form in hiring practices. In fact, it would seem that minority groups would enjoy a preferential treatment in hiring practices. Even on college campuses, blacks seemed to enjoy the rights that they had not known during the previous 10 years.

Although the 1964 Civil Rights Act may not be without faults, the law has become a landmark in the long history of black struggle for equality and justice. The Supreme Court had no intention of going back on the question of African American advancement. Seeing the great period of change coming, a number of colleges and universities in the South signed statements indicating that they would comply with the Civil Rights Act of 1964.

BUSING AND SCHOOL INTEGRATION

In 1852 Massachusetts became the first state to enact a law that made school attendance compulsory, but the lawmakers did not foresee all possible implications or complications that were eventually to arise. One of these came from the fact that the population of the day was scattered and there were a limited number of school buildings. Therefore, some means had to be devised for each pupil, especially from the rural areas, to get to school. In 1869 Massachusetts once again became the first state to provide pupils with transportation at public cost. Again, the legislators were not aware of the possibility of future implications or complications.

Other states in the Union followed the Massachusetts example, so that by 1919 all states were using tax revenue to transport students. The most practical, feasible, and popular means of transportation was the bus. Across the country the yellow school bus has over the years been closely associated with education. Even some private and parochial schools have resorted to the bus to maintain the characteristic feature of their schools. The number of students thus bused to and from school grew rapidly into the 1970s.

Since 1965, when federal courts began to order the use of the school bus as a means of providing quality education which every state promised to its students, busing has become so controversial that its history and purpose have often been forgotten. In the controversy and sometimes the bitterness that have arisen, the bus has been denounced or stoned, although estimates indicate that school children bused for integration purposes accounted for a very small percentage of the total number of students bused. According to a federal survey for the 1969–1970 school year, a total of between 18 million and 19 million students, or 43 percent of all public schools were bused.[16]

The Nixon administration expressed itself about some of the complaints and criticism regarding busing in a statement that accompanied its antibusing measures that it sent to Congress in March 1972. That statement said busing was widespread, costly, harmful to the educational process, and created an unnecessary administrative burden. But Stephen Horn, vice chairman of the Civil Rights Commission, sharply disagreed. He told the House Judiciary Committee in May 1972 that population growth accounted for almost all busing and that the cost of busing had held steady at between 3 and 4 percent of total educational expenditures for 40 years. He reminded the Committee that Secretary of Health, Education and Welfare Elliot Richardson told Congress in 1970 that there had been more busing in past years to preserve segregation of schools than there was in 1970 to desegregate them. Horn said that desegregation could be a means to enable students to spend less time on the bus because some children were no longer bused past one segregated school to another.

THE ROLE OF THE COURTS

The federal courts and the judges who handed down decisions on busing took the brunt of the criticism of busing, because nearly all busing has been a result of some court action. However, one would need to understand that the courts did not order busing, rather it was their approval of the plans including busing that put those plans into effect. Busing was approved as a means of desegregating schools by the Supreme Court decision in 1971 in *Swann vs. Charlotte-Mecklenburg Board of Education*. In that unanimous opinion the Court held that desegregation plans could not be limited to the walk-in school. Busing was permissible as long as it did not risk the students' health or impinge on the education process. The *Swann* decision was the latest in a series of Supreme Court rulings on school desegregation which came out of the 1954 *Brown* decision.

The federal courts came into the desegregation process only when local school authorities had failed to fulfill their obligation to eliminate the dual school system. If school authorities defaulted, as the lower courts found to be the case for the school board of Charlotte, North Carolina, then the federal judges have wide discretion in selecting the means of desegregation of the school system. As an interim measure, the courts may order school districts and attendance zones to pair or group the schools. But without a constitutional violation there would be no basis for court orders directing assignment of pupils on a racial basis. Busing of students has been an integral part of the public education system and was a permissible remedial method when ordered by a court to implement desegregation.

By 1972 the Supreme Court had still not determined the question of whether segregation of schools resulting from residential segregation was also unconstitutional, although a federal court in Denver ruled in 1970 that de facto segregation was in fact unconstitutional. In that case Judge John Doyle ordered implementation of a housing plan to overcome segregation in the schools, so that a busing scheme would not be worked out. In 1973 the Supreme Court asked Doyle to look again to see if discriminatory policies of the school board made the entire system a segregated school system, and if so to order immediate desegregation. Judge Doyle had been given a free hand in the desegregation process.

There have been other cases in the federal courts in relation to busing and desegregation of schools. But the celebrated case of Boston has become famous, and Judge Arthur Garrity has become a national figure in his busing plans as part of desegregation. In the summer of 1974 Judge Garrity ruled that the Boston school committee had maintained a dual school system, one for blacks and another for whites. He said that assigning students to neighborhood schools "cannot achieve substantial desegregation in Boston due to geography of the city."[17] Garrity said the transport alone in 1975 would cost $7.6 million. Bus trips would average 10 to 15 minutes, and the longest trip would last about 25 minutes.

Garrity worked out a plan that would divide Boston schools into eight districts, all but one would contain a portion of the city's predominantly black students. On December 9, 1974, the Court of Appeals upheld Garrity's desegregation plans, which were denounced by Mrs. Mary Louise Hicks, the firebrand of segregation in Boston for over 10 years. Mrs. Hicks and other community members vowed to fight the desegregation plans through busing to the bitter end. There was racial bitterness, there was disruption in the schools, but Garrity would not be moved. In 1975 the Supreme Court refused to hear and review the Garrity decision, and this meant that his decision became the law of the land.

Busing became so controversial in the country that many white parents have moved their children to private schools. But for black students, busing seems to remain a part of their education progress. To them it is one step further to securing the equal opportunity for education. Table 6.1 shows a historical perspective to busing during each five-year period from 1929 to 1970.

SUMMARY AND CONCLUSION

This chapter has presented a discussion of various forms of civil rights activity that were related to African American struggle for development, as part of the process of change and progress of the nation. The focus of

Table 6.1
National Pupil Busing Data, 1929–1930 to 1969–1970

School Year	Total public enrollment	Pupil transported at public expense		Expenditure of public funds for busing	
		Numbers	Percent of enrollment	Total (excluding cost of new buses)	Average cost per pupil
1929-30	25,678,015	1,902,826	7.4	$54,823,000	$28.81
1931-32	26,275,441	2,419,173	9.2	53,078,000	24.01
1933-34	26,434,103	2,794,724	10.6	53,908,000	19.29
1935-36	26,267,098	3,250,658	12.3	62,653,000	19.27
1937-38	25,975,108	3,769,242	14.5	75,637,000	20.07
1939-40	25,433,542	4,144,161	16.3	83,283,000	20.10
1941-42	24,562,473	4,503,081	18.3	92,922,000	20.64
1943-44	23,266,616	4,512,412	19.4	107,754,000	23.83
1945-46	23,299,941	5,056,966	21.7	129,756,000	25.66
1947-48	23,944,532	5,854,041	24.4	176,265,000	30.11
1949-50	25,111,427	6,947,384	27.7	214,504,000	30.83
1951-52	26,562,664	7,697,130	29.0	263,827,000	34.93
1953-54	26,643,871	8,411,719	32.8	207,437,000	36.55
1955-56	27,740,149	9,695,819	35.0	353,972,000	36.51
1957-58	29,722,275	10,861,689	36.5	416,491,000	38.34
1959-60	32,477,440	12,225,142	37.6	486,338,000	39.78
1961-62	34,682,340	12,222,667	38.1	576,361,000	43.59
1963-64	37,405,058	14,475,778	38.7	673,845,000	46.55
1965-66	39,154,497	15,588,567	39.7	787,358,000	50.68
1967-68	40,827,965	17,100,873	42.1	981,006,000	57.27
1969-70	41,934,376	18,200,000	43.4	$1,214,399,000	$66.73

Source: U.S. Office of Education, Department of Health, Education and Welfare, 1971.

this civil rights activity was directed at political rights, social development, economic opportunity, and education. The good thing about this struggle is that African Americans by this time received the support of the three major branches of the federal government, the executive, the legislature, and the courts. It has been seen that the southern whites were not willing to let African Americans enjoy the civil rights which the U.S. Constitution guaranteed them with passage of the Thirteenth and Fourteenth Amendments. Whites wanted blacks to remain in the same condition of servitude as they were in during slavery. But through their

own effort and against formidable odds, African Americans made remarkable progress in seeking to meet their developmental needs. Beginning in 1938 the courts became active in supporting civil rights for
African Americans. Congress took a similar position in 1957. Once this
trend was in place it would not be reversed. Therefore one can conclude
that the promotion of civil rights for African Americans beginning in
1964 was a cooperative endeavor between African Americans and the
American government. Such endeavor was bound to yield a profitable
outcome. For this reason African Americans continued to look to the
future with great expectations. They also waged relentless battles
through a nonviolent philosophy to consolidate the gains they made in
critical areas of their development. The patience and courage with which
they struggled are rarely known in the history of man's struggle for
development.

This kind of story has been told many times in history. Strong groups
of people, empires, kingdoms, and indeed individuals have found it necessary to oppress the weaker, unfortunate people. Sometimes, as we
know in some cases in Africa, the oppressed people have resorted to
violence or blood revolutions to free themselves from their oppressors.
But African Americans resorted to a different method. They loved their
country, the United States was the only land that they knew as theirs.
Efforts made by Marcus Garvey and other leaders before him to have
African Americans go back to Africa were futile because, although they
were black, they were not all Africans. They sought to improve themselves in the context of American society to which they belonged.

Maybe the Supreme Court, in its early decisions from 1857 to 1954,
was not aware that African Americans were fully determined to secure
their rights, and that they would not give up the fight for equality and
justice ever. Then Congress appeared to have misjudged the intention
and determination of African Americans to improve themselves. Over
the years they had been lynched, murdered, and subjected to all forms
of violence and inhuman treatment when they tried to assert their rights.
Still, they kept course on their journey to the promised land.

However the question remains: Is violence a means to secure the rights
of the oppressed people justified in any form? It would be irresponsible
to advocate violence as a method to achieve the ends that people are
struggling to strive toward. But it must also be readily acknowledged
that as situations are different, violence in some situations may be justified, but not in others! The American revolutionaries were justified, as
was the struggle for independence in Africa, to use violence against foreign domination.

However, violence would not be justified in the African American
struggle for justice. They were fighting against the evils of a social sys-

tem; they had no intention of driving out whites, but they felt that a system of justice had to change in order to enable them to feel more at home as citizens. Black and white had to live together. But in an African context, where the white minority deliberately denied the vast black majority of their freedom, violence may be the only means to bring about change, since nothing else would make the oppressive colonial regimes change their policy.

Finally we must attempt to answer the question: Why has it taken so long for African Americans to really feel free after the Civil War was over? It is quite obvious that both Abraham Lincoln and Andrew Johnson, who succeeded him, wanted to have effects of slavery removed as quickly as possible, so that the African Americans would enter the mainstream of American life as smoothly as possible. They had hoped that the American people would soon forget about the horrible past and look to the future as a national goal. African Americans would be a part of that future. The Fourteenth Amendment and the 1875 Civil Rights Act were designed to make African Americans equals of the whites in the eyes of the U.S. Constitution. But after Lincoln's death Johnson was in serious trouble with Congress. His impeachment was a serious setback to his Reconstruction programs. That was the beginning of the slowdown process that has lasted so long in the progress of the African Americans.

By 1954 the United States had been tired of the same old problem. Something radical had to be done: give African Americans their rights. The 1957 Civil Rights Act was a prelude to the momentous Civil Rights Act of 1964, which finally brought about real change. This was positive progress for African Americans; now they began to hope to have a future different from the past.

NOTES

1. P. Blanstein and R. Zangrando, *The Civil Rights and the American Negro* (New York: Trident Press, 1968), p. 474.

2. Ibid., p. 473.

3. Ibid., p. 475.

4. Miles Wolff, *Lunch at the Five and Ten: The Story of the Greensboro Sit-ins* (Chicago: Ivan R. Dee, 1970), p. 7.

5. Blanstein and Zangrando, *The Civil Rights and the American Negro*, p. 480.

6. Ibid., p. 484.

7. Ibid., p. 483.

8. Ibid., p. 485.

9. Ibid., p. 532.

10. Ibid., p. 559.

11. United States, *Report of the National Advisory Commission on Civil Disorders* (Washington, DC: Government Printer, 1968), p. 406.

12. Blanstein and Zangrando, *The Civil Rights and the American Negro*, p. 650.

13. J. S. Payne, *Head Start: A Tragicomedy with Epilogue* (New York: Behavioral Publications, 1975), p. 54.

14. Ibid., p. 55.

15. Ibid., p. 56.

16. U.S. *Congressional Quarterly*, Vol. 3, 1970, p. 512.

17. *New York Times*, May 11, 1975, p. 27.

7

African and African American Struggles in Comparative Perspective

We need a powerful sense of determination to banish the ugly blemish of racism scarring the image of America.

Martin Luther King, Jr., 1964

To set the mind free and to make judgment informed are as important a cause of struggle as the struggle for political and economic emancipation.

Robert Mugabe, 1983

THE MEANING OF HUMAN DEVELOPMENT

When Alfred North Whitehead discussed his ideas of the rhythmic character of educational development as a prerequisite of human development, he saw it as "involving an interweaving of cycles"[1] of events that are related to the general themes of human existence. In taking this line of thinking, Whitehead seems to suggest that one of the fundamental objectives of education is to create a social environment that would make it possible for individuals to utilize their potential to ensure their development and so enable them to play their role in shaping the character of society. Whitehead also suggests that the development of the individual will ensure his own sense of human completion. The question that one must ask is: How does education make a human being complete?

One can consider the answer in the context of the aims of an African 13-year-old girl in a remote rural school in eastern Zimbabwe in 1983.

Having observed the diligence and the unusually high level of interest and enthusiasm with which she approached her schoolwork, this author could not resist the temptation to ask her the obvious question of what she planned to do in the future when her education was completed.[2] Believing that she had a golden opportunity to tell him the true purpose of education, she responded with an assured self-confidence and a measured degree of self-pride:

You really want to know what I want to do after my education is completed? I have absolutely no doubt about that. After my primary schooling here I will go to St. Augustine's School[3] for my secondary education. Then, with a first class pass I will go to the University of Zimbabwe[4] to study to be a doctor. I will then get married and have two children, one boy and one girl. I am sure that as an African you understand that without a family a woman remains incomplete and that without children she is considered to be less than a woman. But without education her sense of self-fulfillment, or better still, her completion, is virtually impossible. I hope that there will come a time when Africans will no longer regard women from this perspective.[5]

What this girl said seems to suggest that human development, as a form of human completion, has two dimensions, the collective and the individual and that education plays a very important role in that human endeavor. This chapter will focus on both dimensions as they relate to the African and African American struggle for development.

Although the odds were heavily against this girl,[6] the level of determination was her own definition of the role of education in her own struggle for development and self-fulfillment. It is quite evident that this girl of humble origin was embracing the individual dimension of her own sense of completion. This is precisely the dimension that, for example, Linda Brown's parents took into consideration when they brought suit against the Board of Education in Topeka, Kansas. But when the U.S. Supreme Court ruled in that case on May 17, 1954, it went beyond the individual dimension to embrace the collective dimension, saying that education was perhaps the most important function of state and local governments. Compulsory school attendance laws and the great expenditures for education both demonstrated a recognition of the importance of education to democratic society. It was required in the performance of most basic public responsibilities. It was the very foundation of good citizenship. It was the principal instrument in awakening children to cultural values, in preparing them for later professional training, and in helping them to adjust normally to their rapidly changing environment.[7]

In a similar fashion, when Rosa Parks refused to give up her seat to a white man on the transit bus in Montgomery, Alabama, in December 1955, she thought she was merely asserting her individual right as she said, "Over the years, I had my own problems with the bus drivers. Some did tell me not to ride their buses if I thought that I was too important to go to the back door to get on. One had evicted me from the bus in 1943."[8] But the result of her action led to a spontaneously collective response that involved an interweaving cycle of events between defining a set of objectives and designing a strategy to fulfill them. This action of a simple woman mobilized African Americans to launch a campaign that led to the civil rights movement, which in turn changed the course of events and history in the United States.

Indeed, the history of human struggle for development is closely related to the history of educational endeavor. It is a history of the search for the means to improve their conditions of life. It is a history for the struggle for self-actualization and to eliminate the conditions that oppress them. Because modern man has recognized that military might alone does not ensure his security, he has espoused a new theory that the ballot is mightier than the bullet. But man has also recognized that to fulfill the purpose of the ballot requires collective action, and that collective action requires dialogue, and dialogue requires skills. These skills come from education. In terms of the collective action, two of the outcomes which education makes possible are the ability to engage in a critical analysis of the issues facing society and to use the individual's intellect as an instrument of solving social problems. The first entails the collective dimension and the second involves the individual dimension.[9]

For society to respect conditions that would enable individuals to fulfill their tasks in the pursuit of their objectives and at the same time meet the needs of society is to recognize the importance of both the collective dimension and the individual dimension. This means that in order to meet these conditions the concept of equality of educational opportunity must be based on the recognition of the importance of the individual and must become a prerequisite of solving human problems. Without an education to sharpen this consciousness to enable individuals to acquire the skills they need to help find solutions to problems of society, society itself remains underdeveloped.[10]

Society must place emphasis on education for individuals because it enables them to play important roles in a collective endeavor to stop society from degenerating. It also helps individuals in formulating a definition of objectives consistent with their understanding of what they need to do to ensure society's development.[11] One must take the reality of these conditions into account in discussing the main purpose of education as a principal instrument of searching for human development.

This chapter examines the interrelatedness of the two dimensions of human development as they pertained to the struggle for development by Africans under colonial conditions and African Americans during the civil rights movement—both of which must be studied to understand the implications of the collective and individual dimensions. This enables one to understand the nature of the environment in which they histori-cally attempted to secure education and the reasons for their endeavor. Although that endeavor is of an individual nature, its effects are felt more profoundly on society as a whole. This means that individuals must remain conscious of the relationship that exists between the indi-vidual dimension and the collective dimension.

In 1900 Booker T. Washington recognized this reality as he argued that the Negro must become aware of the important role he must play in society after he had received education. In characteristic fashion, Wash-ington added,

One of the main problems as regards the education of the Negro is how to have him use it to the best advantage after he has secured it. In his present condition it is important, in seeking after the ideal that the Negro should not neglect to prepare himself to take advantage of the opportunities that are right about his door. Ignorance still prevailing among the Negroes, especially in the South, is very large and serious. But I repeat, we must go farther if we would secure the best results and most gratifying returns in public good.[12]

There is no doubt that Washington understood the importance of edu-cation to the development of the Negroes, both individually and as a group.

THEORETICAL CONSIDERATIONS

Throughout human history the quest for education has always been regarded as a means of bringing about improvement in human condi-tions to make development possible. Human completion occurs when one is satisfied with that improvement. Therefore, what identifies as in-terweaving cycles of the educational process may be regarded as the essential collective and individual dimensions, which constitute an im-perative condition that influences educational endeavor as a prerequisite of development.

Paulo Freire[13] of Brazil and Albert Memmi[14] of Tunisia have developed frameworks of theoretical considerations that have applicability to the African and African American struggles for development relative to both individual and collective dimensions. Both authors discuss the elements of their respective theories that address the effect of the denial of equal educational opportunity as a condition for their development. In this denial both Africans and African Americans were effectively denied an opportunity to define and seek their own sense of development and self-fulfillment.

When Freire concludes that all human beings, no matter how oppressed, and presumed ignorant, are capable of engaging in constructive interaction with other people to make their development possible, he suggests that without education defined in accordance with their desire to improve their conditions of life, they remain incomplete, both as individuals and as a group. But in the process of becoming conscious of themselves, the oppressed embrace the principles of self-liberation embedded in both the collective and individual dimensions.[15] Understanding the elements of this liberation constitutes the elements of development. What Freire seems to suggest is that while this struggle for self-liberation must, of necessity, entail the search for human development, its outcome is a product of both the collective and individual endeavor.

Freire goes on to add that the collective endeavor has meaning only if the individual endeavor is related to it. What one sees as the essential character of Freire's theory as it relates to the educational endeavor of people in the Third World, including Africa, is that there comes a time when their limited educational opportunity makes it possible to reject the notion that they "are inhibited from waging a struggle for freedom."[16] This leads to the conclusion that once the oppressed—indeed, oppressed by various conditions of human existence—become conscious of the importance of education to their own liberation, they will never cease to struggle to secure more of it in order to realize their own definition of their development.

One must understand that in terms of Freire's theory, the oppressor mistakes oppression for the oppressed's inherent lack of intellectual potential. By seeking an education intended to serve their developmental needs, they not only dispel that erroneous impression, but they also find new strength to attain their defined objectives. In this manner Freire's concept of dialogical encounter implies much more than the search for education "viable only as the oppressor-oppressed contradiction is superseded by the humanization of all men,"[17] it also implies the need to design strategies to ensure the development of the oppressed. Indeed, dialogical encounter suggests a mutual collective interaction based on common objectives.

But Freire concludes that because the oppressed are denied an opportunity for education designed to meet their developmental needs, they are unable to engage in critical thinking. This leads the oppressor to the erroneous conclusion that they are ignorant. In that context the oppressor never stops to consider the fact that his conclusion is a result of oppression as an outcome of his denial of equal educational opportunity to the oppressed. Once the oppressed are aware of the strategy of the oppressor, they will design their own strategy to counteract it.

One also sees that when Freire suggests that if education does not make this humanization a reality, or when it fails to occur within the framework of the search for self-liberation, then social conflict of major proportions becomes inevitable, not because the oppressed want to initiate radical social change, but because the oppressor wishes to foil their efforts to gain meaningful education to ensure their development. Further, when Freire argues, "To surmount the situation of oppression, the oppressed must first critically recognize its causes so that through a transforming action they create a new situation, one which makes possible the pursuit of fuller humanity";[18] he recognizes the importance of the relationship that must exist between the two dimensions to make possible the development of the oppressed.

The obvious conclusion one reaches is that this situation constitutes a combination of the two dimensions as a manifestation of the critical duality of human existence that the oppressor forces the oppressed to adopt. Without the one dimension the other cannot be effective as an instrument of promoting the development of the oppressed. The denial of equal educational opportunity to both Africans under colonial control and African Americans before and during the civil rights movement made the task of integrating the two dimensions a very difficult one. But it was an endeavor that both groups concluded in 1955 must continue.

Indeed, Freire is not the only thinker from the Third World to develop a theory about the importance of education as an essential condition of human development. Albert Memmi concludes in his theory of the relationship between the colonizer and the colonized that the interaction between people of different cultural backgrounds and socioeconomic status is heavily influenced by the notion among people of the privileged class that they are superior to those of the other.[19] Memmi's conclusion that the people presumed to be inferior become the colonized and those presuming to be superior become the colonizer suggests the creation of an environment in which race, affluence, and culture heavily influenced the nature of relationships between the white establishment and the African Americans and between the colonial establishment and the Africans during the colonial period.

Applying this theoretical tenet to colonial Africa, one sees that the colonial establishment defined education for Africans to enable them to function in ways that were intended to make their labor cheap in order to provide the comfort that whites sought in accordance with the objectives they defined during the industrial revolution. In the United States the white establishment defined the purpose of education for African Americans to have them remain in their proper place. But the Africans defined it in order to meet their developmental needs, and African Americans defined it in order to ensure their civil rights. In a real sense both Africans and African Americans were colonized and oppressed because slavery in the United States and colonization in Africa had the same effect: control of the thinking process.

Memmi's conclusion is that the essential element in the pattern of behavior of the colonizers is their desire to design and implement an education for the colonized as an instrument of preserving their own position of privilege.[20] Therefore, because colonizers have political power that the colonized do not have, they exploit their education to make themselves the principal beneficiaries of their struggle and to attune them to their own lifestyle. Essentially this is why segregation in education was hard to fight in both the United States and Africa.

From Freire's and Memmi's conclusions, the principle of equality in both the educational process and society, as perceived by the oppressor and colonizer, is rendered meaningless under the condition of their desire to perpetuate the myth of their superiority.[21] This situation suggests serious implications for the educational development of both Africans under colonial conditions and African Americans before the civil rights movement. Memmi suggests that instead of accepting the myth of their inferiority, the colonized will arouse a collective consciousness that influences the emergence of their uncompromising demand for equality of both educational opportunity and rights in general. He argues that meaningful education is a measure of their collective search for their own definition of their struggle for development.

In adopting this strategy the colonized unconditionally reject the colonizer's Machiavellian definition of their educational pursuit.[22] This leads to the conclusion that the act of rejecting a form of education imposed by the oppressor or colonizer constitutes an act of seeking a fuller meaning of human development. The collective dimension of this endeavor is illustrated by the civil rights movement in the United States beginning with the Rosa Parks incident in 1955, and in Africa by the rise of the African nationalist movements in the same year.

THE COLLECTIVE DIMENSION

The theories espoused by Whitehead, Freire, and Memmi offer a viable perspective from which to discuss the objectives that influenced the struggle of Africans and African Americans for development during the colonial and civil rights periods. The political activities that precipitated an unprecedented rise of the civil rights movement in the United States and those that gave rise to African nationalism came as a result of the rise of a new level of consciousness and the desire for collective action as a more potent force to deal with problems of their development, which both groups were denied in the past.

As both groups became aware of their colonial and oppressed conditions, they each rejected the myths of their presumed social inferiority, and, indeed, the Machiavellian definition of their place in society. What they wanted instead was nothing less than equality of educational opportunity to realize their social, political, and economic opportunities as a manifestation of a better life to which they felt entitled. In doing so they embraced Thomas Jefferson's idea that all men were created equal. The question is: How could this be achieved, as individuals or as a group?

Memmi seems to take the view that at the initial stage of their struggle, the colonized must take the route of collective action to realize their goals. He suggests that this level of consciousness is "an actuality of history,"[23] and goes on to conclude that one must accept the argument that the road to political independence in Africa and the attainment of limited civil rights in the United States were both products of events that began to unfold in the 19th century. A case in point: helping to stage a boycott of the school system in Rochester, New York, in 1850 because African Americans were receiving an inferior education, Frederick Douglass argued, "The Negroes are chained together. We are one people with one common degradation. As one rises, all must rise, and as one falls, all will fall. There is no time too precious, no calling too holy, no place too sacred to sacrifice our cause."[24]

It is quite evident that Douglass was in effect rejecting the myth of the inferiority of African Americans and he was reasserting the importance of the collective dimension of their struggle to secure more meaningful education than was given them as a means of their collective development so that the individual dimension could begin to take shape. In short Douglass seems to suggest that before individuals could seek their own definitions of their development, the collective definition must first come into being and that the educational process must help it come about.

While one can conclude that Douglass had a good reason to state this priority, one can also see that it is an irony of historical actuality that the U.S. Supreme Court, ruling in the *Plessy* case of 1896, 16 years after Douglass's plea, elected to follow the collective route to limit the African American search for a definition of development during the next 50 years. When the same Supreme Court used the *Brown* case in 1954 to reverse the *Plessy* decision, it also elected to use the collective dimension to seek a resolution to a problem facing the individual. Neither Homer Plessy nor Linda Brown considered the possibility of a collective action; they merely thought that they were seeking solutions to the problems that they faced as individuals.

The actuality of historical precedence that Douglass addressed is evident in the work that other African American leaders did. Marcus Garvey, Booker T. Washington, and W.E.B. Du Bois are only a few examples that show what African American leaders tried to accomplish to give the collective dimension a new meaning and at the same time attempted to reshape the formation of the individual dimension.

The importance of the interweaving nature of these two dimensions seems to be what Martin Luther King, Jr. fully recognized as the impact of this historical actuality when he argued in 1964 that the denial of equality of educational opportunity to African Americans had created a social environment that had to be reconstructed if they ever hoped to realize their goals as a people. King went on to add, "When the locomotive of history roared through the 19th century and the first half of the 20th century, it left the nation's black masses standing at the dismal terminals. They were unschooled and untrained. We need a powerful sense of determination to banish the ugly blemish of racism scarring the image of America."[25]

King was really suggesting that the United States up to 1964 had actually left African Americans collectively sitting in the shadow of the political, socioeconomic, and educational twilight zone that had engulfed their existence since the days of slavery. He was also suggesting that it was now time to make a new collective effort, as conditions of the time demanded, to give the collective dimension a new purpose. In essence, this was King's call for education to help African Americans realize their quest for development.

King's enthusiasm for African Americans to embrace the collective dimension of their struggle for development was shared by his own father, who was equally clear about the importance of education in that endeavor. This author will never forget what Martin Luther King, Sr. told him in Atlanta in May 1962 when he was a sophomore in college:

The civil rights movement is a call for human actualization, a completion of all men, not just the black people. It is also a movement to free the white people. The freedom of Negroes is the freedom of America itself. The freedom of black Americans is interwoven with that of white Americans. It is a call for freedom to join hands in a collective effort in creating a social environment that enables each one of us to pursue our individual goals.[26]

What deeply touched this author about this great man is the absence of anger or rancor often characteristic of oppressed people. King Sr. was so humble, so dignified, and deeply proud in every aspect of being human. Those who came to know Martin Luther King, Jr. as the disciple of nonviolence must remember the enormous influence that his father had on the development of this philosophy. Both Kings saw all human beings, even those who oppressed them and their people, as precious products of creation, all capable of making a valuable contribution to human happiness based upon mutual respect. This leads to the conclusion that Freire reaches in his theory: in the process of seeking their own freedom and, thus, their completion, the oppressed also collectively seek to liberate their oppressor.[27] King symbolized the nobility of this line of thinking.

The conclusion this action suggests is that the development of society itself is exactly why in 1982 George Wallace, for example, regretted his infamous statement of January 14, 1963, in which he said during his inauguration as governor of Alabama, "I draw the line in the dust and toss the gauntlet before the feet of tyranny, and I say segregation now, segregation tomorrow, and segregation forever,"[28] and began to seek the votes of the black citizens of Alabama, a group of people he once vowed to deny an equal opportunity for education as a means of defining the extent of their self-fulfillment and development. Wallace did not consider the fact that by denying African Americans an opportunity for development he was in effect trying to perpetuate the tyranny that he argued was coming from the federal government in its insistence that they be given equal opportunity for development.

Wallace's line of thinking and behavior are also exactly why Ian Smith, the last prime minister of colonial Zimbabwe, admitted to this author during an interview in 1983 saying, "It was hard for us to believe that the advent of a black government would mean, in effect, freedom of the white man, freedom from fear of reprisals. It is evident that it was not possible to deny the black people an opportunity for self-fulfillment by denying them an opportunity for education."[29] Indeed, Smith faced exactly the same situation with the British government as Wallace did with the federal government.

Since 1957, when it granted independence to Ghana, Britain demanded that the colonial governments in Africa respect its policy of extending equality of opportunity to Africans to ensure their development. This was the policy that Smith repeatedly rejected, forcing Britain to impose economic sanctions and the Africans to take up arms to fight for that opportunity. It was only after the war had ended in December 1979 that Smith, like Wallace, finally came to accept the inevitability of the advent of the African government.

The reality of African struggle for development left him with no alternative course of action but to give way. In 1994, as South Africa was preparing to hold elections in which Africans would participate for the first time, Eugene Terreblanche, an Afrikaner of extreme political views, especially his belief in the political and intellectual inferiority of the Africans, particularly that of Nelson Mandela, adopted the attitude that Wallace adopted in 1963 and Ian Smith in 1964 by threatening violence if whites were not given their own state.[30] Apparently Terreblanche had not learned from the reality of Wallace's and Smith's experiences.

There is no doubt that by 1960 the quest for education by Africans and African Americans to realize their own definition of development was having a profound impact on the dynamics of human relationships in both the United States and Africa. On the African side of the Atlantic, Africans were aggressively seeking an education that they knew would help them in their quest for development as their own way of preparing themselves for the future. In rejecting the ambiguity, or what W.E.B. Du Bois called the twoness of black existence and demanding the right "to attain self-consciousness, to emerge from this twoness, a double self, into a better and truer self,"[31] the Africans saw the ambiguity of their life under colonial conditions from the perspective of its harmful effects, not its claimed benefits.

The historical actuality that Memmi says is essential for the colonized to recognize in order to acquire an education that would help them reshape their life into a more meaningful future is evident in the efforts that leaders like Kwame Nkrumah of Ghana, Jomo Kenyatta of Kenya, Albert Luthuli of South Africa, and Julius Nyerere of Tanzania have all made to help their people erase the ambiguity that imposed serious limitations on both their life and their collective quest for development.[32] Their sense of future was very different from what the past had meant to their endeavor. Their ability to perceive what was real in terms of what was possible became a new motivating factor that enabled them to raise themselves to a level that the colonial governments could not understand. Their claim to know the ultimate in human endeavor combined with their obsession of the inferiority of Africans to the extent that Africans, victims of the colonial myth, seized the opportunity to envisage themselves.

From what has been discussed so far, one must raise two questions: How does the concept of human development affect both society and the individual? Does the collective dimension relate to the individual dimension? One can find answers to these questions from what Africans and African Americans themselves attempted to accomplish in a manner that demonstrated the applicability of the theoretical considerations that Whitehead, Freire, and Memmi espoused.

In 1981, asked to define the objectives of his administration and how he planned to initiate the trust for national development, Robert Mugabe, the new president of Zimbabwe, responded, "We are evolving a system in which the collective dimension will become the major focus of our efforts. In doing so we will leave room for individuality. In seeking a functional balance between these two dimensions we must bring in the love for each other as a component of national life."[33] There is no doubt that Mugabe fully understood how these two dimensions were expected to function in a free nation to ensure national development.

The conceptual perspective of the arguments advanced by Africans and African Americans immediately becomes clear in several examples. In 1962, when the Zimbabwe African Peoples Union (ZAPU) issued a statement of its principles and goals, it left no room for doubt as to how the Africans wished to utilize education to achieve the objectives of a collective dimension, saying

We are concerned only with our determination to end the socioeconomic, political and educational exploitation to which the colonial forces have subjected us. Our self-fulfillment and freedom are the ultimate manifestation of the liberation of our society. The individual Africans cannot be free until we as a people are free. Therefore, we seek a total transformation of Zimbabwe from the colonial status to independence under an African government.[34]

The essence of this statement is also the same line of thinking that King used to speak on behalf of African Americans in 1964 when he concluded that their educational endeavors implied political implications as a manifestation of their struggle for selfhood. Recognizing the impact of the lack of educational opportunity for African Americans, King concluded, "The average Negro is born into want and deprivation. He struggles to escape his circumstances and is hindered by a lack of education and the absence of social and economic opportunity. The shadow of political and intellectual bondage is hidden in subtle disguise."[35]

It is evident that the historical actuality of the importance of the political dimension of education as an instrument giving effect to the collective dimension, to which King referred, had its precedence in the recognition made by President Franklin Roosevelt and Prime Minister Winston Churchill on August 11, 1941, in the Atlantic Charter: "We respect the right of all people to choose the form of government under which they will live."[36] It is logical to conclude that the two leaders had seen that the denial of equal educational opportunity to the Africans in British colonial Africa and to African Americans translated into the denial of political and socioeconomic participation in their respective societies.

There is yet another example of conceptual framework of the applicability of the educational process to the collective dimension of human development relative to Africans and African Americans. On assuming office on January 20, 1961, President John Kennedy appears to have extended Memmi's concept of historical actuality much further when he recognized the need to balance his call for the exploration of space, a new frontier, with his call for equal educational opportunity as manifestation of the freedom of all people.

In stating, "Our basic goal remains the same, a peaceful world community of free and independent states, free to choose their own future,"[37] Kennedy was acknowledging the message contained in the Atlantic Charter and the importance of accepting the call from African Americans for better educational opportunity to enable them to realize their search for their own development. Recognizing that this was essential to the development of society, Kennedy felt it was necessary to adjust the exploration of space to the exploration of the means to sustain the fundamental principles of African American yearning for education to realize their goals.

These developments were why Kennedy fervently responded to the call for the enactment of the most comprehensive civil rights law, which he envisaged as a viable form of the collective dimension of the development of African Americans. The Civil Rights Act of 1964 went further than any other federal legislation since the ratification of the Fourteenth Amendment to the U.S. Constitution in July 1868 in trying to extend equality of opportunity to African-Americans. It was a gallant effort to envisage the emergence of a viable form of collective dimension of the development of African Americans.

This is also why Kennedy's administration confronted Governors Ross Barnett of Mississippi and George C. Wallace of Alabama over the admission of African American students at their institutions of higher learning. Lyndon B. Johnson, Kennedy's successor, carried on the campaign initiated by his predecessor in an effort to create what he called the Great Society based upon the collective dimension of the development of all people. In colonial Africa this kind of national program was totally unheard of, giving Africans a sense of Freire's conclusion that the task of liberation rests squarely on the shoulders of the oppressed.

Two things are clearly distinguishable from Kennedy's role in an effort to provide equal educational opportunity to African Americans. The first is that he had become part of the collective dimension as a more powerful means of realizing the individual dimension in promoting the collective dimension. The second is that once Kennedy saw the importance of the collective process to achieve the individual dimension, he did everything possible to make sure that both dimensions were successful. In this manner the two dimensions developed a reciprocal relationship that meant that the success of the one depended upon the success of the other.

This reality is now being brought to the test in painful ways in the lives of African Americans. The increasing murder rate of African Americans by other African Americans must raise serious questions as to the meaning of this relationship between the two dimensions. The tragedy of governments in Africa where dictatorships, military coups and countercoups, corruption by government officials, poverty of the masses, and exploitation by new elite groups have been the order of things, must raise equally troubling questions about that relationship. Where do Africans and African Americans go from here?

THE INDIVIDUAL DIMENSION

The discussion of the applicability of Memmi's theory of self-actualization and Freire's concept of self-consciousness through education would be incomplete if one failed to recognize an important aspect of the educational process as it is related to the quest for human development evident in the search for education by the individual to ensure his development. One can see that while political freedom is an essential manifestation of collective development, it is the educational development of the individual that evinces the ultimate development of society itself. Some African leaders have recognized this truth in their struggle to ensure the development of their people as a condition of national development.

In 1983 Rev. Ndabaningi Sithole, a founding member of African nationalism in Zimbabwe, told the author during an interview:

Education provides an individual a means of articulating and expressing ideas consistent with his own sense of development. It gives a wider scope, a depth to one's thinking, a comprehensive grasp of who one really is in relation to one's own needs and to society itself. It makes an individual a complete human being. Without education a complete human being is not possible. Without a complete human being society remains undeveloped. Therefore education meets the needs of society only if its meets the needs of the individual.[38]

The essential nature of the relationship that Sithole sees between the collective dimension and the individual dimension is that it helps to explain the clarity of Whitehead's concept of the interweaving character of the struggle for development through education. Indeed, following the revolution of 1917 the former Soviet Union based its developmental programs on the collective dimension, espousing the philosophy that when society was secure, it would then be in position to assist the development of the individual.

This, then, was a fundamental tenet of socialism. It operated under this philosophy until Mikhail Gorbachev came to the scene in 1984. But because Gorbachev was unable to reconcile the two dimensions, his reform movement failed, causing the demise of his nation in 1992, giving the United States reason to reinforce its own belief that the best interests of society are served by the development of the individual. But its application of this ideology to the development of African Americans has yielded marginal results. Many countries of the world have yet to define their approach to this critical aspect of their development.

One sees that education designed to ensure human development in terms of the collective dimension enables individuals to engage in equally important dimensions of their own development as a manifestation society's development. Both Freire and Memmi unhesitatingly conclude that when individuals are oppressed or colonized, society itself pays the price. Therefore, the freedom of individuals, evident in their educational attainment and ability to think critically, builds the foundation on which society must be structured. Both authors argue that mental and intellectual freedom as a product of the educational process cannot occur under oppressed or colonized conditions.

It is equally true that while collective action only comes from individual ability to think creatively, it is the individual action that makes the collective action possible. Therefore, the education of the individual is essential to the development of society itself. The importance of this relationship was recognized by Robert Mugabe, the president of Zimbabwe since 1980. In 1983 Mugabe observed, "To set the mind free and to make imagination creative, to make judgment informed, objective and fair, are as important a cause of struggle as the struggle for political and economic emancipation and cannot be taken for granted."[39] This is the nature of the relationship that education seeks to promote between the two dimensions of the search for human development relative to the African and African American struggles for development. It is not possible to separate these relationships and still have education serve its real intended purpose.

In their struggle for development today, both Africans and African Americans must take new realities of that relationship into consideration. For Africans the scourge of poverty and deprivation has recently combined with the absence of political participation to reduce the masses to new levels of oppression—political, educational, and economic. For African Americans the scourge of violence perpetrated by African Americans themselves robs a people in a way that so disturbed President Bill Clinton to remind them that Martin Luther King, Jr. did not die to have African Americans kill each other.[40] Only by understanding the relationship that must exist between the individual dimension and the collective dimension will both groups have a proper perspective of their struggle for development.

The struggle of African Americans for development must also be seen in the context of events of the past that seem to strengthen negative attitudes toward better race relationships. In 1968 the *Report of the National Advisory Commission on Civil Disorders*, otherwise known as Otto Kerner Commission, seems to indict white America for its role in promoting racial discrimination and segregation when it said, "What white America has never fully understood, but what the Negro can never forget, is white society is deeply implicated in the ghetto. White institutions created it, white institutions maintain it, and white society maintains it."[41] Addressing the nation on July 27, 1967, when he first named the Commission, President Johnson said, "The only genuine, long-range solution to racial disorders lies in an attack mounted at every level upon the conditions that breed despair and violence."[42] This is the reality that both Africans and African Americans had to take in account in launching a crusade for fundamental social change in their respective systems. Part of their challenge was to convince whites to recognize what they were

doing to maintain the social status quo. This was not an easy task. For-
tunately, from the time of John Brown in 1858 in the United States to
that of Garfield Todd in Africa in the 1950s, there were whites who saw
the need to adopt a positive attitude toward African Americans and Africans for the good of race relations. In Africa this meant the end of
colonial governments, and in the United States it meant extending equal
rights to all people.

SUMMARY AND CONCLUSIONS

The discussion in this chapter has focused on the applicability of
Memmi's, Freire's, and Whitehead's theoretical considerations relative to
the struggle for development of Africans during the colonial period and
of African Americans during the civil rights movement. In doing so it
has addressed the importance of the relationships that must exist between the individual dimension and the collective dimension and how
the quest for education strengthens those relationships. From this discussion one reaches four basic conclusions. The first is that education is
essential to both the collective dimension and the individual dimension.
In assessing the efforts that both Africans and African Americans made
to secure education to achieve these two dimensions, it seems that their
ability to adjust and retain the essential elements of their respective iden-
tities is what has positively influenced their development.

While the struggle for their development has by no means been fully
accomplished, Africans and African Americans fully understood what
they would wish to accomplish. As both groups are now struggling
against new formidable problems, one would hope that in time they will
once more see the need to restructure their strategy in order to meet the
objectives they formulate to attain their genuine freedom from violence,
poverty, and political and socioeconomic exploitation by the powerful.
The interweaving cycles of their struggle for education help broaden
their horizon to assist them in setting new goals on both the collective
and individual dimensions. Although both groups came to recognize
that the process of development cannot be reversed, they must now accept new challenges that threaten their very existence.

The second conclusion is that there is a disturbing reality facing both
Africans and African-Americans in their struggle for development. Opposition to such programs as affirmative action in the United States and
positive discrimination in some countries of Africa appears to have had
a negative effect on the development of those who need these programs.
Sadly, opposition has come from among Africans and African Americans
themselves. If this continues, old habits will resurface to reverse the
progress that has been made on this front. Adam Curle takes this line
of thinking when he argues, "Education for liberation is that which at-

tempts to liberate us from the habits of thought, action or feeling which make us less than human."[43] In essence Curle is warning against stereotypes, a definite form of myth that both Freire and Memmi say should be eliminated if meaningful human interaction must take place for the benefit of all as an outcome of the quest for education to make development possible.

The third conclusion is that there seems to be an interesting phenomenon relative to the rise of a new level of self-consciousness among Africans and African-Americans relative to Freire's and Memmi's theories. Once the Africans understood the importance of the collective dimension of their struggle for political independence, they entered a more challenging phase: the search for individual dimension. Robert Mugabe recognized this reality in asking his fellow countrypeople to come forward and unite to meet this new challenge. Although it has remained elusive, it is a challenge that has to be met to give a meaning to collective struggle. Once African Americans reached a stage where they thought the United States had restored to them the rights intended in the Civil Rights Act of 1964, they, redirected their efforts toward the quest for individual development. This, too, has remained elusive.

The problems making it hard for both groups to realize their individual dimension illustrates how education is important in the struggle for their development. The reality of this situation is that both the collective dimension and the individual dimension have not been fully redefined in the context of the forces that oppose their development. The reality of the interweaving cycles of the educational process crucial to its success has not yet been understood by those in positions of power. This understanding is necessary in order to strike a working balance between the two dimensions. What one sees is that regardless of the efforts that are being made to improve the situation, the education of both Africans and African Americans may continue to deteriorate in the future unless something drastic is done to reverse the trend.[44]

The fourth conclusion is that in both the United States and Africa the years 1957 to 1964 seem to give Memmi's concept of historical actuality a new definition, an uncertain future. The collective action that yielded tangible results since 1964 appears to fade away in the face of uncertain hope for individual development. Unless education is designed to meet this fundamental objective, the quest for both dimensions will remain elusive. It is essential that both Africans and African Americans must now view their development from a perspective of new realism that demands the spirit of cooperation that witnessed the birth of Pan-African movement that followed the end of the First World War. It is a strategy that they can utilize with a greater degree of success than in the past, because both groups are much more informed about the common problems that they face. In Africa neocolonialism, aided by severe economic and political problems, is preying upon the life of the people with a vengeance. In the United States economic deprivation of African Americans has equally taken a heavy toll.

The ability of both groups to use the educational process to bring this reality into focus would help accelerate their quest for development. They must realize that the most potent forms of colonization and oppression exist in the continual denial of equal opportunity, both in education and society. While the institutions that control their lives have viewed them as groups, they themselves must now attempt to influence the emergence of a working balance between the collective action and the individual action so that their efforts would yield a broad leverage they need to assist them attain their objectives.

The following are among the problems that both Africans and African Americans face: a lack of meaningful opportunity for employment, a shortage of housing, the breakdown of the family, the increase in the phenomenon of the single family, and an increase in poverty. All these translate into new powerful forms of oppression and colonization, even stronger than the colonial forces in Africa and segregation prior to the civil rights movement in the United States. While the results of this situation have been more evident in the lives of African Americans, Africans have suffered equally severely in various ways, such as extended periods of drought, political and social disintegration, and economic hardships.

There are serious implications to these developments. All these forces have preyed upon people's lives with a forceful brutality. In both Africa and the United States the erosion of self-confidence in the future has combined with the failure of national leaders to inspire their people with confidence for the future. In this setting the spirit of survival has been broken and many Africans and African Americans have given up the struggle because they feel inadequate to fight for their survival. Many have found solace in crime in which to express frustration. For them the future has become an abyss of despair, not a season of hope. If this course continues, it is a matter of time before both the United States and Africa pay the ultimate price: national stagnation and underdevelopment.

The threat to the progress that African Americans have made now comes partly from the negative attitude of many African Americans themselves, as well as of those who oppose the concept of equality in society. In 1982 the Reagan administration appeared to be less sympathetic toward the problems that African Americans were facing. The resurgence of racism, as shown during that time in New York and Georgia (where whites tried to stop African Americans from using public facilities), created a climate of a new form of national conflict that did not contribute to the national efforts to confront problems on a collective basis.

The action taken by the Reagan administration in questioning the effect of affirmative action programs did not help matters. This is how white America may once more strengthen the stereotypes that handicapped African Americans prior to the civil rights movement. To end affirmative action programs is to effectively end the means that African Americans have been using to ensure their development. Since its inception, affirmative action has been the major means of creating viable conditions for African Americans to define the objectives of their development. The threat to the limited progress that has been made through collective action in some countries of Africa, such as Zimbabwe, have yielded limited results due to failure to define a national agenda that would commend the enthusiasm of the people.

The threat to affirmative action in the United States and positive discrimination in Africa appear to constitute what national leaders such as Jimmy Carter and Julius Nyerere defined as bringing into play the elements that have retarded the efforts of the underdeveloped people, who have come to depend upon the viability of the educational process to initiate reform and provide an environment for national development.[45] Indeed, Carter and Nyerere would add that without education to give individuals the skills they need to sustain their own freedom and self-actualization, there would be no freedom for society itself.

During his administration from 1953 to 1960, President Dwight D. Eisenhower fully recognized the need to balance these two dimensions in an effort to promote the development of the nation. The conflict that broke out between him and Governor Orval Faubus in 1957 in Little Rock, Arkansas, shows his determination to extend equal educational opportunity to African Americans. This is why he urged his fellow Americans to accept his argument: "We must be willing, as individuals and as a nation, to pay the sacrifice expected of us."[46] This is the reality of the dimension of human development that Africans and African Americans must take collectively into consideration in designing new strategies of dealing with the problems that they face in today's world. These strategies must embrace both the collective dimension and the individual dimension in order to have interweaving cycles of the educational process that would yield the desired results.

NOTES

1. Alfred North Whitehead, *The Aims of Education* (New York: The New American Library, 1929), p. 373.

2. Many people in far less compelling circumstances ask such questions to children. This author thinks that no child should be subjected to this kind of question because even students in high school are not often able to provided a clear answer. But one would have to put oneself in the position in which the

author found himself to ask the question. As the reader can see from the answer the girl gave, the compelling circumstances of the question yielded tangible results. Even the classroom teacher was quite impressed with her answer as she said to the author later, "That girl is one of the brightest students I have ever had. Students like her are the future of this country."

3. Founded by the Anglican Church in 1898 near Penhalonga, St. Augustine's School is a leading secondary school for Africans in Zimbabwe. Secondary education there began in 1939, the first in Zimbabwe.

4. Founded in 1956 by the British Charter, the University of Zimbabwe was then known as the University College of Rhodesia and Nyasaland. In 1957 the college enrolled 8 African students, including 1 woman, and 60 white students, including 27 women.

5. A 13-year-old girl during a conversation with the author in a rural school in eastern Zimbabwe, July 15, 1983.

6. The girl was sixth in a family of nine children and the two older children were already out of school due to economic difficulties the family was encountering. Her parents were simple peasant farmers. This is a typical situation that one sees at most rural schools in Africa.

7. *Brown vs. Board of Education of Topeka*, 347 U.S 483, 1954.

8. Henry Hampton and Steve Fayer, *Voice of Freedom: An Oral History of the Civil Rights Movement from the 1950s Through the 1980s* (New York: Bantam Books, 1991), p. 17.

9. Assen Balacki, "Conflict and Society," in Thomas Weaver (ed.), *To See Ourselves* (Glenview, IL: Scott, Foresman and Company, 1973), p. 370.

10. Ibid., p. 371.

11. Canaan Banana, *Theology of Promise: The Dynamics of Self-Reliance* (Harare, Zimbabwe: The College Press, 1982), p. 19.

12. Booker T. Washington, *The Future of the American Negro* (Boston: Small, Maynard, and Company, 1900), p. 78.

13. Paulo Freire, *Pedagogy of the Oppressed* (Trans. by M. B. Ramos) (New York: Continuum, 1983).

14. Albert Memmi, *The Colonizer and the Colonized* (Boston: Beacon Press, 1965).

15. Freire, *Pedagogy of the Oppressed*, p. 39.

16. Ibid., p. 32.

17. Ibid., p. 33.

18. Ibid., p. 34.

19. Memmin, *The Colonizer and the Colonized*, p. 9.

20. Ibid., p. 13.

21. Ibid., p. 16.

22. Ibid., p. 42.

23. Ibid., p. 7.

24. Bennet, Jr., *Pioneers and Protests* (Chicago: Johnson Publishing Company, 1968), p. 203.

25. Martin Luther King, Jr., *Why We Can't Wait* (New York: The New American Library, 1964), p. 129.

26. Martin Luther King, Sr., during a conversation with the author at Ebenezer Baptist Church in Atlanta, May 17, 1962. Two weeks before the author made the trip to the South, he bought a sophisticated Japanese camera known as a Tower

with a timer, and which had just come on the market in the United States. For nearly 20 years the author used this camera to take some of his best photographs, including several of Dr. King, Sr. Two of these photographs are included in the photo essay in this book. The author now considers it a high privilege to have taken several photographs of King, Sr., and of John Lewis.

27. Freire, *Pedagogy of the Oppressed*, p. 39.

28. Hampton and Fayer, *Voices of Freedom*, p. 123.

29. Ian Smith, during an interview with the author in Harare, Zimbabwe, July 20, 1983.

30. Bruce, "Spoiling for a Victory," in *Time*, February 21, 1994, p. 35.

31. Eleven Rich, *Africa: Traditional and Modern* (New York: New House, 1972), p. 457.

32. William Smith, *Nierere of Tanzania* (Harare: Zimbabwe Publishing House, 1981), p. 53.

33. Robert Mugabe in "Not in a Thousand Years: From Rhodesia to Zimbabwe," a documentary film, PBS, 1981.

34. Zimbabwe African Peoples Union, Statement of Principles and Objectives, December 19, 1962, Zimbabwe National Archives.

35. King, *Why We Can't Wait*, p. 23.

36. Franklin D. Roosevelt and Winston Churchill, "The Atlantic Charter," in *Public Papers and Addresses of Franklin D. Roosevelt*, Vol. 10 (Washington, DC: U.S. Government Printing Office), August 14, 1941.

37. G. Mennen Williams, *Africa for the Africans* (Grand Rapids, MI: Eerdmans, 1969), p. 30.

38. Quoted in Dickson A. Mungazi, "Educational Innovation in Zimbabwe: Possibilities and Problems," in *Journal of Negro Education*, Vol. 54, No. 2 (1985), p. 209.

39. Robert Mugabe, "Literacy for All in Five Years" (Speech given in launching the National Adult Literacy Campaign), July 18, 1983.

40. For violence perpetrated by African Americans on other African Americans, see, for example, John D. Hull, "Have We Gone Mad?" in *Time*, December 20, 1993, p. 31.

41. United States, *Report of the National Adivsory Commission on Civil Disorders* (Otto Kerner, chairman) (Washington DC: U.S. Government Printing Office, 1968), p. 2.

42. Ibid., p. xiii.

43. Adam Curle, *Education for Liberation* (New York: John Wiley and Sons, 1973), p. 127.

44. For a discussion of some of educational problems that Africans and African Americans are facing, see, for example, Dickson A. Mungazi, *Educational Policy and National Character: Africa, Japan, the United States, and the Soviet Union* (Westport, CT: Praeger Publishers, 1993), p. 129.

45. Smith, *Nyerere of Tanzania*, p. 56.

46. John Chancellor, "The Politics of Change," a documentary film aired by the Discovery Channel, February 21, 1994.

8

The Journey to the Promised Land: Summary, Conclusions, and Implications

The crowdedness in the Negro ghettos, the poverty and the economic insecurity, the lack of wholesome recreation are factors which all work in the direction of fostering anti-social tendencies leading to conflict.

Gunnar Myrdal, 1944

Racial reconciliation is a top priority in the United States of the 21st century. I am going to play a role in efforts to increase African American membership in the Republican Party.

Jack Kemp, 1997

THE PURPOSE OF THE STUDY IN PERSPECTIVE

The purpose of this study was to present important aspects of the struggle of African Americans for development from the end of the Civil War to the present. It is a study of their journey to the promised land. When President Abraham Lincoln issued the Emancipation Proclamation on September 22, 1862, to take effect on January 1, 1863, the Civil War was already under way. During his first inaugural address on March 4, 1861, Lincoln raised the question of slavery in form of rhetorical questions, asking "May Congress prohibit slavery in the territories? The Constitution does not expressly say. Must Congress protect slavery in the territories? The Constitution does not expressly say."[1] Lincoln's position indicates that the new president had long made up his mind that slavery was wrong and that it had to go. There was no room for compromise.

To understand why Lincoln felt that slavery had to go, one must first understand the conditions that produced him. In a letter dated December 20, 1859, addressed to Jesse W. Fell, an official in the Republican Party in Illinois, Lincoln gave an account of how his own background paved the way for the formulation of his views on the question of slavery. Born on February 12, 1809, in Hardin County, Kentucky, Lincoln said he came from an undistinguished family known for its hard work and fairness. His parents were born in Virginia. His paternal grandfather, Abraham Lincoln, emigrated from Rockingham County in Virginia to Kentucky in 1781. A year later he was killed in a skirmish with Indians. As members of the Quaker religion, the Lincoln family embraced religious and moral principles that heavily influenced their lives. Although his father died when he was six years old, Lincoln never lost the importance of the values he began to learn as soon as he was conscious of his world. The Lincoln family did not subscribe to the idea that slavery must be maintained. Although he believed that the Negro was not equal to the white man socially and that he did not have the same intellectual potential,[2] he was a human being who deserved to be treated with respect, and slavery was as humiliating to him as it was to the slave owner.

On August 21, 1858, during the first debate with Stephen A. Douglas, Lincoln argued that as far as human rights were concerned, the slave was equal to the white man. He argued further, "But the right to eat bread without the leave of anybody else, which his own hand earns, the Negro is my equal, and the equal of Judge Douglas,[3] and the equal of every living man."[4] There is no question that in this line of thinking, Lincoln was ahead of his time. He recognized that slavery had been in place many years and that fact convinced him that it was wrong and had to go.

Lincoln then concluded that it was up to his generation to assume the responsibility of resolving the question of slavery once and for all. As soon as he was elected to the U.S. House of Representatives in 1864, he began to make speeches against slavery.[5] As soon as he was elected president in 1860, Lincoln concluded that the question of slavery would be resolved by presidential emancipation proclamation because the issue was too controversial to be resolved by debate and consent of Congress. Once he reached that conclusion he would not reverse the decision that he based on it. It was a matter of time before he took appropriate and decisive action to end slavery. He felt that there was urgency in taking this decisive action because some nations in Europe were considering extending recognition of the Confederacy. The ratification of the Thirteenth, Fourteenth, and Fifteenth Amendments to the U.S. Constitution was intended to give African Americans equal rights as citizens of the United States. But the bitterness that was part of the conflict quickly translated into hostility against African Americans themselves, as Lincoln abandoned his idea of repatriating them back to Africa. His assassination on April 14, 1865,[6] and the formation of KKK in 1868 created a new national climate that cast a long shadow on the future of both the nation and African Americans themselves. The institution of slavery was now substituted for by the institution of racial hatred and discrimination.

In an effort to heal the wounds inflicted on the nation by the Civil War, Congress passed a series of Reconstruction legislation which the federal government hoped to utilize in carrying out Reconstruction programs. But the impeachment of President Andrew Johnson on February 24, 1868,[7] created new ominous political clouds on the national horizon to overshadow Reconstruction itself. To complicate matters each subsequent president, wishing to secure votes from the South, did not pursue Reconstruction programs in the way Congress intended. In 1877 President Rutherford Hayes withdrew federal programs from the South. Immediately the South began to reverse the gains that African Americans had made. The progress that they had made on their journey to the promised land came to a stop.

As they struggled to find a new identity, African Americans knew that they could not rely on either the state legislatures or the U.S. Congress to help them on their journey to the promised land. The passage of civil rights legislation in 1875 did little to assist them in their struggle. Although the campaign to end slavery launched by such people as William Lloyd Garrison strengthened Lincoln's determination, African Americans knew that they had a difficult road ahead. They therefore turned to the federal courts, especially the Supreme Court, to address their problems. But from 1896 to 1938 the Supreme Court was so conservative that it ruled persistently against them. This was a period of 40 years of wandering in the wilderness.

Remembering that the destiny of the struggling people rested squarely on their own shoulders, African Americans decided to rescue themselves. This began a period of time when leadership became important. From Frederick Douglass to Martin Luther King, Jr. some African Americans rose to the occasion to exercise the responsibility for leadership that was critical to the success of their endeavors, their journey. One sees three periods in the struggle of African Americans for development since 1865: from 1965 to 1896, when efforts were being made to ensure their rights as citizens of the United States; from 1897 to 1954, when they were struggling for equal rights; from 1955 to the present, when their struggle acquired new dimensions.

AFRICAN AMERICANS IN CONTEMPORARY TIMES

Since the First World War African Americans have continued to struggle for development by playing important roles in national events. Many have served in the military, others have become scholars. Some have become astronauts, others have become politicians serving in various capacities. One would be led to the conclusion that African Americans have reached the promised land. But the increasing disillusionment with the American dream, the tragedy of violence perpetrated on African Americans by other African Americans and hate groups, increasing numbers of unemployed, lack of interest in formal education, increasing poverty—all would lead to the conclusion that the promised land is in sight but it has not yet been reached.

The outbreak of Second World War in September 1939 transformed the way Americans thought about themselves and their world. The Japanese surpise attack on Pearl Harbor on December 7, 1941, forced the United States to end its neutrality. In January 1942 President Roosevelt underscored the importance of four freedoms he believed must be preserved for all people, saying "In the future day, which we seek to make secure, we look forward to a world founded upon four essential human freedoms. The first is freedom of speech and expression everywhere in the world. The second is freedom of every person to worship God in his own way. The third is freedom from want. The fourth is freedom from fear."[8] Africans under colonial control and African Americans took this message seriously. The application of these four basic principles would ensure their security and would constitute essential elements of their development. But their success would depend upon the goodwill of white America and liberals in Africa. This author recognizes that since he arrived in the United States from Africa for the first time in August 1961, he has observed tremendous change in attitudes for the better toward race and race relations. But the lingering elements of discrimination cast the thrust for national development in doubt.

One must see the struggle of African Americans to reach the promised land from a larger perspective. For example, when France surrendered to Nazi forces on June 22, 1940, Germany launched its blitz against Britain, believing that the British people would not be able to withstand the power and destruction that German military forces unleashed. For several months Winston Churchill pleaded with Roosevelt to come to Britain's aid, arguing that united German and Italian forces would force Britain to surrender, posing serious implications for the United States itself. After meeting secretly the two leaders issued what became known as the Atlantic Charter on August 11, 1941, consisting of eight principles. The third principle stated, "We respect the right of all peoples to choose the form of government under which they will live, and wish to see sovereign rights and self-government restored to those who have been forcibly deprived of them."[9]

This statement shows two things: the United States was now willing to consider its involvement in world events that held implications for its own future, and it implied that the rights of African Americans had to be recognized and that colonial systems in Africa had forcibly deprived Africans of their right to self-determination. Both implications would have serious consequences for the future of both Africans and African Americans as they began to demand better treatment soon after the war. In the United States this meant the beginning of the civil rights movement. In Africa it meant the rise of African nationalism. Both movements had a profound impact on social conditions on both continents.

The passage of the Lanham Act in 1941 made it possible for the federal government to provide funds for school districts to build and operate schools where federal war-related activity created problems that local governments could not resolve. Three years later, in 1944, two events occurred that would have a profound impact on the United States. The first event was the passage of the Servicemen Readjustment Act, better known as the GI bill. This legislation provided education and training for returning war veterans. African Americans who had participated in the war took advantage of it to promote their educational advancement. Later the benefits it provided were expanded to include veterans of the Korean and Vietnam wars. The ability of the United States to initiate educational plans for the future in an environment of war suggests a critical feature of the human struggle for development. The GI bill made it possible for Americans returning from the war to receive the education that they needed to prepare themselves for the future.

The second event that took place in 1944 was the publication of a report entitled *An American Dilemma: The Negro Problem and Modern Democracy* by Gunnar Myrdal, a Swedish sociologist and researcher. In his well-documented study, Myrdal predicted that unless racial discrimination ended soon, the United States was likely to encounter serious racial and social problems in the not-so-distant future and at a level not experienced in the past. Myrdal suggested the causes of this social conflict:

The crowdedness in the Negro ghettos, the poverty and the economic insecurity, the lack of wholesome recreation are factors which all work in the direction of fostering anti-social tendencies leading to conflict. Racial discrimination in the opportunity for school facilities is as spectacular as it is well known. The current expenditure per pupil in daily attendance per year in elementary and secondary schools in ten southern states in 1935 and 1936 was $17.04 for Negroes and $49.50 for white children.[10]

This difference meant that African Americans were receiving less educational opportunity than white Americans, a fact that contributed to both the *Brown* decision in 1954 and the beginning of the civil rights movement in 1955. The war had transformed the way African Americans saw their position in society in relation to that of white Americans, and they decided that they were entitled to equal treatment.

The violent deaths of Adolf Hitler and Benito Mussolini in 1945 meant that only Japan remained determined to continue the war against the Allied forces. After nearly six years of fighting, the world was getting tired of the war. On July 16, 1945, the United States tested an atomic bomb in New Mexico. On August 6 the United States dropped one such bomb over Hiroshima, killing more than 70,000 persons. Three days later a second atomic bomb was dropped on Nagasaki, killing nearly 36,000 people. The use of these two bombs brought the war to an end, but the use of the bomb created conditions of increasing world insecurity and danger. The United States saw its new role in the world in direct relationship to its policy toward its own people, especially African Americans. The atomic bomb had ushered in the era of nuclear technology which posed the possibility of destroying the world itself. In spite of the end of the Second World War, the wars in Korea and Vietnam brought the United States into the arena of international relationships more intimately than in the past.[11] Since that time the world has not been the same. The United States has been involved in seeking solutions to a plethora of world problems. But in doing so it recognized that it must address the problems that its own people face.

AFRICAN AMERICANS IN RECENT DEVELOPMENTS

One year following the end of the war in 1945, dramatic events began to take place rapidly in the United States. In 1946 a 38-year-old conservative Republican politician from Wisconsin, Joseph McCarthy, was elected to the U.S. Senate. Four years later, in 1950, he attracted public attention by accusing some members of the U.S. State Department, colleges and universities, and public schools of harboring Communists. He capitalized on this publicity by writing two books, *America's Retreat from Victory* (1951) and *McCarthyism: The Fight for America* (1952). Although both books were less than successful, McCarthy used them to stage a massive investigation of individuals he suspected of Communist activity. In the process of carrying out his self-assigned inquisition, he initiated a witch hunt that violated the basic constitutional principles that he claimed he was trying to protect. This activity offered indirect encouragement to those whites who were against the development of African Americans. Discrimination and segregation acquired more powerful dimensions at a time when better relationships between the races should have been expected.

When Dwight Eisenhower was elected president in 1952, McCarthy was already at the height of his purported investigations. He singled out teachers and college professors because of their activities during the Depression. During what has become known as the McCarthy Era, careers were destroyed. Eisenhower, fearing to divide the Republican Party, tried to ignore McCarthy and his activities. But, by 1953, he and his administration soon realized that McCarthy was an embarrassment to both the Republican Party and the country.[12] Eisenhower had reached the same conclusion as President Harry Truman, who served as president from 1945 to 1952, that in his purported investigation McCarthy was doing more harm than good to the United States. In all his activity McCarthy never produced a single Communist.

The president tried an approach of quiet diplomacy to have McCarthy cease his activities. In 1954 McCarthy was censured by the U.S. Senate, bringing his infamous activities to a halt. Education scholar Diane Ravitch concluded, "With Eisenhower as President, McCarthy could no longer call upon and sustain an atmosphere of suspicion. The efforts to oust teachers suspected of being Communists continued for a time in some school districts."[13]

Among the dramatic events that had a profound impact on the United States during this time was the Supreme Court decision in *Brown vs. Board of Education of Topeka*. Since the end of Reconstruction and the passage of Jim Crow laws, there had developed a thinking that differences in skin color represented differences in intellectual potential and that the black race was inferior to the white race.[14] A conclusion was then reached that because of this difference, separate facilities must be established for whites and African Americans. This thinking was seen as receiving official approval by the U.S. Supreme Court in its 1896 *Plessy vs. Ferguson* decision. From this decision, the doctrine of separate but equal became the modus operandi until the *Brown* decision of 1954.

From 1952 to 1953 the Supreme Court heard arguments against this policy and the specific application of separate but equal relative to segregation in education. These arguments were directed at schools in South Carolina, Virginia, Delaware, the District of Columbia, and Kansas, which were the objects of similar lawsuits, combined into the *Brown vs. Board of Education of Topeka* case that put John W. Davis in the national spotlight for the last time. In arguing on behalf of his clients, the school boards, in favor of maintaining segregation, Davis cited the *Plessy* decision to conclude that the issue of race had been settled once and for all and that the constitutionality of racial segregation had been substantiated by that decision. He further argued that nothing must be done to change it.

The lawyers in favor of integration, led by Thurgood Marshall, the chief counsel for the plaintiff (and later, in 1968, named by President Lyndon B. Johnson the first African American to serve on the U.S. Supreme Court), argued that segregation did great damage to African American students because separate educational facilities were not equal.

Robert L. Carter, arguing for the plaintiffs, advanced a compelling argument, saying, "No state has any authority under the equal protection clause of the Fourteenth Amendment to use race as a factor in affording educational opportunity among its citizens."[15] Marshall, who had attended the Howard Law School directed by Charles H. Houston, added that "there are no recognizable differences from a racial standpoint between children."[16]

On May 17, 1954, after hearing the arguments, the Supreme Court reached a unanimous decision, stating that the doctrine of separate but equal as enunciated by the *Plessy* decision was no longer applicable to conditions of the day. Chief Justice Earl Warren[17] wrote the decision, posing a fundamental question: "Does separation of children in public schools on the basis of race, even though the physical facilities and other tangible factors may be equal, deprive the children of the minority groups of equal educational opportunity? We believe that it does. Such segregation is a denial of equal protection of the law."[18]

The reaction to the historic decision can be understood in the context of events that began to immediately unfold. The formation of the infamous White Citizens Councils in close cooperation with the Ku Klux Klan to coordinate efforts to disobey the ruling was the beginning of a decade of unprecedented social turmoil. Some U.S. senators from the South, especially South Carolina and Mississippi, were actively involved in efforts to disregard the decision and to maintain racial segregation. James Westland and John Stennis, U.S. senators from Mississippi, both took the center stage in their resistance to the *Brown* decision.

On August 20, 1955, Emmett Till, an African American youth of 14, almost missed his train from Chicago to the Mississippi Delta, where he was going to spend part of the summer with his relatives. Till caught his train but never made it back to Chicago. He was murdered and those responsible for his death were acquitted of the crime. A decade after the end of the Second World War, southern states, especially Mississippi, felt that the *Brown* decision had plunged the United States into "another war to protect its way of life."[19] Those responsible for Till's death did not know that they were helping arouse a new level of consciousness among African Americans about the need to initiate a protest movement to gain their civil rights. In this tragedy the United States was about to enter a dark period in its development.

In the same year Till was murdered, Rosa Parks was arrested in Montgomery, Alabama, for not giving up her seat on the bus to a white person. This led to a lengthy boycott of the bus company, organized by Martin Luther King, Jr. and other black leaders. In September 1957 the crisis over school integration in Little Rock, Arkansas, erupted. The anger and outrage with which the white community responded to the events in Montgomery and Little Rock, in being forced to give up its exclusive power and position of privilege, were manifested in violence against African Americans. While the Supreme Court required the end of discrimination, it did not order integration, and "the Constitution does not require integration as a result of voluntary action, it merely forbids the use of governmental power to enforce segregation."[20] Regardless of this action, African Americans were forging ahead with plans for the future. There was no going back to conditions of the past.

The crisis in Little Rock was placed in the back pages of national newspapers when the Soviet Union launched the first satellite Sputnik (Voyager) on October 4, 1957. The satellite circled the earth once every 95 minutes at a speed of 18,000 miles per hour until it returned to Earth on January 4, 1958. The entire world was caught by surprise. Few people believed that the Soviet Union, coming out of the Second World War weakened to the point where its recovery would take years, was capable of rising above its third-rate development to the status of a major nuclear power in the way that it did.[21] By 1959 Soviet leader Nikita Khrushchev exploited the Sputnik's success for his own political advantage and threatened to bury the West in the intense ideological competition that was rapidly developing as part of the Cold War.

The impact of Sputnik was felt more profoundly by the United States than by any other country in the world. The United States saw the success of Sputnik as a challenge and decided to respond in two specific ways. The first had to do with a change of attitude about the involvement of the federal government in education. Out of this new thinking emerged a national call for the federal government to think of new ways of encouraging development in key areas of research and technology. This in turn required funding for certain academic areas, especially mathematics and the hard sciences. President Eisenhower had vigorously opposed any federal role other than that of offering encouragement in education. Sputnik would change that position. Combined with the crisis in school desegregation, Sputnik had a profound impact on national policy, especially recognizing the need to promote better racial relationships by giving all Americans equal opportunity. That the southern states saw this effort as a way of seeking to impose the *Brown* decision accentuated the controversy surrounding the federal involvement in education that Eisenhower was now seeking in order to ensure its development as a response to Sputnik.

KENNEDY, THE NEW FRONTIER, AND CIVIL RIGHTS

The tragic death of President John F. Kennedy on November 22, 1963, did not slow down the intensity of the arms race and the Cold War in general. Kennedy's successor Lyndon B. Johnson continued the programs Kennedy had started. The installment of the Kennedy administration gave Americans an opportunity to reevaluate the relationship that their country had with other countries. This could be realistically done only in the context of posing fundamental questions about the United States' own national character and domestic programs. This is why, on taking office on January 20, 1961, Kennedy recognized the need to develop a national program that would reach out for improved relationships with other nations.

Kennedy's concept of the New Frontier was born out of this endeavor. It was significant because it acknowledged a basic tenet in human relationships: the freedom of all people is essential to stability and peace among all nations. For Kennedy the exploration of space was only meaningful within the context of seeking to recognize the exploration of the aspirations of all people, both in fulfilling their personal ambitions and in meeting new challenges leading to national enrichment. This is why in 1961 Kennedy enunciated new policies regarding the rise of African nationalism. The appointment of Dean Rusk as U.S. Secretary of State brought a fresh new approach that saw a departure from past policies pursued by the State Department under John Foster Dulles. Until the Kennedy years, prior administrations believed that the consequences of the rise of African nationalism were the sole responsibility of the colonial governments.[22]

Kennedy also fully recognized the momentum that the civil rights movement was gathering in the United States. In it he saw a struggle that gave the country an emerging national character that was necessary to enable the country to recognize its proper role in critical issues of international relationships. His basic conviction was that unless the United States found solutions to problems at home, it would not be able to play an effective role in international developments. The New Frontier demanded the administration take all pertinent factors into account in designing a domestic policy and agenda that were closely related to events abroad. This is why Kennedy submitted to Congress the most comprehensive bill on civil rights, which became law in 1964. The creation of the Peace Corps in 1961, under the direction of Sargent Shriver, Kennedy's brother-in-law, brought the country to the ultimate New Frontier. The Peace Corps became a cultural bridge that helped build international relationships by providing the U.S. government and its people with an opportunity to understand the nature of other cultures and the problems that other countries faced in their struggle for advancement.

Americans from all walks of life were called upon to join the Peace Corps to participate in a national program intended to give Kennedy's transformation vision a practical application to human understanding and cooperation. They were asked to live and work with people in foreign countries, studying and advising them on various aspects of national development. They would immerse themselves in foreign cultures and avoid trying to persuade the people in those lands to adopt the American culture. They symbolized mankind's ability to appreciate cultural diversity as a means toward global enrichment. Kennedy envisioned this as constituting an understanding that was a prerequisite in creating an atmosphere of peace and cooperation. Nurses, teachers, agricultural specialists, engineers, and industrial workers all came forward in the spirit of Kennedy's call to offer their services in this international program. African Americans had an opportunity to live and work in Africa and came to know the people.

This approach to national policy created an environment that helped define a new paradigm, which held new meaning for the United States. This New Frontier manifested itself in a variety of program initiatives at home. The Higher Education Act of 1963 authorized $935 million in matching funds and $360 million in loans extended over a period of five years to institutions of higher education, both public and private, for constructing new educational establishments that included athletic and recreational facilities and buildings for all purposes, even sectarian.[23] At the same time the Vocational Education Act, also passed in 1963, "extended and expanded all previous vocational programs including the Smith-Hughes Act of 1917.[24]

The passage of the Civil Rights Act of 1964 was the high-water mark of President Johnson's term of office. The new law made provisions that extended those of the Civil Rights Act of 1875. In 1965, having won the 1964 presidential election on his own merit against his Republican opponent, Barry Goldwater of Arizona, Johnson set out to define in his own way the New Frontier. On April 11, 1965, President Johnson initiated what he regarded as a new definition of the New Frontier by signing the Elementary and Secondary Education Act. This legislation represented the most comprehensive provisions for education since the National Defense Education Act of 1958. The law provided for annual appropriations for education that enabled students from low-income families to avail themselves of educational opportunities. The implementation of the law began with $100 million for the 1965 academic year. It allowed for the purchase of textbooks, library resources, and other published materials needed in the promotion of education among the children of economically deprived families. States were required to assure that fiscal control of the funds ensured fair and equitable distribution of resources.

On November 8 President Johnson expanded the concept of the New Frontier in the area of higher education by signing the Higher Education Act. Coming one year after the passage of the Civil Rights Act of 1964, this legislation prompted Johnson to acknowledge its importance by saying, "This is only one of more than two dozen educational measures enacted by the first session of the 89th Congress. History will forever record that this session did more for the cause of education in America than all the previous 176 regular sessions of Congress did put together."[25]

While this was happening, African-Americans were trying to define the New Frontier in their own way. Since the *Brown* decision, they were increasingly demanding their fair share of the educational pie. The constitutional conclusion of the Supreme Court in that decision—that separation of children on the basis of color gave them the stamp of inferiority—became the basis of a fresh approach to their quest for educational opportunities. Those who continued to argue that the black race was intellectually inferior, such as Arthur R. Jensen,[26] saw the earlier *Plessy* decision as supporting their line of thinking.

This line of thinking was why from provisions of the Civil Rights Act and of the Economic Opportunity Act, both of 1964, efforts were made to assist students from economically disadvantaged family backgrounds. They received special attention to help them overcome the effects of the denial of equal opportunity. Known as the antipoverty initiative, the Economic Opportunity Act was intended to help students recognize their potential and to encourage them to use it in their educational efforts. In this connection Johnson's understanding of the New Frontier was evident in his desire to initiate Head Start, a program for preschool children, most of them African Americans. The rationale behind Head Start was that a culturally disadvantaged background made it more difficult for a student to learn. This was due to the lack of racially integrated social interaction. This situation also deprived them of access to quality teachers and appropriate educational resources.

This paradigm shift in education held meaning and renewed hope for those responsible for education. They understood that educational materials and adequate environment were critical variables for educational success. The U.S. Office of Economic Opportunity has also argued that this disadvantage can be corrected by appropriate remedial strategies designed early in the life of students.[27] This is precisely the position that African Americans took in their understanding of Kennedy's original concept of the New Frontier. With the passage of this legislation they felt that the concept was within their grasp. With this recognition they felt that they and the country stood on the verge of a new era, an era of social cooperation and acceptance.

The so-called white flight to avoid integration meant that inner-city public schools were rapidly becoming predominantly African American or Hispanic. Albert Shanker saw this development as totally negative because, as Henry Barnard and Horace Mann had envisaged during the reform movement of the 19th century, the purpose of the civil rights movement was to bring about integration of the schools as a means of advancing toward social reform and development. Mann saw racial integration as the balance wheel of the new social order that education was expected to bring about. Sensitivity on the part of many years compelled one to ask: "If it takes four ounces of poison to kill a person, how many ounces would it take to kill your mother, your father, your sister, and your brother?[28]

Although this approach to mathematics was an unfortunate example, it was real and was relevant to human conditions. Four ounces of poison may be the same as behaving in ways that are inconsistent with human expectations or adopting attitudes that may damage relationships between people or demonstrate ignorance about human issues. In this approach teachers hoped to accomplish two objectives: to teach students how to solve mathematics problems and to apply those principles to find solutions to the problems of society.

In 1968 the Ocean Hill-Brownsville dispute in Brooklyn, NY, captured the attention of the national media. When a community board that was fully controlled by black militants dismissed 19 white school administrators and teachers, some white teachers felt that they had an opportunity to confront a major national problem: racial conflict. In a way that was typical of the African American political movement, the board gave a number of reasons for its action. When the city Board of Education reversed the decision of the community board, the students, most of them African American and Hispanic, boycotted classes. A serious crisis was developing that could have serious implications for education in the city as a whole. One white teacher, Albert E. Shanker,[29] feeling that the African American community was accentuating the problem of race, decided to intervene.

While Shanker attempted to mediate this dispute, a militant African American teacher recited an anti-Semitic poem over the local radio station. Shanker felt that the poem was directed at him personally and tried to bring the two sides together to resolve the dispute through dialogue. Things came to a head when a white pregnant teacher was hit in the stomach, threatening the life of her unborn baby. Shanker refused to give up efforts to mediate between the administration and the African American communities, arguing that both groups had so much to lose by division. While he saw no clear possible solution to the crisis, Shanker simply appealed to both sides to apply common sense. He encouraged dialogue, rather than confrontation; understanding, rather than placing demands; cooperation, rather than competition; reason, rather than rancor; persuasion, rather than threats. He advocated what Jesse Jackson later used in the Rainbow Coalition, consisting of dispossessed and disenfranchised people who, he said, needed cooperation and unity to bring about meaningful change.

Through his insistence that solutions to the problem lay in the dialogical process, Shanker succeeded in convincing his political antagonists about the real cause of the dispute in the Ocean Hill-Brownsville district. He argued that the situation was not caused by dispute over whether the school board should be controlled by militant African Americans under the local control principle recommended by McGeorge Bundy, then president of the Ford Foundation. Rather, the cause of the dispute was that, as members of a profession, teachers must no longer continue to teach in any school or district in which decisions involving their professional functions and operations are made by groups of people who have no knowledge of the educational issues, but are purely influenced by political considerations. He also succeeded in convincing the parties in the dispute that when political considerations heavily influence educational decisions, the result is and has always been that the educational process suffers. This is why he vehemently argues that teachers must be allowed to make decisions relative to education.

In September 1974, Shanker appeared before the U.S. House Education and Labor Committee to advocate enforcement of hiring policies in higher education. Shanker took the opportunity to take his mission to new heights in urging the adoption of affirmative action to enhance educational opportunity for all students. He suggested an approach that had not been thought of before, saying, "Our view of what an affirmative action program should be is to start with open admission, free tuition, interest-free loans, and grant money which will not only open the doors of educational opportunity to minority students, but would also encourage their pursuit of professional careers."[30]

In arguing in support of affirmative action, Shanker took the position that any significant increase in minority hiring on faculties must start with a significant increase in the pool of available personnel. He knew that four years earlier, in 1970, approximately 10.6 percent of all undergraduate admissions were African Americans, Native Americans, and Hispanics combined. These groups collectively constituted 16.8 percent of the U.S. population. Shanker also knew that of the bachelor's degrees awarded in 1970, 5.2 percent were awarded to African American students, 1.2 percent to Hispanic students, and 1.0 percent to Native American students.

AFRICAN AMERICAN RESPONSE TO CURRENT NATIONAL DEVELOPMENTS

The enactment of the Civil Rights Act of 1964 was considered a major milestone. It was, and is, an unprecedented national recognition that all Americans must be treated equally. It was also believed, at the time, to be the ultimate solution to the problem of social injustice that African Americans and others felt was overtly expressed when Rosa Parks was ordered to give up her bus seat to a white male passenger in Montgomery, Alabama, in 1955. The Civil Rights Act of 1964 was also considered to be the quintessential panacea for racial conflict in the United States. It was more comprehensive in its provisions than the civil rights legislation of 1875 and 1957. In the Civil Rights Act of 1964, Americans thought that their nation had at long last found a permanent solution to the problems of inequality and injustice. They optimistically and prematurely believed that the country could now look into the future with great expectations and excitement, putting the past behind them in order to concentrate on making the future the best that it could possibly be.

In 1965, when Americans thought social utopia was within reach, a violent riot erupted in the Watts area of Los Angeles, caused by discontent that stemmed from unfulfilled community expectations. This was a prelude to equally violent eruptions in Detroit in 1967. What had gone wrong? Americans thought the Civil Rights Act of 1964 was an instrument for eliminating racial inequality. They discovered that old practices die hard, but they believed that the country was embarking on a new era of changed racial attitudes. They soon found out that racial prejudice was entrenched and emerging in new and profound ways. They mistakenly thought that the country had adopted a new idealism that would ensure national development, only to find that the era of goodwill that the Civil Rights Act of 1964 was expected to create had actually never materialized. They thought that racial integration would bring all ethnic groups together in cooperation to create a new society with shared values. They learned that racial conflict remained the modus vivendi of the nation.

Americans also believed that the Civil Rights Act of 1964 would make it possible for all people to trust one another, only to find that distrust and suspicion had even intensified. They thought that the Civil Rights Act would help extend the concept of equal economic opportunity to all people, yet they discovered that the country continued to grow apart. This is precisely what the Otto Kerner Commission of 1968 took into account when it reported that the United States was moving in two opposite directions, that African Americans were being impoverished at the same rate that white Americans were getting richer. The Kerner Commission warned, "What white Americans have never fully understood, but what the Negro can never forget is that white society is deeply implicated in the ghetto. White institutions created it, white institutions maintain it, and white society condones it."[31]

Jonathan Kozol's *Death at an Early Age* (1967) showed the extent to which African American youth felt isolated and alienated from the socioeconomic life of the country. The book was also an account of a generation lost in the shuffle of social disintegration and the malaise it endured in a rapidly disintegrating urban environment. Marjorie Murphy concluded that the educational process, considered the salvaging instrument of a society in dire straits, was seen in a negative light because "teachers were perpetuating a racist class-based system of education."[32] While this was happening, black organizations were conducting intense self-examination.

As a result of this exercise, several black groups adopted a more militant and confrontational position on the issue of race. For example, Stokely Carmichael, who later changed his name to Kwame Toure,[33] the chairman of Student Nonviolent Coordinating Committee, concluded that seeking racial integration should not be part of the objectives of African Americans. The Congress of Racial Equality (CORE) acquired a new level of popularity among African Americans as a result of its insistence that American society recognize the need for minority groups to aggressively demand their rights. Both the NAACP and the Urban League were compelled to reexamine the traditional relationships they maintained with liberal whites.

The Black Panther Party, led by Eldridge Cleaver, Huey Newton, Bobby Seale, and H. Rap Brown, began to advocate black power in a way that frightened most white Americans. The violent confrontation that erupted in Oakland, California, between the members of the Black Panther Party and the police was indicative of how seriously strained racial relationships had become. When put together, these events show that in spite of the hope for improved social relationships expressed by the Civil Rights Act of 1964, the United States was heading directly toward further major racial conflict unless all segments of the society made a concerted effort to resolve the issues that deeply divided them.[34]

In 1965, only one year after passage of the Civil Rights Act, observers concluded that the failure to establish clear lines of communication between African Americans and white Americans was having an adverse effect on the needed dialogical interaction between them. Americans recognized that the future of the country was in doubt unless they came to an understanding of the real problems that divided them and then cooperated in seeking solutions. The decade between 1955 and 1965 saw the Reverend Milton Galamison conduct a series of workshops on racial communication and understanding on behalf of the NAACP. In the process Galamison was able to convince school officials that African Americans and white Americans could establish lines of communication by identifying issues that were adversely affecting relationships between them, such as inequality in educational opportunity, the unrepresentative character of the political process, deteriorating community facilities, and wide differences in socioeconomic opportunity.

CONCLUSIONS

To understand the problems that African Americans have encountered on their journey to the promised land, one needs to understand their origin. When the educational reform movement initiated by Horace Mann became a reality, the central question that everyone asked was how education in the common schools would be financed. The consensus that taxation was the best form of support created a new level of controversy because, at the time, the argument that not every member of the community had children in school was a powerful factor in the decision. Although the practice evolved over the years to use a property tax to support public education have been accepted, it has left a trail of controversy that has not been fully resolved to this day. African Americans have been caught in that controversy because, until recently, their contributions to financial support of education have been small compared to the contributions that white Americans have made. This is a result of discrimination in economic activity.

Across the United States today communities have wrestled with this problem without finding an adequate solution.[35] If at the inception of the reform movement the federal government had assumed greater financial responsibility for education than it did, an equitable system of supporting education and related activity would have been worked out to meet the developmental needs of African Americans. Today some school districts are not able to meet their financial obligations simply because the economic base on which the system of taxation is structured is not equitable.

Since the addition of the Fourteenth Amendment to the U.S. Constitution on July 28, 1868, granting equal rights to former slaves, the United States has not been able to solve its racial problems. The controversy surrounding the proposed holiday honoring Martin Luther King, Jr. in some states, especially Arizona, testifies to the degree to which race has remained a factor of American national life. In 1991 a professor at a leading university spoke to the author about the turmoil in South Africa under apartheid:

It is ironic that while the United States has condemned South Africa for maintaining the notorious policy of apartheid, the United States itself has not been unable to resolve its racial problems. One of these days the United States will have to seek the help and advice of F. W. de Klerk, the leader of a country whose racial policy the United States has rightly attacked. But after South Africa has solved its racial problems, the United States will be the only country in the world to have a racial problem. This is a frightening reality.[36]

The *Plessy* decision seemed to underscore the thinking that even though the Fourteenth Amendment explicitly stated that equal protection of the law for all people must be an operative principle of national life, the Supreme Court's interpretation of it in *Plessy* left no doubt that it was still operating under the thinking of distributive justice based on race.

When the Court tried to function by the intent of the Fourteenth Amendment in its ruling in *Brown* in 1954, it created an entirely new racial situation that had not existed before—an intensity of white opposition to the idea of racial equality. Formation of the White Citizens Councils in response accelerated the deterioration of a situation that was taking a heavy toll on national purpose. The crisis in Little Rock in 1957 and at the University of Alabama in 1963 showed that the United States was entering a new phase of racial conflict that threatened to sabotage the journey to the promised land. The increase in racial violence among young people, an age group that is traditionally intolerant of racism, troubles many people. An American educator told the author in Florida in November 1990:

Racial unrest in the United States has taken a more serious twist than in the past. Young people who are generally known for their liberal political views, have turned into extreme racists who are creating a dangerous situation for the country. It is painful to see that in the United States, young people are in the front line of promoting racial intolerance and violence. Any nation that fails to teach its young to understand their social responsibility spells it own demise. I am afraid that this seems to be the direction we are moving as a nation. Why can't our young people learn lessons from the social movements of the 1960s?[37]

The enactment of the Civil Rights Act of 1964 made it possible for the United States to see other dimensions of the race issue as a major factor of national development. In the same way, the Elementary and Secondary Education Act of 1965 provided funds to assist the expansion and improvement of educational programs for the benefit of all students. Title V of the same law provided funds to state departments of education and gave them power to distribute them as they saw fit. This was done to allay fears of those who were concerned that with increased funding the federal government would have more power than it should have in controlling education.[38]

In their study conducted in 1972, *Education in the U.S.S.R.*, N. Kuzin and M. Kondokov argued that problems of race in the United States continued to handicap efforts of African Americans in their struggle for development. They concluded that the reason for this situation was that a capitalist system was designed to protect the political, social, and economic interests of white Americans at the expense of African Americans. This in turn caused so much social conflict that has remained permanently part of the American system. Kuzin and Kondokov added:

In the United States the Supreme Court as early as 1954 came out in favor of school integration. But to date only a small fraction of black children have received the opportunity of studying together with white children. Every year the press brings new evidence of recurring outbreaks of racial hostilities in U.S. schools. In October, 1974 in Boston a racial storm broke out. Local racists joined by KKK and storm troopers from the local organizations incited major disorders in the city to prevent the instruction of black children together with white children. Blacks have twice as great a probability of being unemployed. The capitalist system is at the center of this serious social conflict.[39]

While there is substance to the observation of these two Soviet authors about the problems of educational development for African Americans, one has to conclude that their views provide no solace to the agony of economic and social dysfunction that the Soviet Union has endured for nearly seven decades due to unrelenting pursuit of socialist ideology. This is why in 1986 Mikhail Gorbachev decided to chart a new course. But the process of change from a socialist economy to one entailing elements of free enterprise involves the painful pangs of frustration in the same way the need to preserve free enterprise in the United States creates serious problems of development for African Americans. Is there a happy medium between socialism Soviet-style and capitalism U.S.-style? Must one conclude that the problems of race in the United States will never be resolved?

In 1902 William E. B. Du Bois predicted that the major problem in the United States of the future would be the problem of race. It is amazing to see that since definitive action was taken in 1865 to put an end to the question of race, it has still persisted to this day. White Americans have accepted the fact that racial equality is essential if race relationships must develop for the good of everyone. However, the decision of the federal court in California on April 8, 1997, to support the action of the voters in the state in a referendum in November 1996 to end affirmative action is a sad reminder of the end of Reconstruction.

IMPLICATIONS

Although this author has seen remarkable effort and progress to eliminate race as a factor of national life, there are still lingering elements of it in a variety of ways. For example, in his study, *Being Black, Living in the Red: Race, Wealth and Social Policy in America*, Dalton Conley, Professor of Sociology and African American Studies at Yale University, concluded in 1999 that differences in income between white Americans and African Americans is still considerable. Conley gives the following figures to substantiate his conclusion:

At the lower end of the income spectrum the median African American family with $15,000 per year has no assets, while the equivalent white family holds $10,000 worth of equity. At upper income levels, greater than $75,000 per year, white families have a median net worth of $308,000, almost three times the figure for upper income African American families of $114,600.[40]

Regardless of this obvious inequality, a number of African Americans have distinguished themselves by the quality of their service and performance. A few examples will illustrate the accuracy of this conclusion. Besides Frederick Douglass, Martin Luther King Jr., Malcolm X, Thurgood Marshall, and W.E.B. Du Bois, there are quite a number of African Americans who rose to the occasion to lead the journey to the promised land. These include Jackie Robinson, the first African American to play for the Dodgers in a major baseball league. In 1947 *Time* described him as "the most artful Dodger who never backed down."[41] Louis Armstrong and Ray Charles distinguished themselves as musicians of rare ability. Ralph J. Bunche was a very successful official of the United Nations. He was named director of the division of trusteeships for the UN Secretariat. He also carried out several important missions on behalf of the UN. In 1950 Bunche received a Nobel Peace Prize for his efforts to bring peace to troubled areas of the world. Colin Powell distinguished himself as a military official and author. Carole Simpson was named anchorwoman for Saturday evening news at ABC. Maya Angelou and Alex Haley became successful authors. Her *I Know Why the Caged Bird Sings* and his *Roots* provoked the conscience of the nation about social issues.

There are other examples of successful African Americans. Marian Wright Edelman was the first African American woman to be admitted to the bar in Mississippi. She later founded Children's Defense Fund in Washington, DC. Andrew Young was named U.S. Ambassador to the UN during the Carter administration and later served as mayor of Atlanta. Bill Cosby became a successful comedian and later donated $20 million to Spelman College. Patricia Roberts Harris became a successful ambassador to Luxembourg. Michael Jordan and Scottie Pippen led the Chicago Bulls to two successive championships in the National Basketball Association. Controversial and conservative Clarence Thomas[42] was named a member of the U.S. Supreme Court by President George Bush to replace liberal Thurgood Marshall. These examples show that when given the opportunity African Americans can become successful in all areas of human endeavor for the benefit of the nation.

However, in a real sense some African Americans have sometimes undermined their own cause and development. For example, in 1994 a major crisis developed within the ranks of the NAACP, an organization that since 1909 has been dedicated to the struggle for development for African Americans. In June 1994 Mary Stansel, former administrative assistant to NAACP President Benjamin Chavis, sued the organization for sexual harassment and discrimination. Chavis decided to pay her $332,400 without the knowledge and approval of the board of directors.[43] The board then voted to ask Chavis to submit his resignation. This action divided the black community and the NAACP itself into two opposing camps, paralyzing its operations. Since its founding the NAACP had not experienced a crisis of this magnitude. It was imperative to find a solution to it quickly if the organization hoped to carry out its responsibility of directing the journey to the promised land by promoting the development of African Americans. But we cannot measure success or failure of all African Americans by these examples of failure.

One is led to the conclusion that the crisis within the NAACP was symbolic of the crisis that African Americans have been facing in recent years. Difference of opinion about programs, disagreement about methods or approach, conflict in political activity and ideology, increase in violence perpetrated by some African Americans on other African Americans—all have placed African Americans at the crossroads to the extent that their vision of the journey to the promised land has become blurred. The action of Texaco reported in 1996 to continue discrimination, the conservative opinions that Justice Thomas has expressed on the U.S. Supreme Court, especially on affirmative action, are among events that show that the journey to the promised land can be derailed by a combination of forces that oppose it.

However, since 1964 some African Americans have achieved remarkable accomplishments. In 1962 Edward W. Brooke won the highest state elective office held by an African American when he was elected Attorney-General in Massachusetts and later to the U.S. Senate. In 1964 Martin Luther King, Jr. won the Nobel Peace Prize for his role in leading the civil rights movement. In 1965 President Lyndon B. Johnson appointed Thurgood Marshall to the position of solicitor general and in 1967 to the Supreme Court. In 1966 Robert C. Weaver became a member of the Johnson administration with responsibility for housing. Following the congressional elections of 1998, J. C. Watts, a conservative African American from Oklahoma, was elected chairman of the Republican congressional caucus.

These appointments have done a lot to improve race relations in the United States. But unfortunately race relations have a long way to go to create a real nonracial society. This is why, speaking on CNN on April 12, 1997, Jack Kemp, the Republican candidate for vice president in 1996, said that racial reconciliation was a top priority in the United States for the 21st century. He indicated that he was going to play a role in seeking an increase in African American membership in the Republican Party. But before the Republican Party hopes to bring more African Americans into its own ranks, it must endeavor to build a vibrant segment of the

African American community itself. So far this has remained distant and far removed from the mainstream of American political, social, and economic life. Current leadership is either controversial or fragmented. As long as the African American community remains divided, its members will not fully experience the joy of arriving in the promised land, and Jack Kemp's idea of increasing African American membership within the Republican party will remain as distant as it has ever been.

One must see Kemp's idea of rebuilding the Republication Party in a larger social and political context. On November 30, 1998, this author wrote a letter to Senator Orrin Hatch (R. Utah) to say:

Soon after the elections of earlier this month you appeared on NBC to discuss your reaction to the results. You expressed disappointment that the Republican Party in both the House and the Senate did not gain more seats than was previously predicted. Speaker of the House, Newt Gingrich, had predicted that the Republican Party in the House would gain more than 20 seats and the Senate would have 67 seats. Not only was this prediction wrong, the Republican Party also lost five seats to Democrats in the House, and there was no significant change in the number of seats in the Senate.

As I watched you on NBC, I concluded that these were the circumstances that influenced your decision to appear on TV. You seemed worried by the fact that the Republican Party has not attracted significant numbers of African Americans to its ranks. The question now is: Why do most African Americans stay away from the Republican Party? You may recall that after the presidential elections of 1996 Jack Kemp recognized this fact and indicated that the Republican Party must do more to attract African Americans.

Let me suggest why most African Americans do not support the Republican Party:

1. The Republican Party has sought to promote very conservative African Americans who do not have the support of their own people. Clarence Thomas is a clear example. His presence on the Supreme Court will remain a reminder to African Americans that the Republican Party does not care about the issues that are important to their development.

2. The Republican Party has eliminated programs that African Americans consider important to their development. An example is affirmative action. During the past few years Governor Pete Wilson of California took the initiative to kill affirmative action. He succeeded at the cost of deciding not to run again, and his possible successor lost to a Democrat. The African American vote made a difference in California in the victory scored by Barbara Boxer in her reelection bid to the U.S. Senate. This is the same reason why Senator Alfonse D'Amato lost to Charles Schumer in New York.

3. Mexican Americans are equally disappointed by the action the Republican Party took to kill bilingual education. Republicans fail to realize that bilingual education poses no threat to English and that Mexican Americans want to utilize bilingual education as transition only.

4. While the Republican Party wants to draw blood from Bill Clinton, African Americans see that action as a front for action against their developmental interests. As long as

Republicans pursue the impeachment, African Americans have serious questions about the Republican ultimate motive.[44]

Geraldine Peten, an African American educator in the Phoenix area, understands the struggle of African Americans and the need to arrive at the promised land in terms of relationships that must emerge between them and white Americans. She stated her belief that racial relationships and values are interrelated with the subjects in an attempt to identify and eliminate false consciousness. "Accomplishing this feat is intended to raise African Americans to the level of true consciousness for trans-formational emancipation."[45]

The truth of the matter is that the Republican Party cannot expect on the one hand to act in ways that African Americans consider against their interests and to seek their support on the other hand. The author is not arguing that all African Americans must belong to the Democratic Party, but that the Republican Party has a long way to go before it can hope to attract significant membership of minority groups, especially African Americans, in its ranks. If the Republican Party wants to attract more African Americans, it would have to abandon its policy of exclusion to embrace policies that reflect their interests to ensure their development. Only then will it attract their membership.

Any benefit that the Republican Party sees in attracting African Americans to its ranks is the same benefit that the United States must see for the advancement its own journey to the promised land. Since the Civil War African Americans have surveyed the direction of that journey. Now, it is the responsibility of the country to construct the highway that leads to it. Unless national resources are utilized to initiate that journey, the country will remain in the wilderness for a longer period of time than the time it has taken African Americans to be where they are today on that journey. In short the progress that African Americans have made so far on that journey is on behalf of the United States itself. America, be well advised and be wise!

NOTES

1. John Gabriel Hunt, *The Essential Abraham Lincoln* (New York: Random House, 1993), p. 217

2. Ibid., p. 181.

3. Stephen Arnold Douglas was a popular and skillful orator. He was a Democrat born in Vermont, but moved to Illinois as a child. He served as a member of the supreme court of Illinois from 1841 to 1843. He was elected to the U.S. House of Representatives in 1843 and to the U.S. Senate in 1847. That is why during the debate Lincoln addressed him as Judge Douglas.

4. Hunt, *The Essential Abraham Lincoln*, p. 129.

5. Lincoln served a single term in the House of Representatives from 1846 to 1848 and did not seek reelection.

6. History says that John Wilkes Booth shot Lincoln a little after 10:00 p.m. on April 14 and that he was pronounced dead at 7:22 a.m. the next day, April 15. Booth was hunted down and shot in Bowling Green, Virginia, for the crime.

7. On that date the House of Representatives voted 128 to 47 to impeach Johnson, who succeeded Lincoln and served from 1865 to 1869. On March 13, Chief Justice Salmon P. Chase presided as the U.S. Senate began the impeachment trial of Johnson. Conviction required two-thirds or 36 votes out of the 54 senators. The vote was 35 for conviction and 19 for acquittal. This means that the impeachment failed by a single vote. This made Johnson ineffective in carrying out Reconstruction programs. His term of office as president did not accomplish much.

8. Franklin D. Roosevelt, *The State of the Union Message*, January 6, 1941 (Washington, DC: U.S. Government Printing Office, 1941).

9. Franklin D. Roosevelt and Winston Churchill, "The Atlantic Charter," in *The Public Papers and Addresses of Franklin D. Roosevelt*, Vol. 10, August 11, 1941 (Washington, DC: U.S. Government Printing Office, 1941).

10. Gunnar Myrdal, *An American Dilemma: The Negro Problem and Modern Democracy* (London: Harper and Brothers, 1944), p. 332.

11. For example, since the United States recognized the formation of the government of Israel in 1948, it has tried to mediate between Israel and its Arab neighbors. Its efforts remained unsuccessful until September 14, 1993, when the government of Israel and representatives of the Palestine Liberation Organization met in Washington, D.C., to sign an agreement that they had reached.

12. Diane Ravitch, *The Troubled Crusade: American Education, 1945–1980* (New York: Basic Books, 1983), p. 110.

13. Ibid., p. 111.

14. For a detailed discussion of this thinking, see Dickson A. Mungazi, *The Mind of Black Africa* (Westport, CT: Praeger, 1996).

15. Leon Friedman (ed.), *Argument: The Oral Arguments Before the Supreme Court in Brown vs. Board of Education of Topeka, 1952–1955* (New York: Chelsea House, 1969), p. 14.

16. Ibid., p. 15.

17. Warren had been named chief justice by President Dwight D. Eisenhower in 1953 to replace Frederick Vinson, who died suddenly.

18. *Brown vs. Board of Education of Topeka*, 347 U.S. 483 (May 17, 1954).

19. Henry Hampton and Steve Fayer, *Voices of Freedom: An Oral History of the Civil Rights Movement from the 1950s Through the 1980s* (New York: Bantam Books, 1991), p. 2.

20. Diane Ravitch, *The Troubled Crusade*, p. 165.

21. Ibid., p. 228.

22. Dickson A. Mungazi, *The Struggle for Social Change in Southern Africa: Visions of Liberty* (New York: Taylor and Francis, 1989), p. 100.

23. Robert E. Potter, *The Stream of American Education* (New York: American Book Company, 1967), p. 406.

24. Ibid., p. 402.

25. U.S. Senate, Committee on Labor and Public Welfare, *Enactment by the 89th*

Congress Concerning Education and Training (Washington, DC: U.S. Government Printing Office, 1966), p. 18.

26. William van Til, *Education: A Beginning* (Boston: Houghton Mifflin Company, 1974), p. 346.

27. U.S. Public Law 88–482, Economic Opportunity Act (1964).

28. Timothy Noah, "The Fiery Unionist as Educational Leader: Albert Shanker," *The New Republic*, June 24, 1993.

29. For detailed discussion of this remarkable American educator, see Dickson A. Mungazi, *Where He Stands: Albert Shanker of the American Federation of Teachers* (Westport, CT: Praeger Publishers, 1995).

30. "Shanker Urges Affirmative Action Through Better Training and More Jobs," *The American Teacher* (October 1974), p. 22.

31. United States, *Report of the National Advisory Commission on Civil Disorders* (Otto Kerner, Chairman). Washington DC: U.S. Government Printing Office, 1968), p. 2.

32. Marjorie Murphy, *Blackboard Unions: The AFT and the NEA, 1900–1980* (Ithaca, NY: Cornell University, Press, 1990), p. 232.

33. After Kwame Nkrumah of Ghana and Sekou Toure of Guinea.

34. Quoted in Hampton and Fayer, *Voices of Freedom*, p. 399.

35. A case in point: in April 1991, local school districts in Arizona attempted to organize a discussion forum involving members of the legislature to find a formula for equitable distribution of funds to support the schools.

36. An American professor of comparative sociology during an interview with the author, March 15, 1991.

37. An American professor during a conversation with the author, November 2, 1990.

38. Joel Spring, *American Education: An Introduction to Social and Political Aspects* (New York: Longman, 1993), p. 154.

39. N. Kuzin and M. Kondokov, *Education in the U.S.S.R.* (Moscow: Progress Press, 1977), p. 18.

40. Dalton Conley, *Being Black, Living in the Red: Race, Wealth and Social Policy in America* (Berkeley: University of California Press, 1999), p. 1.

41. *Time*, September 22, 1947.

42. On July 29, 1998, Thomas delivered a speech to a conference of black attorneys held in Tennessee in which he defended his right to express his conservative views, both as a member of the Supreme Court and as an individual.

43. *Time*, August 29, 1994, p. 40.

44. Dickson A. Mungazi, letter addressed to Senator Orrin Hatch, November 30, 1998. Senator Hatch did not respond.

45. Geraldine Peten, "Paradigm of Skin Color," paper written for a graduate course at Northern Arizona University, 1999.

Selected Bibliography

BOOKS

Bailyn, Bernard. *Education in the Transformation of America Society: Needs and Opportunity for Study*. New York: Borton and Company, 1972.

Banana, Canaan. *Theology of Promise: The Dynamics of Self-Reliance*. Harare, Zimbabwe: The College Press, 1982.

Banks, James A., and Cherry A. McGee Banks. *Multicultural Education: Issues and Perspectives*. Boston: Allyn and Bacon, Inc., 1989.

Bardolph, Richard. *The Civil Rights Record: Black Americans and the Law, 1949–1970*. New York: Thomas Crowell, 1970.

Barnes's Historical Series. *A Brief History of the United States*. New York: American Book Company, 1899.

Baulware, M. H. *The Oratory of Negro Leaders, 1900–1968*. Westport, CT: Negro Universities Press, 1969.

Bennet, L., Jr. *Pioneers in Protest*. Chicago: Johnson Publishing Company, 1968.

Bennet, L., Jr. *What Manner of Man: Martin Luther King, Jr.* Chicago: Johnson Publishing Company, 1968.

Berube, Maurice R., and Marilyn Gittell (eds.). *Confrontation at Ocean Hill-Brownsville: The New York School Strikes of 1968*. New York: Praeger, 1969.

Binder, Frederick M. *The Age of the Common School, 1831–1865*. New York: John Wiley and Sons, 1974.

Blanstein, P., and R. Zangrando, *Civil Rights and the American Negro*. New York: Negro Trident Press, 1968.

Bleiweiss, R. M. *Marching to Freedom: The Life of Martin Luther King, Jr.* New York: The New American Library, 1969.

Bordolph, R. *The Civil Rights Record: Black Americans and the Law, 1849–1970.* New York: Thomas Crowell, 1970.

Boyer, Ernest L. *High School: A Report of Secondary Education in America.* New York: Harper and Row Publishers, 1983.

Brameld, Theodore (ed.). *Workers' Education in the United States.* New York: Harper and Brothers, 1941.

Brubacker, John S. *Henry Barnard on Education.* New York: McGraw-Hill Book Company, 1931.

Bunzel, John H. *Challenge to American Schools: The Case for Standards and Values.* New York: Oxford University Press, 1985.

Carter, Barbara. *Pickets, Parents and Power: The Story Behind the New York City Teachers' Strike.* New York: Citation Press, 1971.

Cash, Wilbur Joseph. *The Mind of the South.* New York: Alfred Knopf, 1941.

Coleman, J. S. *Equality of Educational Opportunity.* Washington, DC: U.S. Office of Education, 1966.

Conant, James B. *The Education of American Teachers.* New York: McGraw-Hill Book Company, 1963.

Conant, James B. *Slums and Schools.* New York: McGraw-Hill Book Company, 1961.

Conley, Dalton. *Being Black, Living in the Red: Race, Wealth and Social Policy in America.* Berkeley: University of California Press, 1999.

Counts, George. *Secondary Education and Industrialism.* Cambridge, MA: Harvard University Press, 1929.

Counts, George. *The Selective Character of America Secondary Education.* Chicago: University of Chicago Press, 1922.

Counts, George. *Social Foundations of Education.* New York: Charles Scribner's Sons, 1934.

Cremin, Lawrence. *The American Common School.* New York: Teachers College Press, Columbia University, 1951.

Cremin, Lawrence. *The Republic and the School: Horace Mann on the Education of Free Man.* New York: Bureau of Publication, Teacher's College Press, Columbia University, 1957.

Cruse, Harold. *Plural but Equal: A Critical Study of Blacks and Minorities and America's Plural Society.* New York: William Morrow and Company, 1987.

Cubberley, E. P. *Changing Concepts of Education.* Boston: Houghton Mifflin, 1909.

Cunningham, Noble E., Jr. *In Pursuit of Reason: The Life of Thomas Jefferson.* Baton Rouge: Louisiana State University Press, 1987.

Curle, Adam. *Education for Liberation.* New York: John Wiley and Sons, 1973.

Davis, Angela. *Angela Davis: An Autobiography.* New York: International Publishers, 1989.

Dennis, R. E. *The Black People of America.* New York: McGraw-Hill Book Company, 1970.

Doherty, Robert (ed.). *Employer-Employee Relations in the Public Schools.* Ithaca, NY: Cornell University Press, 1967.

Douglass, Frederick. *Narrative of the Life of Frederick Douglass: An American Slave Written by Himself.* New York: American Library, 1845.

Downs, Robert B. *Horace Mann: Champion of Public Schools.* New York: Twayne Publishers, 1974.

Du Bois, W.E.B. *The Souls of Black Folk: Essays and Sketches*. Chicago: A. C. McClurg and Company, 1903.

Duck, Lloyd. *Understanding American Education: Its Past, Practices, and Promise*. Burke, VT: Chetelaine, 1996.

Eaton, William Edward. *The American Federation of Teachers, 1916–1961: A History of the Movement*. Carbondale, IL: Southern Illinois University Press, 1975.

Elam, Stanley M. *Readings on Collective Negotiations in Public Education*. Chicago: Rand McNally, 1967.

Esedebe, P. Olisanwuche. *Pan-Africanism: The Idea and Movement, 1776–1963*. Washington, DC: Howard University Press, 1982.

Fantini, M. D. *Alternative Education*. Garden City, NY: Doubleday, 1976.

Fawcett, L. A. *Life of W.E.B. Du Bois: Cheer the Lonesome Traveler*. New York: Dial Press, 1970.

Fellman, D. *The Supreme Court and Education*. New York: Columbia University Press, 1969.

Fox, S. R. *The Guardian of Boston: William Monroe Trotter*. New York: Atheneum, 1976.

Franklin, John Hope, and Alfred A. Moss, Jr. *From Slavery to Freedom: History of African Americans* (7th ed.). New York: McGraw-Hill Book Company, 1994.

Frazier, E. F. *Bourgeoisie: The Rise of the New Black Middle Class*. New York: The Free Press, 1965.

Freire, Paulo. *Pedagogy of the Oppressed* (Trans. by M. B. Ramos). New York: Continuum, 1983.

French, William M. *American Secondary Education*. New York: The Odyssey Press 1957.

Friedman, Leon (ed.). *Argument: The Oral Arguments Before the Supreme Court in Brown v. Board of Education of Topeka, 1952–1955*. New York: Chelsea House, 1969.

Gillespie, Judith, and Stuart Lazarus. *American Government: Comparing Political Experiences*. Englewood Cliffs, NJ: Prentice-Hall, 1979.

Gitlin, Todd. *The Sixties: Years of Hope, Days of Rage*. New York: Bantam Books, 1987.

Glazer, Nathan, and Patrick Moynihan. *Beyond the Melting Pot*. Cambridge, MA: M.I.T. Press, 1963.

Gorton, Jacob U. *The African American Male*. Westport, CT: Praeger, 1999.

Graham, Hugh D. *The Uncertain Triumph: Federal Education Policy in the Kennedy and Johnson Years*. Chapel Hill, NC: University of North Carolina Press, 1984.

Grant, Gerald. *The World We Created in Hamilton High*. Cambridge, MA: Harvard University Press, 1988.

Grayson, K. "Human Life vs. Science," in Thomas Weaver (ed.), *To See Ourselves: Anthropology and Modern Social Issues*. Glenville, IL: Scott, Foresman, 1973.

Greene, John C. *American Science in the Age of Jefferson*, Ames: Iowa State University Press, 1984.

Greven, Philip J. *Child-Rearing Concepts, 1628–1881: Historical Sources*. Itasca, IL: F. E. Peacock Publishers, Inc. 1973.

Grobman, Arnold B. *Urban State Universities: An Unfinished National Agenda*. New York: Praeger Publishers, 1988.

Gutek, Gerald. *American Education in a Global Society: Internationalizing Teacher Education*. New York: Praeger Longman, 1993.

Gutek, Gerald. *An Historical Introduction to American Education*. Prospect Heights, IL: Waveland Press, 1991.

Hampton, Henry, and Steve Fayer. *Voices of Freedom: An Oral History of the Civil Rights Movement from the 1950s Through the 1980s*. New York: Bantam Books, 1991.

Harlan, Louis R. *Booker T. Washington: The Wizard of Tuskegee, 1901–1915*. New York: Oxford University Press, 1983.

Harley, Sharon. *The Timetables of African American History: A Chronology of the Most Important People and Events in African American History*. New York: Simon and Schuster, 1995.

Harris, R. J. *The Quest for Equality*. Baton Rouge: Louisiana State University Press, 1960.

Henry, R. S. *The History of Reconstruction*. Gloucester, MA: Free Press, 1963.

Hook, Sidney. *In Defense of Academic Freedom*. New York: Bobbs-Merrill Company, 1971.

Hughes, Langston. *Fight for Freedom: The Story of the NAACP*. New York: W. W. Norton and Company, 1962.

Hunt, John Gabriel. *The Essential Abraham Lincoln*. New York: Random House, 1993.

Johnson, Charles, and Patricia Smith. *Africans in America's Journey Through Slavery*. New York: Harcourt Brace and Company, 1998.

Jones, James. *Prejudice and Racism*. New York: Addison Wesley Publishing Company, 1972.

Kallen, Horace M. *Cultural Pluralism and the American Ideas*. Philadelphia: University of Philadelphia Press, 1956.

King, Martin Luther, Jr. *Why We Can't Wait*. New York: The New American Library, 1964.

Krug, Mark. *The Melting of the Ethnics: Education of the Immigrants, 1880–1914*. Bloomington, IN: Phi Delta Kappa Educational Foundation, 1976.

Kuzin, N., and M. Kondokov. *Education in the U.S.S.R.* Moscow: Progress Press, 1977.

La Noue, George R., and Bruce L. R. Smith. *The Politics of School Decentralization*. Lexington, MA: D. C. Heath, 1973.

Lapan, Stephen, and Sam Miner (eds.). *Perspectives: Dimensions of Diversity*. Flagstaff, AZ: Center for Excellence in Education, 1996.

Lee, Gordon C. *Crusade Against Ignorance: Thomas Jefferson on Education*. New York: Bureau of Publications, Teachers College, Columbia University, 1962.

Lemann, Nicholas. *The Promised Land: The Great Black Migration and How It Changed America*. New York: Alfred A. Knopf, 1991.

Lieberman, Myron. *The Future of Public Education*. Chicago: The University of Chicago Press, 1960.

Luria, A. R. *Cognitive Development: Its Cultural and Social Foundations*. New York: Longman, 1989.

Madsen, David L. *Early National Education, 1776–1830*. New York: John Wiley and Sons, 1974.

Majors, Richard G., and Jacob U. Gordon. *The American Black Male*. Chicago: Nelson-Hall Publishers, 1991.

Marable, Manning. *How Capitalism Underdeveloped Black America: Problems in Race, Political Economy, and Society*. Boston: South End Press, 1983.

Marable, Manning. *W.E.B. Du Bois: Black Radical Democrat*. Boston: Twayne Publishers, 1986.

Meier, August, and Elliott Rudwick. *From Plantation to Ghetto* (3rd ed.). New York: Hill and Wang, 1976.

Memmi, Albert. *The Colonizer and the Colonized*. Boston: Beacon Press, 1965.

Messerli, Jonathan. *Horace Mann: A Biography*. New York: Alfred A. Knopf, 1972.

Mezu, S. O., and R. Desai. *Black Leaders of the Centuries*. Buffalo, NY: Black Academy Press, 1970.

Miller, James. *Democracy Is in the Street: From Port Huron to the Seige of Chicago*. New York: Simon and Schuster, 1987.

Miller, Lynn. *The Global Order: Values and Power in International Politics*. Boulder, CO: Westview Press, 1994.

Miller, W. R. *Martin Luther King, Jr., His Life, Marytrdom, and Meaning to the World*. New York: Weybright and Talley, 1968.

Moreland, Willis D., and Erwin H. Goldenstein. *Pioneers in Adult Education*. Chicago: Nelson-Hall Publishers, 1985.

Mungazi, Dickson A. "Education and the Quest for Human Completion: The African and Afro-American Perspectives Compared," in *ERIC Clearinghouse for Social Studies and Social Science Education*. ref. Ed 292/713/MF01/PCO2. Bloomington: Indiana University, 1987.

Mungazi, Dickson A. "Educational Innovation in Zimbabwe: Possibilities and Problems," in *Journal of Negro Education*, Vol. 54, No. 2. Howard University, Washington DC, 1985.

Mungazi, Dickson A. *Educational Policy and National Character: Africa, Japan, the United States, and the Soviet Union*. Westport, CT: Praeger Publishers, 1993.

Mungazi, Dickson A. *The Evolution of Educational Theory in the United States*. Westport, CT: Praeger Publishers, 1999.

Mungazi, Dickson A. "The Interpretation of Booker T. Washington's Contemporaries of His Work." Paper written for Graduate Seminar on Problems of National Development, Lincoln: The University of Nebraska, Summer 1977.

Mungazi, Dickson A. *The Struggle for Social Change in Southern Africa: Visions of Liberty*. New York: Taylor and Francis, 1989.

Mungazi, Dickson A. *Where He Stands: Albert Shanker of the American Federation of Teachers*. Westport, CT: Praeger Publishers, 1995.

Murphy, Marjorie. *Blackboard Unions: The AFT and the NEA, 1900–1980*. Ithaca, NY: Cornell University Press, 1990.

Myrdal, Gunnar. *An American Dilemma: The Negro Problem and Modern Democracy*. London: Harper and Brothers, 1944.

Noll, James W. *Taking Sides: Clashing Views on Controversial Educational Issues*. Guilford, CT: Dashkin Publishing Group, 1983.

Northrup, David. *The Atlantic Slave Trade*. Lexington, MA: D.C. Heath, 1994.

Osborne, C. *I Have a Dream: The Story of Martin Luther King, Jr*. New York: Time-Life Books, 1968.

Pathfinder Publications. *The Constitution of the United States with the Declaration of Independence.* Boston: Pathfinder, 1973.

Payne, J. S. *Head Start: A Tragicomedy with Epilogue.* New York: Behavioral Publications, 1975.

Peirce, Neal. "Obstacles to Change in Schools," in *The Arizona Republic,* October 16, 1989.

Perkinson, Henry. *The Imperfect Panacea: American Faith in Education, 1865–1990.* New York: McGraw-Hill Book Company, 1991.

Ploski, H.A., and R.C. Brown. *The Negro Almanac.* New York: Bellwether Publishing Corporation, 1967.

Potter, Robert E. *The Stream of American Education.* New York: American Book Company, 1967.

Pulliam, John D. *History of Education in America.* New York: Macmillan, 1991.

Ravitch, Diane. *The Troubled Crusade: American Education, 1945–1980.* New York: Basic Books, 1983.

Ray, James Earl. *Who Killed Martin Luther King Jr.?* New York: Marlowe and Company, 1992.

Reed, Wornie (ed.). *African-Americans: Essential Perspectives.* Westport, CT: Praeger Publishers, 1993.

Rich, Eleven. *Africa: Traditional and Modern.* New York: New House, 1972.

Riche, John Martin. *Innovations in Education: Reformers and Their Critics.* Boston: Allyn and Bacon, Inc., 1988.

Roosevelt, Franklin D. *State of the Union Message.* Washington, DC: U.S. Government Printing Office, 1941.

Roosevelt, Franklin D., and Winston Churchill. *The Atlantic Charter,* in *Public Papers and Addresses of Franklin D. Roosevelt.* Washington, DC: U.S. Government Printing Office, 1941.

Rouceck, J. S., and T. Kierman. *The Negro Impact on Western Civilization.* New York: Philosophical Library, 1970.

Rudwick, E. M. *Propagandist of the Negro Protest.* New York: W. W. Norton and Company, 1962.

Silberman, Charles E. *Crisis in Black and White.* New York: Vintage Books, 1964.

Sims, William E. *Black Studies: Pitfalls and Potential.* Washington, DC: University Press of America, 1979.

Sizer, Theodore R. *The Age of Academies.* New York: Bureau of Publications, Teachers College, 1962.

Sizer, Theodore. *Horace's Compromise: The Dilemma of the American High School.* Boston: Houghton Mifflin Company, 1984.

Smith, William. *Nyerere of Tanzania.* Harare: Zimbabwe Publishing House, 1981.

Spencer, S. R., Jr. *Booker T. Washington and the Negro Place in the American Life.* Boston: Little, Brown and Company, 1955.

Spring, Joel. *American Education: An Introduction to Social and Political Aspects.* New York: Longman, 1985.

Spring, Joel. *Conflict of Interest: The Politics of American Education.* New York: Longman, 1993.

Spring, Joel. *Deculturalization and the Struggle for Equality: A Brief History of The Education of Dominated Culture in the United States.* New York: McGraw-Hill Book Company, 1997.

Spring, Joel. *Wheels in the Head: Educational Philosophies of Authority, Freedom, and Culture from Socrates to Paulo Freire*. New York: McGraw-Hill, 1994.

Thornbrough, E. L. *Booker T. Washington*. Englewood Cliffs, NJ: Prentice-Hall, 1969.

Thursfield, Richard E. *Henry Barnard's America Journal of Education*. Baltimore: John Hopkins University Press, 1945.

Tiedt, Sidney W. *The Role of the Federal Government in Education*. New York: Oxford University Press, 1966.

Tussman, J. *The Supreme Court on Racial Discrimination*. New York: Oxford University Press, 1968.

van Til, William, *Education: A Beginning*. Boston: Houghton Mifflin Company, 1974.

Washington, Booker T. *The Future of the American Negro*. Boston: Small, Maynard and Company, 1900.

Washington, Booker T. *Up From Slavery*. New York: Doubleday, 1916.

Washington, Booker T. *Working with the Hands*. New York: Doubleday, Page and Company, 1902.

Weaver, Thomas (ed.). *To Know Ourselves*. Glenview, IL: Scott, Foresman and Company, 1973.

Webster, S. W. *The Education of Black Americans*. Berkeley: University of California Press, 1974.

Weinberg, M. *W. E. B. Du Bois: A Leader*. New York: Harper and Row, 1970.

White, Anne T. *George Washington Carver: Boy Scientist*. New York: Randolph House, 1954.

White, John. *Black Leadership in America*. New York: Longman, 1990.

Whitehead, Alfred North. *The Aims of Education*. New York: New American Library, 1929.

Williams, G. Mennen. *Africa for Africans*. Grands Rapids, MI: Eerdmans, 1969.

Wolff, Miles. *Lunch at the Five and Ten: The Story of the Greensboro Sit-ins*. Chicago: Ivan R. Dee, 1970.

GOVERNMENT MATERIALS

Brown v. Board of Education of Topeka, 347 U.S. 483, 1954.

"Early Childhood Education: A National Program," October 20, 1976. AFT Files, Washington, DC.

Economic Opportunity Act. U.S. Public Law 88–482. Washington, DC: U.S Government Printing Office, 1964.

National Commission on Excellence in Education. *A Nation at Risk*. Washington, DC: U.S. Department of Education, 1983.

National Defense Education Act. U.S. Public Law 85–864, 85th Congress. Washington, DC: U.S. Government Printing Office, 1958.

Report of the National Advisory Commission on Civil Disorders (Otto Kerner, chairman). Washington, DC: Government Printer, 1968.

OTHER MATERIALS

Berg, J. Otto. "America Faces a Choice." Lecture to a graduate class in education at Northern Arizona University, December 3, 1992.

Chancellor, John. "The Politics of Change." Documentary film aired on the Discovery Channel. February 21, 1994.

King, Martin Luther, Sr. Interview with Dickson A. Mungazi, Atlanta, Georgia, May 17, 1962.

Lewis, John. Interview with Dickson A. Mungazi, Atlanta, Georgia, May 18, 1962.

Mugabe, Robert. "Not in a Thousand Years: From Rhodesia to Zimbabwe." Documentary film. PBS, 1981.

Mungazi, Dickson A. "Crisis in Literacy in the World after the Second World War." Paper presented at the Literacy Volunteers of Coconino County, Flagstaff, Arizona. October 23–24, 1992.

Mungazi, Dickson A. Interview with Albert Shanker, President, American Federation of Teachers (1974–1997). Washington, DC. May 17, 1993.

Mungazi, Dickson A. Interview with Ian Smith, former prime minister of colonial Zimbabwe, Harare. July 20, 1983.

Mungazi, Dickson A. Letter to U.S. Senator Orrin Hatch (R.-Utah) on Reflections of Congressional Elections of 1998. November 30, 1998.

Mungazi, Dickson A. "The March to the Promised Land: The Development of Black Education in the U.S., 1875–1975." Paper written for Graduate Class, University of Nebraska. 1975.

NAACP. "Biographical Sketch of Julian Bond." Baltimore, 1999.

NAACP. "President's Corner: Kweisi Mfume, President and Chief Executive Officer of the NAACP." Baltimore, 1999.

NAACP. "What You Should Know About NAACP." Baltimore, 1999.

Peten, Geraldine. "Paradigm of Color." Paper written for Graduate Class, Northern Arizona University. 1999.

Sacks, Eve, Secretary to AFT, "Shanker's Impact on American Education and Society," interview conducted by Dickson A. Mungazi. Washington, DC, May 17, 1993.

Simitar Entertainment, Inc. *The Civil War: Struggle for Freedom.* Vols. 1 and 2. Documentary Film. Plymouth, MN. 1993.

ZAPU. Statement of Principles and Objectives, Harare. December 19, 1962.

Index

About the Author

DICKSON A. MUNGAZI is Regent's Professor of Education and History at Northern Arizona University. His numerous publications include *In the Footsteps of the Masters: Desmond M. Tutu and Abel T. Muzorewa* (Praeger, 2000), *The Last British Liberals in Africa* (Praeger, 1998), *The Mind of Black Africa* (Praeger, 1996), and *Educational Policy and National Character* (Praeger, 1993).